STAGES *The*
Fifty-Year
Childhood
of the
American
Theatre

Also by EMORY LEWIS

CUE'S NEW YORK:
A Leisurely Guide to Manhattan

STAGES

The Fifty-Year Childhood of the American Theatre

EMORY LEWIS

PRENTICE-HALL, INC., ENGLEWOOD CLIFFS, N.J.

STAGES

The Fifty-Year Childhood of the American Theatre by Emory Lewis

Prentice-Hall International, Inc., London
Prentice-Hall of Australia, Pty. Ltd., Sydney
Prentice-Hall of Canada, Ltd., Toronto
Prentice-Hall of India Private Ltd., New Delhi
Prentice-Hall of Japan, Inc., Tokyo

ACKNOWLEDGMENTS

I wish to thank all those involved in the realization of this book, most particularly Stanley Corwin, who prodded me into writing it. Cecile Grossman, an editor of penetrating mind and unfailing courtesy, has provided me with invaluable suggestions. As to a bibliography, I am stymied, since a list of the books, magazine articles, and newspaper reports I have noted during past seasons would fill yet another volume. I have learned much from hundreds of theatre chroniclers, from Walter Prichard Eaton to James A. Herne to John Rankin Towse. I am delighted, however, to pay special homage to the New York Public Library's Theatre Collection, over which Paul Myers presides with uncommon erudition and wit. It is the best of its kind anywhere in the world.

For

LILA,

who occupies the other seat

CONTENTS

INTRODUCTION: A POINT OF VIEW

THEATRE IS A social art, intimately tied to the world outside the auditorium. One cannot separate theatre from man's other activities. A good critic is keenly aware of the currents swirling around the theatre and of the stage's necessary relation to life. Unless theatre criticism goes beyond a study (and I do not disparage that study in itself) of acting, direction, costuming, set design, and the myriad backstage elements of a drama in production and considers the political, social, and philosophical implications of a play, that criticism will remain fragmentary, kaleidoscopic, and, in the long view, unsound. In our country, this total way of looking at theatre is seldom practiced.

This book, then, is suffused with a point of view. Nowadays that phrase has an out-of-fashion ring to it. Everyone is trying rather desperately, it sometimes appears, *not* to have a point of view. Partisanship is in intellectual disrepute in the barren sixties. The mode in the arts is a capricious faddism, whether it be demonstrated by paintings and sculptures which seemingly take over from the artists and create (or destroy) themselves or by pieces of music which are mere accidents occurring on stage and have no ending other than an arbitrary decision by the performer to come to a halt. Many artists are concerned solely with technique, with new ways with new materials, with "spontaneous play," with anything different from last night's fad. Much of this is healthy, even though one might be irritated by some of the experimenters' cultist pomposities and incessant, murky verbiage. Only a Babbitt (he still exists under assumed names) would wish to throttle experimentation or creative play. Obviously, it is vital to artistic development.

But fashionableness, in our current cultural scene, has been elevated to a way of life, an artistic end in itself. In our pragmatic culture (though it is far more manipulated than many would like to believe), goals, planning, or a passionate end toward which one might work are increasingly suspect formulations. Voguish vagaries have replaced a vivid, yea-saying sense of direction. Form alone is today's god. This growing tendency in all the arts has resulted in a blurred focus, widespread examples of spiritual starvation, and a vast amount of energy with no particular place to go.

In the following pages about the contemporary American theatre, a number of unfashionable phrases will reappear. That invaluable word, *content,* which has been scornfully cast aside by some of the more frantic experimenters, will be employed. Is all art supposed "to be," and not, horrors, "to mean"? *Commitment* shall also be reintroduced. In short, my point of view is not altogether removed from the language of the thirties, as evoked so sensitively in Harold Clurman's remembrance of things past, *The Fervent Years.* (Surprisingly, these terms have sometimes been borrowed in the sixties by the most reactionary forces and their misuse, in turn, has led to repugnance against these words by the avant-garde. Words —and their stubborn resistance to clear communication between men—have been the subject of a number of witty comedies by Eugène Ionesco. But to give up talking, to give up words altogether would be yet another futile experiment. Actually, it has been tried in the theatre. Absolute silence on stage—with a paying audience out front.)

This book turns to focus on the grand tradition, the mainstream of humanism from the cultural flowering of the Chinese, the Greeks, and Arabs through the Renaissance and the Enlightenment. Not, to be sure, the same old humanism, with the stultified phrases and slogans with which any point of view is bound to become encrusted. We live in an electronic age, a space age, an atomic age, an age in which the world (or, at least, the planet on which we live) may very well come to an end. Organized murder (in the Congo, Guatemala, Vietnam, and dozens of key points) continues in its ugly way, and everyone is tensely aware that it might flame into global suicide. No age has been in such total danger. Naturally, today's humanism must find new idioms to express new terrors and new visions. Fortunately such bold innovators as Bertolt Brecht, Antonin Artaud, Marshall McLuhan, Jan Kott, Jerzy Grotowski, and the Becks have given us new eyes, new ears, new tools with which to know and enjoy the arts and to communicate with each other with fresh awareness. Jean-Claude van Itallie's *Motel*, with its wild rock music, its psychedelic lighting, and its half-dressed moronic lovers feverishly scrawling graffiti on motel walls, is a most telling comment on the quality of American life today, though its approach is vastly different from that of yesterday's thesis play. Humanism has many faces, and no one would advocate a return to the rather simplistic credos of the thirties. But the clear path for the arts is nonetheless something termed humanism. Art, whether it be theatre, opera, sculpture, dance, or collage, is social, and its direction affects the future of the world just as much as the deposition of the Bomb.

In the United States, a disheartening number of persons in the theatre and elsewhere have childishly opposed the idea that art is political. Yet every play has a "message." No message is a message. Ostrich-like attitudes unwittingly constitute messages. If one consciously avoids commitment, that too makes a comment about society. "If you have a message, send it by Western Union" and "satire is what closes Saturday night" are two of the most repeated capsule comments on the American theatre, both usually attributed, incidentally, to the late George S. Kaufman. However, they are more indicative of what is wrong with our theatre and culture than they are reliable guidelines. The message, or content, of our annual theatre productions is a gauge of the state of the union, a mirror of our times. From these, we can gain great insights into our political and even our sexual patterns. Social scientists study the theatre with avidity. All theatre has something to say, a message of one kind or another, be it direct or oblique, a shout or a sigh. The only valid area of debate is not over whether theatre art is social, but rather over what a particular drama says and whether one agrees with it or not. The discussion inevitably returns to politics, or the fine art of living together. One must take sides. England's Kenneth Tynan, one of the most trenchant theatre critics of our times, has often pointed out that the good critic and great art are always partial. I heartily concur. Art for art's sake is, in practice, an impossibility. As a theory, it has led us into ever-changing, ever-new blind alleys. The resident of the ivory tower merely chooses, in effect, to align himself with the gods of unreason and war. In an era of biological warfare and overkill, on a Lear-ish heath of butchering Belsens and blasted Hiroshimas, most of our theatre seems an evasion of the political realities raging around us. Are our playwrights doodling during the holocaust?

Perhaps the American playwright of our time who comes closest to saying what I am trying to convey is Lorraine Hansberry. This brilliant young Negro writer, who died of cancer in January of 1965, has one of her characters in *The Sign of Sidney Brustein's Window* clarify his own commitment: "Yes, I care. I care about it all. It takes too much energy not to care. Yesterday, I counted twenty-six gray hairs on the top of my head, all from trying not to care . . . The 'why' of why we are here is an intrigue for adolescents; the 'how' is what must command the living. Which is why I have lately become an insurgent again." No contemporary playwright, it seems to me, has captured so vividly the fervor and *Angst* of certain big-city intellectuals now in their thirties and forties, men and women vaguely of the political left, dallying with fashionable art isms, playing now with Zen and now with Camus, flirting with the idea of commitment, engaged and disengaged all at once. In this sense, *The Sign in Sidney Brustein's Window*, flawed though it is, is a key play in the history of modern American drama.

Great artists are always subversives and dreamers. By subversives, I mean not adventurers but rather those whose dedication is to questioning the conventions of time and place, to defying the status quo, to a divine discontent. And by dreamers, I mean those who have a fresh and imaginative realization that tomorrow could be better, that the world need not end with either a bang or a whimper.

It is sometimes difficult to convey this to today's young. Many of them are deeply involved with their own very personal revolt against the pious platitudes and clichés of their elders. Thus all fancy words and preachments smell of hypocrisy to them. They are understandably wary of men with answers or solutions; they dislike heavy-handed dogmatisms of both right and left. Their own revolt against their middle-aged masters is healthy and welcome. But these youngsters and the young of every generation must find their way into the mainstream of revolt, the mainstream which includes Euripides and Aristophanes, Molière and Shakespeare, Ibsen and Shaw, O'Casey and Lorca, Ghelderode and Brecht, Dürrenmatt and Weiss.

The fascinating processes of revolt never cease. The revolt against the Establishment, whether in the United States, France, Russia, England or China, is inexorable. It is the law of change, the only constant. *Struggle* is a key word in life as well as in the theatre. With this revolt, this subversion, there is always the dream, sometimes stated and sometimes implied, of a world without war and with intelligence and love. The subversion contains the dream. If there is bias in this book, it is a bias toward revolt. I am not, of course, referring to crude theatre propaganda. Nobody wants dull, obvious tracts on stage. The Russians, under Stalin, went grievously astray with their elephantine, bureaucratic application by rote of that catch-phrase, Socialist Realism. Theatre must never be imprisoned in a single mold. To flourish, art must come in a rich variety of styles and surprising packages.

However, it should be remembered that propaganda can be artistic as well as inartistic. I am not at all opposed to propaganda if one means using the stage in a skillful, powerful, imaginative way as a platform. Propaganda is only an epithet among confused esthetes. Our dramatists today are often so scared of being thought propagandists that they mumble and stammer with maddening incoherence. So much so that one longs to yell "Speak up, speak up!"

Of course, the vital element in the theatre and in all arts is the quality of the subversion and the dream. Merely to write a play about a lynching or a book-burning or a baby seared by napalm does not automatically insure that the play is good. Indeed, such a play in incompetent hands might be vulgar, insensitive, or shoddy. An artist is not simply a recorder of headlines. By depicting a small act of kindness or compassion in an original manner, an artist can evoke a greater revolutionary spirit than many a dogmatist's clichéd manifesto. Content must always be shaped by form and style. One role of the artist is to inspire qualitative change. Wit, daring, imagination, poetry, beauty—these are the intangibles that turn subversion and dream into great art, that enrich mankind's precious heritage of revolt.

Armed with a viewpoint toward the theatre which sees art and politics as intricately entwined, which sees art as a luminous transfiguration of man's social consciousness, I have been led to a number of positions about our drama which are, I fear, minority opinions. I cannot join the chorus who gush without restraint or scruple over the glories of the American drama. My stomach has been turned not only by the facile overglorification of our nation but by our pathetic eagerness to overpraise our cultural tidbits. Far too much of our current babbling about theatre is Fourth-of-July, Chamber-of-Commerce self-advertising. It is a touched-up portrait, designed to convince the rest of the world that we Americans are just about perfect, that our theatre, like everything else in our vast land, is the best that money can buy. Constant self-congratulation, however, will never lead us into the realm of art. Our national bad habit of using a superlative where a more exact word would do has blinded us to perdurable greatness.

In bitter actuality, our theatre is most often mere titillation, mindless divertisement, cotton candy. Cotton candy is fine, but not as a steady diet; there are more flavorsome foods and more exciting kinds of entertainment. Despite the ballyhooed "cultural explosion," our cultural growth has simply not kept pace with our awesome military power, no matter how convincing the editorial pap might be. Nor can I regard Broadway as a "fabulous invalid" who has known great days, an indomitable *grande dame* who will gallantly survive. Broadway is not a fabulous invalid at all: she is still in her childhood—gawky, cheeky, and unfinished. We have not come anywhere near a Golden Age of the American stage. To think so is to demean the dramatic arts.

There are a few portents, however faint, that the child may be growing up. But the easy talk of greatness tossed around the Broadway arena should be saved for the future, not squandered on the past or present. In a sense, all that has gone before is a rehearsal. Art waits in the wings.

CHAPTER 1

GESTATION

THEATRE IN THE United States began only yesterday. Incredibly, our theatre—and by that I mean American drama as literature and the use of the stage as a platform for art—is just a little over fifty years old. To overrate the past is mere flag-waving and a falsification of history. The American drama was born in 1915. How can a specific year be pinpointed to mark cultural change? It is, of course, a far more complex matter than that. History is process, ever-changing, ever-zigzagging, ever-evolving. So, although for the sake of clarity I have chosen 1915 as the birth date of native drama, there is also something preposterous about choosing a single year.

The drama was born after one of the longest gestation periods on record. The three hundred years before the birth are here considered briefly and summarily. After wading through reams of plays and earlier critical comment, I am certain that these centuries will constitute a mere footnote in the history of American drama. As artists, most of the earlier playwrights were embarrassingly inept, not to be placed for one instant in the same company with Shakespeare, Marlowe, Jonson, Racine, Molière, and a continent of others. In fact, the great European tradition of theatre was somehow forgotten in the settling of North America. Most of our early dramas were not only graceless, they were puerile—an all-too-accurate index of our cultural values.

In the beginning, there was Sin, or so it seemed in the day of Cotton Mather and his fellow-colonists. The public, most particularly in the northern colonies, was sobersides (at least in its official poses), and deemed theatre the most brazen child of Sodom and

Gomorrah. This attitude has not altogether deserted our land, and many men as well as women still giggle rather nervously when they encounter something labeled Sin in our theatre.

The most interesting accounts of early theatre have come from the more cavalier Southern colonies. One of the first recorded descriptions is of a crude English production, *Ye Bare and Ye Cubb*, in Accomac County, Virginia, in 1665. Other early plays were offered in Charleston, South Carolina, and Williamsburg, Virginia. But theatre was sporadic and the pleasure of a few. The busy colonists had little time for cultural pursuits. In 1787, *The Contrast* was produced at the John Street Theatre in New York. Royal Tyler's script is often cited as the first drama written by an American and performed by professionals. A study of social pretension, the play sides with an unlettered but shrewd Yankee against his more polished contemporaries. It is a theme recurrent in our history, sound in its espousal of democracy, unsound in its frequent anti-intellectual echoes. *The Contrast* is merely an amusing museum piece today.

In the nineteenth century, Shakespeare was a staple of our serious theatre, with leading English and American actors competing for the patrons' loyalties. But it was a Shakespeare bowdlerized, abridged, emasculated, and ravaged beyond recognition. The guts were gone, and Shakespeare's decidedly unpuritanical passions were reduced to mere rhetoric and bombast. European drama was imported in a steady flow and shamelessly altered by the producers to suit our audiences. Between 1861 and 1881, actor-manager Lester Wallack ran an elegant and superior stock company in New York, never once producing an American play. They were not good enough, he haughtily decreed. In the main, he was right. Actually, the actor and not the play was the thing. Critics and public alike were much more fascinated by Edwin Forrest, Edwin Booth, Joseph Jefferson, E. H. Sothern, Richard Mansfield, and John Drew than by the vehicles in which they performed.

Were there any important American playwrights? Absolutely not. Reading nineteenth-century drama is painful work today. Even then, some critics were outraged. Walt Whitman, writing in *Democratic Vistas* in 1869, asserted: "Of what is called drama, or dramatic presentation in the United States ... I should say it deserves to be treated with the same gravity and on a par with the questions of ornamental confectionary and public dinners." True, uncritical audiences sat enthralled before Dion Boucicault's *The Octoroon*, and later they thrilled to Olive Logan's *Surf*, subtitled *Summer Scenes from Long Branch*. In 1845, Anna Cora Mowatt's *Fashion*, a study of the *nouveau riche*, was hailed as a masterpiece; a lone dissenting opinion by Edgar Allan Poe in the *Broadway Journal* shortly after the play's opening had no effect whatever on the busy box office. Revivals of these works today succeed only as affectionate and stylish spoofs. Theatre managers often wrote and directed their own scripts. These were usually lifted, boldly and without reference to sources, from the works of both foreign and American authors. Many a playwright was merely a hired scrivener, a ghost-writer—with no billing at all. The Dramatists Guild—designed to protect the American playwright—was then unknown.

The century's religiosity, sentimentality, and persistent emphasis on the smiling aspects of life were mirrored in one crude melodrama after another, with not a hint of criticism directed toward a robber-baron society. Moreover, public prudery still reigned, so that even as late as 1905, Shaw's *Mrs. Warren's Profession* was officially suppressed in New York. A purported critic of the New York *Sun* declared that Shaw's purpose was "to glorify debauchery." In every age and in every country, the public gets the kind of drama it deserves, and New Yorkers didn't yet deserve George Bernard Shaw.

The greatest successes of the nineteenth century were, predictably, the forerunners of the modern musical comedy. The most popular of these was *The Black Crook*, which opened in New York's Niblo's Gardens in 1866. It was a combination of ballet, melodrama, and spectacle. From accounts of the day, Hollywood spectacle specialists would have loved its elaborate scenic effects. (Our theatre concealed its lack of subtlety with eye-popping tricks. Often, the hit of a show was a realistic gorge across which the hero leaped, or a stupendous buzz saw threatening the heroine, or a three-alarm fire destroying the old manse.) That musical extravaganza ran over a year and grossed more than a million dollars. Its revivals (and its imitators) continued for many decades. Only *Uncle Tom's Cabin* (1852) and *Rip Van Winkle* (1866) equaled the extraordinary popularity of *The Black Crook*.

There was vitality, and sometimes artistry, in a variety of popular diversions—"museums" (curious showcases combining animals, freaks, variety acts, and refreshments), the minstrel show (mostly white entertainers in blackface), pantomime (George L. Fox and his *Humpty-Dumpty* ran forever), the tents and showboats (*Ten Nights in a Barroom*, 1858, and *East Lynne*, 1863, were perennials), and vaudeville (its origins were even earlier, but the great impetus came with the opening of Tony Pastor's Opera House on New York's Bowery in 1864). The *tableaux vivants* presented showgirls seemingly nude but actually dressed in daring skintight, one-piece silk costumes. As often happens in a raw culture, these unassuming entertainments were sometimes more truly artistic than the more respectable and overdressed efforts. For example, Edward Harrigan's comic and unpretentious genre pictures of German and Irish immigrant life in New York were sounder art than many a fancier mess of arty antimacassar and plush.

Now the curtain rises on the twentieth century. The box-office hits of 1900 in New York, which had become the nation's theatre capital, were *Ben Hur*, *Quo Vadis*, and *Floradora*. As the century evolved, there were a few hints of that promised birth in 1915. Clyde Fitch showed a spark of genius, though most of his considerable output was hack work. Fitch became a millionaire in a time of no income taxes. More important, he was the first American dramatist to gain even a small amount of artistic acclaim in Europe. But most of his work was bright and superficial, cleverly designed to make him a fortune. Whenever a theme of depth or social significance occurred to him, he skated carefully away from its center to the safe edges. However, in *The Truth* (1906) he did create a fairly honest study of an inveterate liar.

William Vaughn Moody's *The Great Divide*, which opened in New York in 1906 with Henry Miller and Margaret Anglin, was another drama of more than routine interest, contrasting Eastern effeteness with Western frontier openness. There are those who mark Moody's work as the birth of the American drama. Others choose Langdon Mitchell's 1906 *The New York Idea*, a more worldly glance at divorce and remarriage than provincial Americans were accustomed to. Or Rachel Crothers' *A Man's World* (1909), a fairly daring and effective jab at the double standard. Or Percy MacKaye's *The Scarecrow* (1910), a poetic examination of the New England witch trials, a subject to be explored again by Arthur Miller in the Age of McCarthy. Or Edward Sheldon's *The Nigger* (1909), a trifle—but only a trifle—more penetrating look at racism than the usual white man's stereotype. (Sheldon was, incidentally, the first graduate of George Pierce Baker's celebrated Harvard workshop in playwriting which was later to produce, among others, Sidney Howard, S. N. Behrman, Philip Barry, and Eugene O'Neill.) But none of these plays, unfortunately, marked a significant advance. They did contain, however, subtle shifts, indications that the playwright was becoming an independent force. Passing were the days when the theatre manager-director rewrote the playwright's work at will.

Other forces were also preparing for the birth of the American theatre. Often it was the actor who fought for quality. Minnie Maddern Fiske emerges as an important pioneer, not yet given her due in theatre chronicles. Though she acted in her youth in such drivel as *Ten Nights in a Barroom* and continued in only slightly better rubbish, she did come out of retirement at the turn of the century to establish perhaps the best resident company New York had ever seen or would see—until the visit of the Abbey Theatre troupe in 1911. Incidentally, one of the members of her fine troupe was London-born George Arliss. Mrs. Fiske's company performed at the Manhattan Theatre, located on the present site of Gimbels' department store, and here New Yorkers saw a number of Ibsen productions (Ibsen was widely held to be an unhealthy foreign influence on American morals) as well as the best of the American writers. The great lesson Mrs. Fiske taught theatregoers was to listen to and respect the play itself, not merely to applaud star performances. Another actor, the mercurial and silver-tongued Irish-American Arnold Daly, fought for theatre of distinction. In the early 1900's, Daly produced a number of Shaw plays (he was arrested for putting on *Mrs. Warren's Profession*). Shavian wit and irony provided necessary ingredients for the birth of American drama. Alla Nazimova was yet a third performer who brought culture to a nation which had lingered far too long in a cocoon of sterile provincialism. When Paul Orleneff and his Russian company first came to Broadway in 1905 and met rebuffs, they promptly fled to the sympathetic audiences of European immigrants in the crowded slums of the Lower East Side. The company's star, Mme. Nazimoff, was later celebrated on Broadway as Nazimova. This lithe, dark, ardent actress became a dominant figure in New York, waging and winning the battle for Ibsen, the battle Minnie Maddern Fiske had inaugurated.

Actors were also fighting on other fronts. They had long been regarded as immoral waifs, tainted with sin and poverty (both equally reprehensible in polite circles) and never, of course, to be invited to one's home. After many premature skirmishes, a union, Actors' Equity Association, was founded in 1913 and was the first step in giving the actor a sense of respect and professionalism, as well as some control over his destiny. Producers had always considered actors as mere baggage on the show train. With the founding of Equity, the actor, to some degree, freed himself from the great syndicates which controlled the theatres, the bookings, and the choice of performers. At last the actor had an organization to represent him and his craft. Later, in the bitter strike of 1919, the actor finally won certain clearly defined economic rights in the American theatre.

Slowly—we have always lagged a bit behind Europe's cultural timetable—the obvious, melodramatic American theatre began to respond to the stage ferment sweeping the Continent. Europe had waged the struggle for the New Realism in the 1880's and 1890's, mainly through the Little Theatre movements with such partisans as the Freie Bühne in Berlin, the Théâtre-Libre of André Antoine in Paris, and the Independent Theatre in London. Others were searching for even bolder paths. Jarry had shocked Paris in 1896 with his surrealist *Ubu Roi*—a portent of Artaud's Theatre of Cruelty. The French director-critic-dramatist Jacques Copeau was beginning his creative ascent from dull and overdressed naturalism, and his quest for purity and poetry influenced actors from Jouvet

[6]

to Barrault. The brilliant labors of Stanislavsky in Russia and Max Reinhardt in Berlin were stimulating the most advanced theatre minds here. Stanislavsky was to carry realism beyond realism to a point where ensemble acting became poetry, or—better—orchestrated music; Reinhardt was to show the world how poetic spectacle could give theatre a new dimension. Those in the United States who followed trends abroad with especial diligence noted that Russia's Vsevolod Meyerhold was conducting even more daring experiments in the direction of abstraction.

New theories were being promulgated everywhere. The Swiss philosopher and scene designer Adolphe Appia had published in the 1890's his sweeping new theories on stagecraft. The English theatre pioneer Gordon Craig, who died at the age of ninety-four in 1966, was at his peak in the seminal 1910's. The first exhibitions of this actor-turned-designer had been held in 1902, and his revolutionary dicta were published in a unified form in 1905. Craig was one of the first theorists to free the stage from the limitations of painted scenes. He suggested screens, architectural outlines, and fluid spotlighting (ending the reliance on footlights) to replace yesterday's dull flats. His designs carefully created a mood for a play or scene; they were not Belasco-literal settings. His book, *On the Art of the Theatre*, published in 1911, was to become a guide to a generation of directors, designers, and producers. In that same year, he was invited to Russia to create a Moscow Art Theatre production of *Hamlet*. Craig saw the play as a search for the true in a world of falsehood, and he clothed all the characters except Hamlet in sheaths of gold.

All these influences were filtering into the New York theatre. In the Lower East Side slum areas, Tolstoy and Andreyev were performed in German, Yiddish, and Russian. During the 1890's and early 1900's, invaluable productions in German were offered at the vital Irving Place Theatre. Those fortunate enough to know German saw provocative new dramas by Shaw and Schnitzler long before they were presented in the English-speaking theatre. The Irving Place, which will some day be awarded its proper key role in the history of American theatre, also gave New Yorkers rare opportunities to view dramas by Hauptmann, Ibsen, Gorky, Maeterlinck, Wilde, and Molnar. By 1912, the Yiddish theatre had become a vital force on the Lower East Side, introducing great stars from Europe and providing the American stage for decades to come with some of its best actors, directors, and teachers. Foreign visitors to Broadway were of inestimable value, too. In 1911, the Irish Players of the Abbey Theatre introduced plays by Shaw, Yeats, and Synge and such fine performers as Sara Allgood, J. M. Kerrigan, and Una O'Connor. Americans were becoming more intensely aware of how deprived theatrically they were. Some of them learned that theatre could be a more exciting temple of art than anything they had imagined. A not-insignificant event was the founding (in Chicago in 1914, largely through the efforts of Mrs. Starr Best) of the Drama League, a pioneer effort by theatregoers to promote and support superior drama.

The impetus for better theatre also came from the nation's rich and powerful. Many affluent Americans had traveled abroad; they had seen at first hand the prestige that theatre of genuine quality brought to European cities and nations. America's new millionaires, bulging with fat purses and vast political power, now wanted the cultural imponderables as well. A group of the nation's wealthiest men, most of them prominent in the care and feeding of the Metropolitan Opera Company, were determined to do something about the sad state of American theatre. J. P. Morgan, John Jacob Astor, the Vanderbilts, Thomas Payne Whitney, Otto Kahn, and others led the effort to establish a "permanent national art theatre" in New York. (This has its echoes in today's Lincoln Center, with its monies coming from millionaires—notably the Rockefellers— private foundations, and giant corporations.) In 1909 these lucre-laden gentlemen, yearning for a native culture, built a palatial playhouse, the New Theatre, on the west side of Central Park. Costing three million dollars, the house was enormous and had a baroque horseshoe of boxes for its anticipated patrons. The stage equipment was said to be the best in the world. A cultivated Bostonian, Winthrop Ames, was put in charge, and he produced Galsworthy's *Strife*, Sheldon's *The Nigger*, plays by Sheridan, Shakespeare, and Maeterlinck. The dream lasted only two seasons. For one thing, the opulent playhouse was too far from the theatre district. Basically, however, the board of directors was too dilettantish, with no driving force or conviction in the search for elusive culture. The most elaborate of houses will not create a permanent theatre company if a group with passionate purpose and artistic unity does not emerge. Fervor is not to be purchased; it must be created out of a point of view and years of disciplined work. While the New Theatre group was a public acknowledgment of our artistic limitations in the world of drama, it was an important pioneering effort.

Other theatres were going up all over America. At the turn of the century, hundreds of legitimate theatres and stock companies were in existence, and troupers could play six weeks of one-night stands in Texas alone. Broadway boomed with new showcases. In 1900, there were twenty theatres on Broadway; by 1925, there were eighty, an all-time high. In fact, practically all of today's Broadway houses (thirty-three, at last count) were built in that pre-television age. However, in a culture still confused about quantity and quality, about monetary versus artistic success, theatre scholars have tended to write too glowingly of the increase in buildings. I am not so sure of its significance in the advancement of American drama. Certainly, I do not for a moment believe the construction boom was a sign that theatre of quality was being presented, just as success at the box office has never been an indication of a play's worth. Nonetheless, the many new buildings did imply a burgeoning interest in theatre, and out of this busy activity sometimes came quality.

More important than the mushrooming playhouses on Broadway was the astonishing nationwide growth of the Little Theatres (an odious term widely used at the time). As early as 1906–07, there was remarkably varied Little Theatre activity in Chicago. Thomas H. Dickenson founded his Wisconsin Dramatic Society in 1911; Mrs. Lyman Gale's Toy Theatre of Boston appeared in 1912. In that same year, Winthrop Ames established himself in his own Little Theatre on New York's West Forty-fourth Street, and he was an outstanding leader in the growth of Little Theatres everywhere. Many theatre buffs were fed up with commercial theatre, and some were becoming aware of the excitement in Europe. The best of them were rebellious amateurs deeply concerned with

[9]

dramatic reform. Often these groups sprang from a rather incongruous mixture of local social-climbing and idealism. Whatever, they were a growing force across the land, and by 1915 they had developed some nineteen hundred theatres of varying degrees of quality.

There was much pretension in the Little Theatre movement, much old-fashioned heavy breathing about Culture, but out of it all came new writers, new ideas in staging, and a belief that theatre can offer more than trivia. Indeed, it was off and not on Broadway, in certain Little Theatres of New York, that the actual birth of the American drama took place. The Little Theatres were to prod and to fertilize Broadway in every decade to follow.

But it was not just better playwrights, exceptionally adventurous actors, and Little Theatres that prepared the way for the 1915 birth. Vital forces were at work on much larger stages. No longer can one study any art form in a social vacuum. All the arts are intricately interrelated, each one a part of the total social and political tapestry. An entire nation, and its unique position in the world community, must be studied at the same time one analyzes any particular art. Certainly theatre critics should be at home in all the arts and in international politics as well.

In the early 1900's the United States was alive with new ideas and new passions. No period in this century has been so fecund in the creation of nothing less than a new kind of American. For one thing, Europe was being discovered. Better still, Europe was here— physically as well as spiritually. The mass immigration of Italians, Russians, Poles, and Jews in the 1880's and 1890's had immeasurably enriched American culture, just as the earlier immigrations of the Irish had done. Two events sparked this exodus from Europe: in 1881, the most vicious of the many pogroms against the Jews rampaged across Russia; in the 1890's, phylloxera invaded the vineyards of Sicily. At the same time, a booming America needed cheap labor to build its railroads and man its factories. Someday, a monumental study will lovingly detail just how this influx of millions propelled American culture out of its gawky and flaccid provincialism. For these Europeans added a yeasty sophistication to our land. Most particularly, the East European Jews, from Hungary,

Poland, Romania, and Russia, brought with them a fierce love of justice and an insatiable thirst and respect for culture. They most certainly changed the face of New York City. Cultural development moves in incredibly complex ways. Ironically, we must thank Czarist Russia and its cruel pogroms for an enormous enrichment of American life in drama, music, dance, painting, sculpture, philosophy, and poetry.

The European immigrants also contributed new and challenging ideas to politics and economics, most especially anarchism and socialism, fiery concepts which in turn stimulated America's groping intellectuals. The militant International Workers of the World, better known in the lore of the rebels as Wobblies, were loosely organized in 1905. Socialist minded immigrants found a native-born champion in Eugene V. Debs. A man of integrity and personal magnetism, Debs was the Socialist Party's nominee for the Presidency in 1900, 1904, and 1908. By 1912, he had become such a popular figure that he received almost a million votes for President.

A new worldliness—questioning and tough—was coming into our everyday political life. It was nothing less than a revolt of the American conscience; it marked a revulsion against the mindless overglorification of those titans whose fortunes were made in the post-Civil War industrialization of the nation. Ida M. Tarbell, Ray Stannard Baker, and Lincoln Steffens were muckrakers (it was a word President Theodore Roosevelt plucked out of Bunyan's *Pilgrim's Progress*). In the bright and brash *McClure's Magazine* in the early 1900's, this new breed of journalists probed behind the smiling façade of American life. Steffens, particularly in his penetrating analyses of the actual workings of city governments (he ignored the elected front men), penned scalpel-sharp, scathing indictments of St. Louis, Minneapolis, Pittsburgh, Philadelphia, and other cities that shocked a nation. These pieces, later published as *The Shame of the Cities*, are still fresh and painfully relevant today. The book was dedicated "to the accused, to all the citizens of all the cities in the United States." Steffens later continued his incisive, salutary muckraking in the *American* and *Everybody's* magazines until 1910. In that year another muckraker, scholarly Gustavus Meyers, published his fearless and carefully detailed

History of the Great American Fortunes. It has remained a pivotal volume for students of social history. The witty and iconoclastic professor, Thorstein Veblen, was writing about economics in an unorthodox, unsettling way. At the turn of the century, he had already published his *Theory of the Leisure Class*, in which he coined the phrase "conspicuous consumption," which was destined to become a familiar part of our language. It was an era when profits and greed went hog wild, but it was also an era when intellectuals were increasingly articulate about the sad state of the nation. Americans were becoming, to a degree, self-conscious and critical.

America seemed to be seeking new intellectual frontiers now that the physical frontier was closing. Inspiriting experiment and vigorous reappraisal dominated the vanguard in all of the arts. In 1908, a rebel group of painters called The Eight swept away the cobwebs of the Victorian era with a daring exhibit at the old Macbeth Gallery in New York. The Eight, or the Ashcan School as they were sneeringly dubbed, were Arthur B. Davies, Maurice Prendergast, Ernest Lawson, William Glackens, Everett Shinn, Robert Henri, John Sloan, and George Luks. They were fervently united in the belief that the official Academy ideal of gauze-draped pseudoclassical nymphs offered a sterile direction for American art. Some of The Eight looked instead to the crowded city streets, the unkempt backyards, and the neighborhood saloons for inspiration; they offered a bold and irreverent vision. Some members of The Eight were also involved as committeemen in the second bombshell to fall on the astounded American art world: the color-splashed Armory Show (so-called because the vast exhibition was held in a New York armory) of February, 1913. Here the art *isms* of Europe were introduced to a baffled and, at first, angry, New York. Picasso, Brancusi, Duchamp (including his famed "Nude Descending a Staircase"), and Rouault vied for attention along with some American modernists. Teddy Roosevelt, never a man to mince words against trusts or esthetes, angrily denounced the art as "lunatic." Enrico Caruso sat on a stool and made mocking copies. One local art critic included in his review a jab at the immigrants of recent decades by sneeringly calling the works "Ellis

Island art." The show stayed in New York for a month, then went on to Chicago and Boston. It was front-page news wherever it appeared. It was nothing less than a new way of looking at the world, and in a few decades everything from advertisements to eggbeaters to bank buildings was to be influenced by this International Exhibition of Modern Art. The 69th Regiment Armory, at Lexington Avenue and Twenty-fifth Street in New York, is hallowed ground for many American artists.

In another direction, pioneer Alfred Stieglitz and his devoted follower, Edward Steichen, were proving that photography could be art long before museums ever thought of offering photography exhibitions. The amazing Stieglitz was also one of the early advocates of modern art and in 1905 he founded the Photo-Secession Gallery in New York. Here he introduced the newest and best in European and American art. In 1912, Picasso sent Stieglitz a large sampling of his work. Only one drawing was sold—for $12. But change—though agonizingly slow—was in the wind.

The gay colors of revolt were also brightening the world of dance and music. Isadora Duncan was impudently taking off the Victorian corsets—and her shoes and stockings as well. She danced barefoot in a filmy and abbreviated Greek tunic; indeed, she danced in the nude for select gatherings. Performing mostly in Europe in self-imposed exile, she angrily denounced an "artistically ugly" America as not ready for her. But in her dance concerts in the U.S. in 1908, 1911, 1915, and her last in 1922, she represented a New America to the young. True, many Americans were not prepared for Isadora and her modern dance, her scandalous personal life (she bore three children out of wedlock, scorning the convention of marriage), and her lectures in later years extolling the flaming red flag of revolution. (Incidentally, one of her children, Deirdre, was born of a tempestuous liaison with theatre theorist Gordon Craig.) But she was a sweeping, irresistible force in the new feminism, and she was directly responsible for the flood of barefoot dancers on two continents prior to and after 1910.

In America, she also influenced countless numbers of painters and sculptors. Isadora was, of course, the mother of Modern Dance, offering movement from what she called the "soul," free, spontaneous, emotional dancing. She influenced ballet as well as Modern Dance, and Michel Fokine once stated she was an inspiration for his own revitalization of Russian choreography. Fokine's work was introduced to Americans at the same time Isadora was expressing her "soul." His *Dying Swan* was danced by Anna Pavlova in New York in 1910, during the first of her many American tours. When Diaghilev's Ballets Russes, which had burst upon a startled and delighted Paris in 1909, finally came to New York in 1916, it was Fokine's *Petrouchka, Scheherazade,* and *Les Sylphides* which captivated the natives, as did the riotously colored, opulent costumes and settings by Leon Bakst and, of course, the stunning performances of a muscular young dancer named Nijinsky.

Isadora's influence on American culture was incalculable. So was that of Ruth St. Denis, Modern Dance's second mother. St. Denis danced barefoot, too, creating at first somewhat spurious, highly imaginative Oriental dances. After a brief stint as an actress with Mrs. Leslie Carter's company, she gave her first complete dance recital in New York in 1906 and then toured the world. She married dancer Ted Shawn in 1914, and together they founded the Denisshawn School. The most significant of their artistic children were Doris Humphrey and Martha Graham.

Vital critic in this pioneering time was Carl Van Vechten, who died in 1964 at the age of eighty-four. Between 1906 and 1913, primarily as critic for *The New York Times,* Van Vechten was of enormous assistance in interpreting the puzzling new forms of art to Americans. He was one of our first cosmopolitan critics, surpassing his elder rival, James Gibbons Huneker, in his amazing catholicity of taste and interests. He wrote knowingly of the theatre designs of Appia and Craig. Read today, his critiques of Isadora Duncan's concerts in New York vividly recreate an era. Perhaps even more important, however, were his music pieces. He could write with equal brio and keen appreciation about opera's Mary Garden or Parisian music-hall artist Yvette Guilbert. He praised Stravinsky, Satie, and Schoenberg in a period when they were practically unknown in America. Widely traveled, he knew Europe's musical counterpoint in intimate detail; he was the first

American critic, for example, to make a thorough study of the music of Spain.

The most searching of all the critics of this pregnant period was a misshapen dwarf named Randolph Bourne, who wrote pieces for a large number of the little magazines. Had he not died prematurely in 1918 at the age of thirty-two, he would undoubtedly have emerged as the finest social-cultural critic our nation has produced. In Bourne's four slender volumes and his many magazine essays, he explored American education, city planning and the lack of it, our shoddy cultural values, and institutionalized religions with a perception, daring, and erudition that were breathtaking. In the field of literature, he was one of the first to offer warm, generous appreciation for Maxim Gorky's work abroad and Theodore Dreiser's at home. When the United States entered the "war to end all wars" in 1917, he attacked our official policy with courage, bitterly and eloquently opposing such esteemed intellectual organs as *The New Republic* and such eminent thinkers as John Dewey in their base capitulation to Mars.

This remarkably fertile era encompassed in a momentous world view both the Mexican Revolution of 1910 and the Russian Revolution of 1917. It was a hospitable, germinal time for American culture—and for the birth of the theatre arts. In the whirling kaleidoscope of change, note David Wark Griffith, producing his extraordinary silent films which created nothing less than a grammar of film-making. The greatest of the celluloid comics, Charles Chaplin, made his first film in 1913. Upton Sinclair's crusades, the unvarnished novels of Frank Norris and Dreiser, Jack London's heady mixture of socialism and melodramatic adventure—these were a few of the forces sweeping away the cobwebs of McKinley Era mustiness. In 1912, Harriet Monroe started her magazine, *Poetry*, in Chicago, and it was at its best in those early years. Too, *The Little Review* was edited in Chicago by Margaret Anderson and her constant companion, jane heap (she preferred the lower case). This very literary magazine nurtured such unusual talents as poets Hart Crane and Lola Ridge and novelist Djuna Barnes, and first introduced James Joyce to American readers. Amy

Lowell, Vachel Lindsay, Carl Sandburg, and Edgar Lee Masters were, in differing ways, injecting vitality into American poetry. The accomplishments—in every sector of the arts—were myriad and often splendid. In brief, a nation was in labor, and the next event was inevitable. The stage was set for a most dramatic birth.

CHAPTER 2

THE BIRTH

THE ACTUAL BIRTH of American drama took place in New York's Greenwich Village, the indisputable center of cultural ferment in the 1910's. There have been other Bohemias in America—in Chicago, San Francisco, Taos, Big Sur, and Venice, but the Village remains the mother of them all, the national symbol of revolt and freedom for the artist. The Village's finest hours were in its early years as a Bohemia, when rents were low, the Federal and Greek Revival houses were not threatened by skyscraping apartment-buildings, and commercialized Bohemianism was unknown. Too, the resident artists lacked the self-conscious "I-am-a-Bohemian" attitude so prevalent today. Their rebellion was bracing and fervent. One can capture some of that gay and bold spirit in the early poems and stories of playboy-reporter-rebel John Reed, who came from Seattle via Harvard to make Greenwich Village his school and his playground.

Perhaps that elusive state of mind, the Village, began about 1910, for it was in that year socialist Piet Vlag started plans for *The Masses,* which impudent journal, a curious mixture of Karl Marx and Puck, became recognized as the leading Village voice. Art Young, George Bellows, Jo Davidson, Robert Minor, William Carlos Williams, John Sloan, Max Eastman, Floyd Dell, and John Reed were among its talented and gaily irreverent contributors. *The Masses,* as Floyd Dell explained years later, stood for "fun, truth, beauty, realism, freedom, peace, feminism." There were a number of other little magazines, too. Edited by poet James Oppenheim, *The Seven Arts* was one that called for a cultural revolution in America, rather than a political one, as advocated by *The Masses*. Its editorial associates included Van Wyck Brooks and Waldo Frank. Some busy writers contributed to practically all the fertile journals; for example, Randolph Bourne, whose luminous spirit was destroyed by the first Great War, wrote for *The Masses, The Seven Arts, The Dial, The New Republic,* and several less familiar ones.

Two Village meeting places were the cradles of American drama —one an elegant abode on lower Fifth Avenue and the other a somewhat seedy club on MacDougal Street. First, a visit to Mabel's room. Mabel Dodge, a rich, ambitious hostess from Buffalo, New York, presided over the most successful literary salon in the United States. The time, 1913; the scene, a soignée apartment in a building at the northeast corner of Fifth Avenue and Ninth Street. In an all-white drawing room filled with delicate French antiques and dominated by a lovely Venetian ceramic chandelier, pale, aristocratic Mabel Dodge listened intently to her collected celebrities. As Edith Dale, this remarkable lady figures in Carl Van Vechten's *Peter Whiffle,* one of the bibles of Upper Bohemia. She also appears in Max Eastman's novel, *Venture,* as Mary Kittridge. After suffocation in provincial Buffalo (so she said) and a decade of luxurious living in a villa near Florence, Mabel was determined to bring culture to America. The lady Maecenas befriended many struggling artists. She even gave one of them, Robert Edmond Jones, a room to work out the scenic ideas destined to make him the nation's greatest stage designer. Later, this eloquent designer-director-producer became one of our most persuasive theorists for a new theatre of the imagination.

Mabel (a cut flower, Hutchins Hapgood called her) managed to bring every conceivable sort of person to her weekly soirées. Soon everybody wanted to be invited to 23 Fifth Avenue, from cigar-smoking Amy Lowell to jealous uptown hostesses. But nobody could successfully copy Mabel's original pattern. When there was an IWW strike, she would get tough, one-eyed tabloid headliner Big Bill Haywood to hold forth. When anarchism was in the news, she had Emma Goldman tell her startled uptown guests about that. When psychoanalysis became news, selected guests led discussions on the ego and the id. (Young Walter Lippmann presided at one such discussion.) Guests at the celebrated Wednesday evenings talked about everything—birth control, the single tax, cubism, socialism, and the latest ideas from abroad on music and the theatre. "They are a kind of propaganda for free speech," Mabel Dodge once described her Wednesday gatherings to an inquiring reporter. (Incidentally, years later she married a Pueblo Indian and lived in New Mexico until her death in 1962.)

Her tumultous love affair with John Reed, the handsome, strapping, rich hero of the Left, is now romantic legend. Mrs. Dodge met young Reed when she helped him financially with a theatre pageant for strikers. (The gilded Reed, once a Harvard Tory, had discovered the working man through muckraker Lincoln Steffens and his own uninhibited experiences in Greenwich Village.) In 1913, the passionate pair rented Madison Square Garden to publicize the strike by silk weavers in Paterson, New Jersey, for an eight-hour day. Two thousand strikers and their families were in the cast, and Robert Edmond Jones designed the panoramic factory settings with the Garden's aisles representing Paterson's streets. Fifteen thousand people packed the Garden. The pageant was an enormous success, the talk of the town. It was, too, a new kind of theatre, a landmark in drama as meaningful spectacle. But the significant thing about the ebullient Mabel, her loves, and her ever-changing causes was not only her direct influence on theatre and theatre people: more important was the fact that her salon cleared the air for experiment and for unfettered new ideas in every arena of American life.

A short distance from the Dodge drawing room was a much less grand meeting place on MacDougal Street. Often one met the same cast of characters at the Liberal Club one had just left at Mabel Dodge's salon, especially among the artists and writers. One would not, of course, find many of Mabel's rich friends. There was no perfumed, cut-flower ambience here, but rather the hearty conviviality of young, struggling artists with just enough money for a cup of coffee. It is astonishing that more has not been written about the Liberal Club, for it is supremely important in the history of modern American drama. When the club moved from the

Gramercy Park area to 137 MacDougal Street in 1913 after a split in which these Village leftists emphatically stated that Negroes were to be admitted, it became the center for all the fiery young rebels of the Village and, by extension, of America. Perhaps the unifying motif was a kind of vague belief in socialism or a left-of-center philosophy. Whatever, all sorts of new ideas burned bright on MacDougal. (Today, the same street is permeated with a slick Beatnik commercialism, peopled by uptown gawkers, motorcycle cultists, and rumpled, long-haired youngsters with a very fuzzy sense of rebellion against the American Way of Life.)

The Liberal Club occupied two large rooms and a sunroom on the parlor floor of a small house next door to what later became the Provincetown Playhouse. The walls were covered with the latest examples of modern art by members and their friends. There were high ceilings, open fireplaces, and magnificent mahogany portals. The furnishings were sparse—nobody had much money. But there was a piano and someone was always playing ragtime, the music of the moment. Dancing was spirited, and all-night Pagan Routs were held. These dances grew so popular they were eventually moved to a large commercial ballroom. Pagans were everywhere. Indeed, "free love" was the cry of the moment. Some Village girls fought the bourgeois institutions of marriage and prostitution (two sides of the same coin, they declared) by sleeping with practically everybody, and no one dared insult the girls by offering to pay for their pleasures. There was a kind of purity in the dedication to free love.

In the basement of the same building, Polly Holladay, a determined anarchist from Evanston, Illinois, served delicious food at low prices to members and their guests. Some people never bothered to pay at all. The cook and waiter was another anarchist, chubby, curly-haired Hippolyte Havel, whose chief claim to fame was that he had been the lover of the nation's number one anarchist, Emma Goldman. Havel was likely to denounce guests he did not like with the vilest epithet of all—"Bourgeoisie!" Next door to the Liberal Club was Albert and Charles Boni's casual, charming Washington Square Book Shop, where all the new and adventuresome books the Liberal Club members discussed could be bought. Most people came into the shop to browse and talk, however. Indeed, a passage-way was cut through the wall from the Liberal Club to the book-shop so that in a sense the club had its own library.

Perhaps never before or since have so many artists, so many "movers and shakers" congregated in one place in any American city. During the club's incandescent career, one might have met there John Reed, Lincoln Steffens, Max Eastman, Charles Demuth, Jo Davidson, Susan Glaspell, Marsden Hartley, Mary Heaton Vorse, Sinclair Lewis, Art Young, Theodore Dreiser, Louise Bryant (later busy with love affairs with John Reed and Eugene O'Neill simultaneously), George Cram Cook, Inez Haynes Gill-more, Helen Westley, Sherwood Anderson, and Big Bill Haywood. Everyone looking for new directions in American life seemed to find his way to 137 MacDougal. Lawrence Langner, a young patent attorney in love with the arts, often visited there, fascinated more by the artistic discussions than by the politics. Harry Scher-man (later to found the Book-of-the-Month Club) was a regular. Saxe Commins, a dentist who years afterward became the editor-in-chief at Random House, was a frequent visitor. (Commins was Eugene O'Neill's dentist long before he became his literary adviser.) The Village troubadour, tall, distinguished, Harvard-accented Bobby Edwards, entertained with his cigar-box ukulele. Young Harold E. Stearns, later to lead a celebrated band of ex-patriates to Paris, gratefully haunted the unconventional club. Even Upton Sinclair, that fastidious rebel, dropped by briefly but found it a bit too blowzy for his ascetic tastes. These were merely a hand-ful on the amazing ever-changing guest list at the Liberal Club.

Each week there was a lecture by a celebrity. Slender Alfred Kreymborg analyzed the new poetry. Vachel Lindsay chanted "The Congo." Alexander Berkman pontificated on anarchism. Christabel Pankhurst, the English suffragist, spoke enthusiastically of equality for women. Margaret Sanger discussed birth control. Along with these informal talks, the club staged sensational exhibits of the latest cubist art from Paris. Everything from abortions to Zoroastrianism was probed, analyzed, evaluated.

Shortly after its 1913 move to Greenwich Village the Liberal Club became the parent of several rather impromptu, loosely organized dramatic groups within its membership. Young aspiring actors, playwrights, and directors seemed to congregate here, then repair in small groups to Village apartments for experimental presentations of hastily written one-acters. (This kind of home theatre had been a growing trend in the Village for several years. In 1912, painter Everett Shinn, a member of the Ashcan School, had transformed his Village studio into a little theatre, writing and producing his own burlesques.) The Liberal Club became the center of some tenacious talents fed up with the commercialism and dullness of uptown theatre. Out of their arguments and dreams eventually came two revolutionary companies destined to transform American theatre—the Washington Square Players and the Provincetown Players. These off-Broadway theatres did not just happen. They were nurtured by a precious heritage of revolt.

As one triumphantly focuses first on the assembled Washington Square Players and then on the haloed George Cram Cook, the spiritual father of the Provincetown group, appropriate background music of hallelujahs should be played. Perhaps—for ironic contrast—a commentator might state that in the year 1915, when American drama was born off-Broadway, the following were hits in the Broadway quarter: *Fair and Warmer, Hit-the-Trail Holiday, Common Clay, Sinners, The Unchastened Woman,* and *Potash and Perlmutter in Society.*

And now—the Washington Square Players.

The Players really got under way in 1914 as a casual dramatic group within the Liberal Club and without a formal identity. These amateurs had performed a one-acter by Floyd Dell at the club, with a trial run-through at the apartment of Theodore Dreiser. Soon a number of the ambitious actors and writers in the group wanted a theatre all their own—a professional showcase. After a great deal of searching, they could find no suitable playhouse in the Village. On February 15, 1915, the Washington Square Players gave their first professional performance at the cramped Bandbox Theatre, which was well off Broadway on East Fifty-seventh Street. They had a capital of a few hundred dollars contributed by enthusiastic members. In the beginning, the admission charge was fifty cents. Plays were given twice a week. No one was paid. In the second season, however, there were salaries of twenty-five dollars, and plays were given three times a week.

The first director of the Players was Edward Goodman, who had been active in the Socialist Press Club and who wrote one-acters himself. Lawrence Langner and Albert Boni were the business managers. The organization was pleasantly casual, and everyone had a say about everything, even the office boy. Naturally, the group issued a manifesto of aims, and it read in part: "The Washington Square Players, Inc.—an organization which takes its name from the district where it originated—is composed of individuals who believe in the future of theatre in America, and includes playwrights, actors, and producers, working with a common end in view. The fact that the Drama League can recommend at the present time, as worthy of the attention of its members, only three plays running in New York (of which two are by foreign authors, while two productions are by English and part-English companies) is an incisive comment upon the present condition of the American drama. The Washington Square Players believe that a higher standard can be reached only as the outcome of experiment and initiative."

Just about everyone in the Liberal Club and in the Village submitted one-acters, and the Players produced more than sixty-five experimental one-act dramas during their heady existence. They produced plays by John Reed, Edward Goodman, Percy MacKaye, Lawrence Langner, Zoë Akins, Philip Moeller, Lewis Beach, Susan Glaspell, Elmer Rice, Ben Hecht, Zona Gale, George Cram Cook, Theodore Dreiser, Murdock Pemberton, and Rose Pastor Stokes. Nor did they neglect foreign authors, presenting, in the main, playwrights who did not stand much chance in the Broadway maze: Maeterlinck, Andreyev, Schnitzler, Chekhov, Molière, Ibsen, Benavente, and Shaw. The Players introduced a number of fine actors to the public too, including Roland Young, Frank Conroy, Glenn Hunter, and a young novice named Katharine Cornell. They did not neglect the scenic arts. For their first bill of one-acters, Robert Edmond Jones did the set for Maeterlinck's *Interior*. His fee, to cover expenses, was thirty-five dollars. The Players proudly nurtured another enormously gifted scenic artist, Lee Simonson.

Their existence was always precarious. In June of 1916, the group moved to the Comedy Theatre on West Thirty-eighth Street, a deserted playhouse leased from the Shuberts on remarkably reasonable terms. They continued here until the middle of 1918, when financial problems, the loss of key personnel to the army, and the general war hysteria forced their demise. They were resurrected, however, in April of 1919 under a new name, The Theatre Guild. For the next three decades, the Guild offered the best American and foreign plays of any management in the nation, and they competed directly with the commercial wizards of Broadway. But more later about that remarkable child of the Washington Square Players.

Perhaps the most valuable of the Players' contributions was to show the public what it had been missing, and they found an intensely appreciative following. If their partisans were not so numerous as they hoped for, they could console themselves with the fact that they were pioneers. And they could be pleased that some critics understood their purpose. A quirky man with an appetite for quality, George Jean Nathan supported many of their efforts with erudite jubilation. They found friends, too, among young critics Alexander Woollcott, Heywood Broun, and George S. Kaufman, who not only praised their experimental efforts but found time to argue and drink with them after hours. The Players showed a backward, conservative theatre world that entertainment could be more than a time-killer, that the stage could be alive and exciting to the mind and senses, and that drama could be literature.

A second landmark in the development of the American theatre was the Provincetown Players. This group is perhaps of even greater consequence than the Washington Square Players, since it nourished our foremost American playwright, Eugene Gladstone O'Neill. With O'Neill, American drama came into its own. Today, a Broadway theatre is named in honor of that gaunt, brooding, intense original, and it is appropriate, for he is the father of American drama, the first of our playwrights to be performed and studied around the world as a significant literary artist. Indeed, O'Neill remains—in the 1960's—our major contribution to world drama. No one has yet matched—in range and consistency—his passion and his power, though Odets, Hellman, Miller, Williams, and Albee have waited in the wings and offered, on occasion, brilliant turns on our stages. Unfortunately, this giant pioneer lacked the verbal gifts, a felicity of style; at times, an overwrought, schoolboy romanticism marred his scripts. But he gave American drama a new dimension, a grandeur. O'Neill had a sense of mission, and he pondered the human condition with exalted fervor.

But now, the Provincetown Players and 1915. This group, like the Washington Square Players, was an outgrowth of the amateur theatre activity within the Liberal Club. Many of the Provincetown founders and early participants were also members or camp-followers of the Washington Square Players. The connections between the two groups were many and tangled.

The Provincetown's parents and unquestioned leaders were George Cram Cook and his wife, Susan Glaspell, who lived in Greenwich Village's quaint Milligan Place. Both had participated in the formation of the Washington Square Players in 1914. Cook was an extraordinary person. Tall and powerfully built, Jig Cook was a university professor from Davenport, Iowa; he left wife and children to marry Susan Glaspell, a promising writer. Delicate, subtle, she was a perfect counterpoint for her robust, vibrant husband. A Greek scholar, Cook was a socialist with an Athenian accent, for he tried to relate the glories of Greece to the modern American theatre. His socialism was a modern interpretation, perhaps, of Plato's *Republic*.

Playwright-director Cook was not happy with the Washington Square Players—they were not experimental enough for his ambitious dreams. He was consumed by a desire more powerful than box-office success: he sought to revolutionize the American stage. Cook did not want to improve Broadway; he wanted to destroy it. He was primarily interested in developing new American playwrights, and referred to his dream as "a threshing floor on which a young and growing culture could find its voice." This rebel asked his fascinated listeners to ignore all the rules of Broadway, to create something entirely new. During late 1914 and early 1915, he urged his friends to write one-acters for the noble experiment, and in time, all sorts of Villagers, most of them Liberal Club members, responded to the idea.

The nebulous group, held together by Cook's dream, found their first showcase not in the Village, but in Provincetown, Massachusetts, which had become a small summer colony popular with Villagers. There they took over a fish wharf owned by Mary Heaton Vorse. The fish house was fifty by one hundred feet with a door at the back which opened to the sea and often made a perfect backdrop. The actors made their own sets. The earliest performances were lighted by four oil lamps held by hushed acolytes in the wings. A five-dollar donation by each of the Players (totaling thirty at the time) paid for the equipment. In the first season of 1915, there were no seats and the members of the audience were expected to bring their own chairs. The productions at the Wharf Theatre were a great success, most notably *Suppressed Desires*, by Susan Glaspell and husband Cook. A company which was to change American drama forever was born. They were to demonstrate that more often than not amateurs, rather than professionals, took the giant steps toward the future. (Many forget that such groups as the Moscow Art Theatre and the Abbey's Irish Players were started by gifted amateurs).

During their second summer at Provincetown, in 1916, the group introduced plays by a then unknown, unimpressive, hard-drinking vagabond, Eugene O'Neill. He had cautiously followed them to Cape Cod from the Village. He had two purposes in mind: one, he was pursuing Jack Reed's girl, Louise Bryant, and two, he wanted someone to read his trunkful of unproduced plays. O'Neill was both painfully shy and uncannily astute. That summer, he won both his objectives: he captured Louise Bryant, at least temporarily, and he saw two of his one-acters, *Bound East for Cardiff* and *Thirst*, produced with the kind of special fervor reserved only for major discoveries.

Armed with the playwright of the century, Cook and his associates rushed excitedly back to Greenwich Village. Cook found a theatre for his company on that same September day, a parlor floor at 139 MacDougal, conveniently next door to the Liberal Club and the Washington Square Book Shop. After several meetings in Jack Reed's apartment on Washington Square South, the group decided to open with O'Neill's *Bound East for Cardiff,* Louise Bryant's *The Game,* and Floyd Dell's *King Arthur's Socks.* O'Neill's début in New York in October, 1916, impressed a discriminating audience and won converts for the Playwrights' Theatre (the more formal title of the Provincetown Players). The success of the company was assured.

Under Cook the gallant group was not at all concerned with monetary success. Evangelists of the future, they were entirely engrossed in experiment and revolution. Their productions often lacked uptown polish. Sometimes a curtain failed to go up on cue; often props were lost. Rehearsals were sporadic. There were court troubles, because the theatre was run as a private club and was not licensed. Someone was always spending valuable time in court, vainly trying to prove to unenlightened bureaucrats that the theatre was not a commercial venture.

The Playwrights' Theatre continued as a dedicated Cook group until he departed for Greece in 1922. (He died there in 1924, and he was buried, most appropriately, at Delphi.) After his journey to Greece, the group at the Provincetown Playhouse was torn by petty squabbles; it was revived in 1923 with a new and quite different format, as a producing company led by Eugene O'Neill, Robert Edmond Jones, and critic Kenneth Macgowan. Plays were offered both at the Provincetown on MacDougal and at its sister stage, the Greenwich Village Theatre. The new organization continued sporadically in this altered guise until the late 1920's, when O'Neill joined forces with the Theatre Guild.

The pioneering Provincetowners presented most of ONeill's outpouring of great plays until the Guild's *Strange Interlude,* including *The Emperor Jones, The Hairy Ape, All God's Chillun Got Wings,* and *Desire Under the Elms.* They also produced scripts by Alfred Kreymborg, Maxwell Bodenheim, Paul Green, Wilbur Daniel Steele, Edna St. Vincent Millay (her *Aria da Capo* won enormous success), Djuna Barnes, Theodore Dreiser, Michael Gold, Lawrence Langner (his forgotten *Matinata* was the curtain raiser for *The Emperor Jones*), John Reed, and John Dos Passos. Jasper Deeter, who later founded a country playhouse not far from

Philadelphia, was a director. During various periods of the Province-town's history, the actors included Paul Robeson, Jules Bledsoe, Norma Millay (Edna's sister), Rudolph Schildkraut, Ann Harding, Walter Huston, Rose McClendon, Louis Wolheim, Walter Abel, Erin O'Brien-Moore, and Bette Davis. But the Provincetown's greatest gifts were a visionary, George Cram Cook; our leading theatre theorist, Robert Edmond Jones, who both directed and designed settings for the company; and our finest playwright, Eugene O'Neill. Riches enough.

Though it does not seem so vital in the saga of the American theatre's birth as the two groups just saluted, the Neighborhood Playhouse must be mentioned as more than a footnote. This theatre was established in a New York slum on the Lower East Side in 1915 by the wealthy Lewisohn sisters, Alice and Irene. A direct result of the Lewisohn family's philanthropic interest in Lillian Wald's model Henry Street Settlement House, the theatre was first intended as a diversion for the neighborhood children. Soon, ticket-buyers were coming from all over New York. Under the Lewisohn girls' guidance (Alice was interested in drama; Irene in dance), the off-Broadway playhouse became one of the city's most exciting shrines of the New Theatre. The Lewisohns attracted the best teachers from Europe; they employed such imaginative set designers as Robert Edmond Jones and Aline Bernstein. From 1915 to 1927, they offered a synthesis of the arts in theatre form. Here one could view a Japanese Noh play, a Norse fairy tale, a lyric drama drawn from a Walt Whitman poem, Burmese rituals, *The Dybbuk*, a ballet inspired by Andreyev, a medieval French mystery play in an Yvette Guilbert adaptation, along with Dunsany, Shaw, Yeats, and Joyce. In the later years, one could see a young Martha Graham dance in her own creations or a young Aline MacMahon perform in the rollicking and satirical *Grand Street Follies*. The Neighborhood Playhouse taught many New Yorkers to search for theatre in unfamiliar guises.

The heroic labors of these bold innovators did not go unimpeded to the next generation. The strident Kill-the-Hun atmosphere of the Great War (especially after our entry in 1917) stifled but could not altogether crush the New Theatre. Max Eastman, Floyd Dell, and John Reed were indicted for articles in *The Masses* said to have obstructed recruiting and enlistment. (That witty and benign cartoonist, Art Young, snored through the whole trial!) *The Masses* and *The Seven Arts* folded during the war hysteria. Still later came the holier-than-thou vigilantes and the severe repression of intellectual radicalism. The blood lust aimed at all varieties of socialists after the Russian Revolution was as fierce as the wild stampede against Huns and pacifists a few years earlier. The shameless hunting of International Workers of the World members was capped by the particularly brutal lynching of logger Wesley Everest in Centralia, Washington in 1919. A mob cut off his genitals with a razor and hanged him from a bridge. These years were pocked, too, by a series of bloody race riots, starting in East St. Louis in 1917 and coming to a frenzied pitch all over the nation in 1919. Hundreds of Negroes were killed and wounded in the rioting. It was all familiar to the gods of war.

But the New Theatre miraculously continued. The bridges that the new companies off Broadway had created could not easily be destroyed. A number of most happy events between 1916 and 1920 heralded a relatively healthy future. In 1916, Robert Edmond Jones was commissioned by the Ballets Russes to create settings and costumes for Nijinsky's new *Tyl Eulenspiegel*, a signal honor for an American. In that same year, *Theatre Arts*, one of the most stimulating drama magazines ever published in this country, was inaugurated: it continued its brilliant course until 1948. Arthur Hopkins, an unusual Broadway producer with *both* artistic sensibility and business acumen, had visited the European theatres, and his eyes were opened to the newest stage techniques. In 1919, Hopkins presented on Broadway Lionel and John Barrymore in Tolstoy's *The Redemption* and Benelli's *The Jest*. He hired Robert Edmond Jones as designer-costumer. Especially in *The Jest*, Jones proved himself the master of the new stagecraft, on as well as off Broadway. It was a sparkling event which afforded a larger public a glimpse of the New Theatre. Rereading Dorothy Parker's rave in the old *Vanity Fair* is to salute Jones's greatness. How well Jones had learned the lesson of Gordon Craig when he wrote in *The Dramatic Imagination:* "A good scene set is not a picture. It is something seen, but it is something conveyed as well, a feeling, an evocation." In that bountiful year, producer-into-artist Hopkins also presented on Broadway Gorky's *Night Lodging* (now known as *The Lower Depths*), with Pauline Lord, Alan Dinehart, and a promising young actor billed as Edward G. Robinson.

Theatre as an intellectual force, as an art of passion and commitment, was here to stay. It had been a long gestation, but the birth itself was lusty, a cry of joy and wonder. The new child miraculously survived the war and found new strength in its best years, from 1920 to 1940.

CHAPTER 3

ROLLED STOCKINGS AND BOOTLEG GIN

THE MOST VIVID, fervent, and fruitful years of the American theatre were the 1920's. Perhaps this was so because these were the earliest years of promise. Certainly the prevailing ambience was one of great expectations. Reread Oliver Sayler's *Our American Theatre* or Kenneth Macgowan's *Footlights Across America*, both published in the twenties, and your heart will break a little. For the intellectuals of the period saw a splendid theatre future just around the corner. Today, our theatre is bleak and arid, and only implacable optimists can discern outlines of any promise at all for tomorrow.

The twenties were a glorious time of revolt, a rebellion against the stuffy middle-class conventions of the pre-war world. It was not a political revolt in the obvious, sloganeering sense; it was a gay, bright, festive revolt against provincialism, pomposities, and false sermonizing of all kinds, most especially against hypocritical sex. The twenties were that saucily cheerful time of bobbed hair and short skirts, women with the vote, bootleg gin and the speakeasy, the flapper and the sheik, the Charleston and the Black Bottom, and nearing the decade's end, a time of intellectual and emotional sympathy for anarchists Sacco and Vanzetti. Following the follies and brutalities of World War I, hedonism, disillusion with the Establishment's proprieties, religious skepticism, and a general thumbing of the nose at inflated misleaders were the new values—or non-values, if you prefer—of the Lost Generation, the Flaming Youth of the Jazz Age. Emancipated ladies were insolently drinking and smoking in public to a degree hitherto unknown. Insouciant Clara Bow replaced inscrutable Theda Bara as the popular girl of one's dreams. Movies bore such piquant titles as *The Perfect Flapper, Rolled Stockings,* and *Our Dancing Daughters.* "Makin' Whoopee" and "Yes, Sir, That's My Baby" were the new hymns of joy.

Internationally, strutting Benito Mussolini had become the Duce of Italian fascism, but only a few discerning minds saw fascism's inherent threat to the world. A shaky, impoverished Weimar Republic was struggling for solvency and freedom in Germany, and the victorious Bolsheviks were trying to repair a ravaged Union of Soviet Socialist Republics. In the United States, the decade started badly. President Wilson's third attorney general, A. Mitchell Palmer, aspired to the White House himself and divined that the way to that Irish Palladian mansion was to create a witch-hunt. His crude illegalities and midnight raids on private homes and labor headquarters alike remain one of the more infamous escapades in our history. Thousands of innocent persons—socialists of all stripes, anarchists, IWW'ers, and a mixed bag of liberals— were thrown into jail on vague charges, only to be released later. Palmer then stated that on May 1, 1920, the radicals planned to overthrow the government. The National Guard was called out, and in New York the entire police force was on twenty-four-hour duty. When nothing at all happened, the country suddenly began to laugh at Palmer's aberrations. One felicitous event came out of these paranoid forays: the American Civil Liberties Union was founded in 1920 to fight for the constitutional liberties of liberals and radicals falsely arrested. After Palmer's incredible overture, the decade settled down to fun and games. After all, everybody with a thirst for drink was happily breaking the law. And, after all, handsome Warren Gamaliel Harding and his breezily corrupt pals were in the White House, and Harding's "normalcy" meant enterprise at its most free for the boys with the gift of grab. Harding was followed by silent and ineffectual Calvin Coolidge, who practiced a breathtakingly magnanimous laissez-faire policy in dealing with trusts and cartels. Herbert Hoover and the Wall Street Crash were both to come in 1929, and Hoover was to order Federal troops to shoot veterans clamoring for bonuses. But why bother with politics? Politics, to this gay generation, was merely a silly game for politicians.

Perhaps the literary tone of the times was established by two magazines, *The Smart Set* and *The American Mercury*. Under H. L. Mencken and George Jean Nathan, *The Smart Set* continued from 1914 until 1923, whereupon the duo devoted themselves to *The American Mercury*. Mencken, the Bad Boy of Baltimore, was the greatest debunker of them all. (William E. Woodward, in a 1923 novel called *Bunk*, had coined the word, "debunking.") Mencken and Nathan attacked the "booboisie," the genteel tradition in culture, and the Puritanical ethos in morals. *The Smart Set* published F. Scott Fitzgerald's first short story. Fitzgerald's 1921 novel, *The Beautiful and the Damned*, supplied the youth of the twenties with a romantic image suitable for imitation. In 1925, Fitzgerald was to create, with more discipline and sharper insight, his masterly portrait of the bootleg generation—*The Great Gatsby*. Sinclair Lewis, in 1920, published his subversive (or so it seemed to outraged conservatives) novel, *Main Street*, to be followed two years later by *Babbitt*. Babbittry became as much a part of the language as debunking. Theodore Dreiser, that lumbering, brooding giant of a novelist, continued his epic labors from an earlier period and offered in 1925 *An American Tragedy*. A new spirit was abroad, not just among a handful of intellectuals, but among an ever-widening audience. Certainly, John Dos Passos' *Three Soldiers* (1921) and e. e. cummings' *The Enormous Room* (1922) were war novels far removed from earlier heroic posturings and frenzied flag-waving.

A remarkable book of 1921, *Civilization in the United States*, was pivotal in the era's intellectual life. In it, a couple of dozen American writers called the nation to account as a land of boobs. They angrily declared that the U.S. was poor soil for art and culture, and many of them, including the book's editor Harold Stearns, set sail for Paris. The expatriates wrote for a series of rather precious, self-conscious little magazines, including *Transition*, *Broom*, *Secession*, and the *Transatlantic Review*. Gertrude Stein, or so the legend now goes, told Ernest Hemingway: "You are all a lost generation." F. Scott Fitzgerald called the time "the greatest, grandest spree in history." Urbane, cautious T. S. Eliot, too fastidious for the Left Bank, found a home in England, and his poems, *The Waste Land* (1922) and "The Hollow Men" (1925), provided rallying cries for these young Americans abroad, vaguely anarchist, rebels without a cause. They examined Joyce, Proust, the Bauhaus, cubism, Freud, and the Third Sex. Some dabbled in the surrealist and Dada movements of Paris, applauding when the Dadaists held a meeting and an art show in a public urinal. Some secretly dreamed of home, while many of their counterparts at home dreamed of Paris.

New York's Greenwich Village, which had pioneered new ideas and the New Theatre in the teens, burst into national prominence in the twenties. Suddenly, everybody had to visit the Village—at least once. Some came to gape and snicker; some came to wonder. But the Village forever after was to be plagued by tourism and commercialism. The twenties provided, in a sense, a watered-down acceptance by ever-larger groups of the burning, bright ideas of the earlier decade. The rebel pioneers quietly left the Village, leaving their Bohemia to newer and more self-conscious followers. Edna St. Vincent Millay became a safe saint.

A new critic emerged in the twenties, a man who rivaled the earlier Randolph Bourne in his astonishing range of culture. He was, of course, Edmund Wilson, and his urbane, reasoned, and iconoclastic opinions were to influence American letters into the 1960's. Receptive to new ideas, he wrote for a variety of little magazines. He praised F. Scott Fitzgerald but deplored his lack of control and his occasional sloppiness. He handsomely lauded *This Side of Paradise*, adding that it was "one of the most illiterate books of any merit ever published." He encouraged the early Hemingway but not without reservations. Wilson was an early admirer of Ring Lardner not only as a deft humorist but as a bitter, caustic critic of American life. Sympathetic to John Dos Passos' play, *Airways, Inc.*, performed at the New Playwrights' Theatre in the Village in 1929, he understood that it was a cleansing attack on soggy middle-class values; but he also was highly critical of its simplistic approach. In time, Wilson was to become the most perceptive all-around critic the nation has yet produced, unparalleled in the catholicity of his literary taste and erudition and in his broad social vision.

But the man who best captured the authentic flavor of the period was Carl Van Vechten, who in the 1910's had been largely instrumental in introducing Americans to the new cultural directions of Europe. In the twenties, critic Van Vechten turned novelist, the archetypal advocate of hedonism. Somewhat elderly persons today can quote lines and entire passages of his *Peter Wiffle* (1925) and *The Blind Bow-Boy* (1923). These and subsequent novels espoused pagan pleasures with a gay twenties' amorality deftly touched up with Old World curlicues of culture. If there was something a bit artificial in his work, something a mite too glossy, it at least marked a welcome advance over the earlier hypocrisy. Van Vechten performed another overlooked service. In a time when whites were patronizingly slumming in Harlem, loudly and offensively "discovering" the Negro, he applauded Negro culture with sensitive insight and genuine respect. He immortalized Harlem artists in his 1926 novel, *Nigger Heaven*, an ironic title referring to the theatre balconies into which Negroes were segregated. He was singularly free of color prejudice. At his celebrated parties of the twenties, he was likely to ask both Bessie Smith and Metropolitan Opera star Marguerite D'Alvarez to sing, and to present both guests simply and without fuss as great vocal artists.

In the theatre, the unquestionable star was Eugene O'Neill. He was the first major playwright to emerge from what is now a familiar movement, the rebellious theatre groups located outside the Broadway enclave, removed from Broadway by temperament and ideals as well as geography. Perhaps the greatest local splash of the Provincetown Players and their discovery, O'Neill, came with the production in 1920 of *The Emperor Jones*, with a sometime elevator operator, Charles S. Gilpin, in the title role. The play was directed by George Cram Cook, with designs by Cleon Throckmorton. Everyone came down to Greenwich Village to see what the crazy group on MacDougal Street was up to this time. Even the top New York newspaper critics came down to rave—on the third night. (They had been busy opening night with some now-forgotten Broadway fluff.) *The Emperor Jones* was significant in countless ways. The most vital was that it was the first widely successful attempt by an American playwright to defy the strangle hold that a petty, unimaginative literalism held on our theatre.

In the same year that O'Neill won fame off Broadway with his expressionist *The Emperor Jones,* he also startled the commercial theatre on its own grounds and its own terms. *Beyond the Horizon* was produced at the Morosco on Broadway by John D. Williams, one of those rare men of the commercial stage who exhibited both taste and a passion for new ideas. George Jean Nathan had brought the play to Williams' attention. With *Beyond the Horizon,* O'Neill made a breakthrough into a deeper and more honest realism, no longer concerned with "good" and "bad" characters, with un-believably pure heroes and impossibly wicked villains, with con-ventional happy endings of goodness triumphant over evil. He dared introduce men and women who were neither saints nor sinners, but human beings involved in a complex everyday struggle. In *Anna Christie* (1922) he was to develop this new kind of realism further, even capturing the boozy, blurred smell of a waterfront saloon. Thus, O'Neill in these dramas and the prolific outpouring that followed in the twenties, won battles on two fronts: express-ionism and realism. By his immense vanguard efforts, he was the spiritual father of Miller, Williams, Hellman, Albee, and other playwrights to come.

In the twenties, O'Neill was produced everywhere, on and off Broadway, uptown and downtown, and he dominated both land-scapes. *The Hairy Ape,* first presented in the Village in 1922, was another excursion into expressionism, with Louis Wolheim as the unforgettable brutish, brutalized American. O'Neill defiantly pointed to class divisions within democracy. *All God's Chillun,* at the Provincetown Playhouse in 1923, was a pioneer drama about a mixed marriage, with Paul Robeson as the husband. *Desire Under the Elms,* premiered by the Provincetown Players at the Greenwich Village Theatre in 1924, was later moved to Broadway. The police intervened, and the immoralists were taken to court for depicting lust on a New England farm. Reason prevailed, however, and the play went on. In *The Great God Brown,* produced in 1926 by O'Neill himself, with Kenneth Macgowan and Robert Edmond

Jones, the Greek mask was introduced in those passages portraying man's idealized self in contrast to man as he really is. *Strange Interlude* (1929) began O'Neill's collaboration with the Theatre Guild, and that giant drama was the talk of New York, with its startling and frank soliloquies, its unusual asides, and its commanding star, Lynn Fontanne. It was really three three-act plays. One went to the theatre in the afternoon, returned after a dinner intermission, and then stayed on into the long night.

Once-backward Broadway was now dominated by Eugene O'Neill, graduate of the off-Broadway avant-garde. Broadway hacks observed the unfamiliar scene in disbelief. Perhaps I paint too rosy a picture. The Babbitts were still everywhere and all-important. Only the Pasadena Playhouse was unafraid in 1928 to tackle O'Neill's *Lazarus Laughed,* a wild excursion into the mind's interior, a fantasia of the unconscious. Broadway wouldn't touch it. However, O'Neill had won an epochal battle for all of us. He gave to his contemporaries and to future generations new perspectives for the theatre. Others were encouraged to write for the stage as a serious art form. O'Neill is one of the handful of American playwrights who may be said to have "size." Even his failures were on a grand scale. He proved that American plays could also be literature. Too, he was the first American playwright to win enthusiastic acceptance abroad as a major world artist. In fact, Europe was astonishingly quick to accept him. By 1925, his works were being performed in London, Berlin, Paris, Stockholm, Dublin, and Moscow.

Just as O'Neill was the decade's paramount playwright, so the Theatre Guild was the supreme producing organization. The Guild was now determined to beat the commercial theatre of Broadway in its own territory. And for a couple of exhilarating decades, it did just that, presenting both new American and European plays and classics with a force and a passion and a distinction no longer with us. Indeed, the Guild list of dramas in the twenties, incredibly varied, rich, and cosmopolitan, has never been surpassed by any other producing group. From 1919 to 1929, this organization offered a variety of Shavian works, including the antiwar masterpiece, *Heartbreak House,* and the shimmering *Saint Joan,* along with plays by Kaiser, Toller, Werfel, Tolstoy, Andreyev, Strindberg, Claudel, Molnar, Čapek, Copeau, Pagnol, and Obey. The Guild's American list included, in this and succeeding decades, Robert E. Sherwood, Sidney Howard, S. N. Behrman, Philip Barry, Maxwell Anderson, and William Inge, as well as the towering O'Neill. In its first miraculous decade, the group offered seventy productions, with a subscription list of more than thirty-two thousand members. In the early years, the Guild had been ensconced in the old Garrick Theatre on Thirty-fifth Street, leased to them by financier-philanthropist-art patron Otto Kahn for a nominal fee. By 1925, they were so successful they built their own splendid showcase in Fifty-second Street near Eighth Avenue. It is today the ANTA Theatre.

In its first heroic years, the Guild attempted to form an acting company and hold it together. It was a noble if unsuccessful attempt. Equally unsuccessful was its short-lived acting school (the students included Lucia Chase, Sylvia Sidney, Arlene Francis and Cheryl Crawford). The Guild remained a sterling producing company. It never became permanent in the sense of a solid nucleus of actors; it was never a repertory troupe. But the roster of mummers in Guild productions was remarkable for both its stars and minor performers, including Eva Le Gallienne, Joseph Schildkraut, the Lunts, Dudley Digges, Armina Marshall, Helen Westley, Harold Clurman, Philip Loeb, Edward G. Robinson, Morris Carnovsky, Sanford Meisner, Laura Hope Crews, Margalo Gilmore, Beryl Mercer, and Winifred Lenihan. Some have since prospered as directors, teachers, and producers; a few have helped found additional theatre groups.

Other producers of the twenties, sensing profits in the Guild's shrewd sponsorship of quality theatre from abroad, brought over welcome attractions. The list is a long and distinguished one—Nikita Balieff's gay Russian vaudeville known as *Chauve-Souris;* André Charlot's *Revue of 1924,* which introduced Beatrice Lillie and Gertrude Lawrence to lucky Americans; Max Reinhardt's awesome *The Miracle;* the Irish Players, with O'Casey's *Juno and the Paycock, The Plough and the Stars,* and *The Silver Tassie;* Moscow's Habimah Players in *The Dybbuk;* Michio Ito's Players from Japan; Mei Lan-fang and his company in Chinese classics. Perhaps the most seminal event was the New York début in 1923 of the Moscow Art Theatre led by the great Stanislavsky himself in inspired performances which shook the local performers; many learned for the first time what ensemble playing could be.

One of the gems of the period was Eva Le Gallienne's Civic Repertory Theatre. Its career, extending from 1926 to the dismal depths of the Depression in 1932, was disappointingly brief but astonishingly vital. Miss Le Gallienne, who had charmed New York in the Theatre Guild's production of Molnar's *Liliom*, was in her twenties and at the summit of her success. But she dreamed of repertory and ensemble acting and that intangible, theatre as art. So she sought backers for her own showcase. One backer who wished to remain anonymous gave her $50,000; Otto Kahn contributed $10,000; others chipped in lesser amounts. Miss Le Gallienne was determined to sell tickets at a $1.50 top to serve a large and eager new theatre public. She found, however, that not one of Broadway's booming houses was available to her: the owners feared her revolutionary low prices for tickets. Eventually, Miss Le Gallienne set up business in a cavernous, ramshackle theatre on West Fourteenth Street in a seedy, rundown neighborhood. The veteran playhouse, built in the nineteenth century, was large enough to make the $1.50 top practical. The key backers—and this has been true throughout the modern history of drama—were the actors themselves. They worked at a minimum, idealistically supporting a dream. The highest salary went to Alla Nazimova, $400 a week; on Broadway she could command a salary in four figures.

Le Gallienne opened her theatre with Chekhov's *The Cherry Orchard* and a memorable performance by Nazimova. Along with Chekhov, she presented sturdy productions of Shakespeare, Molière, Ibsen, and Tolstoy. The actress-producer did not neglect children's theatre (shamelessly ignored by nearly everyone else in this country), offering fanciful versions of *Alice in Wonderland* and *Peter Pan*. She did not attempt to develop new playwrights; she was content to develop a taste for good theatre. (In the sixties, the indomitable lady toured the nation as an honored guest star with new troupes, the National Repertory Company and the APA. She has much to teach us by her courage and her unswerving allegiance to theatre as art.)

A garland of cooperative ventures was created in the twenties. Most of them are now all but forgotten by the public at large, but they made priceless contributions and created a heritage, an important sense of continuity, for all theatre artists. Today's chief excitements and pleasures, found to a large degree in walkups and churches and cafés labeled off-off-Broadway, are intertwined in complex and fascinating ways with these earlier experiments. The past does create the future. The Actors Theatre, started in 1922, was a cooperative of actors which grew out of Actors' Equity. This group produced the expressionist *Roger Bloomer*, by John Howard Lawson, an American playwright dedicated to social commitment. Plays from abroad included a fine *The Wild Duck*, with Blanche Yurka and Henry Travers in a production staged by Dudley Digges. Though the group lasted only three seasons, it was important beyond its brief existence. Another experiment, the New Playwrights' Theatre, was dedicated to social commentary from the leftist point of view. It was aided by the ubiquitous Otto Kahn. (This singular banker-philanthropist is a key figure in American culture: he gave money to ballet, opera, symphony orchestras, the graphic arts, and modern dance as well as to the theatre.) The ardent if undisciplined company, which also lasted three seasons, explored neglected areas of American life, "discovering" the Negro, the unionist, the immigrant, and the radical long before it became the stage fashion in the thirties. The troupe produced, among other works, Upton Sinclair's *Singing Jailbirds*, John Howard Lawson's *Loud Speaker*, and Michael Gold's *Fiesta*, with joyous choreography by the vivid visionary Helen Tamiris.

The American Laboratory Theatre presented both native and foreign plays under the expert guidance of Maria Ouspenskaya and Richard Boleslavsky, former members of the Moscow Art Theatre. This Slavic duo taught local actors the techniques they had learned from Stanislavsky. Though quite small, the off-Broadway Laboratory Theatre had a profound influence on the future of the American stage. Young Stella Adler was a member of the acting company. Both Lee Strasberg and Harold Clurman studied there. In later decades, the Stanislavsky acting techniques were to be widely misinterpreted as *the* Method, most particularly via Strasberg's Actors Studio. Actually, many teachers and many schools were to present variations on Stanislavsky's methods.

The twenties saw a marked improvement in playwriting. In the main the writers became less glibly moralistic. Stereotyped characters and cliché situations, heavily tinctured with sentimentality, were now to be avoided. True, the sentimental breed did not altogether disappear, and sentimentality remains the bane of Broadway. But to an ever-increasing degree, mother love, glorious heroics in war, the purity and nobility of business, the infallibility of the church, the sacredness of marriage, and the divinity of virginity were re-examined in the harsh spotlight of reality. In addition, writers won important economic demands. The Actors' Equity strike in 1919 had emboldened the lowly scriveners to form a national Dramatists Guild. The authors demanded a standard contract and by 1926, one hundred and twenty-one dramatists announced that the theatre producers must accept a contract universal to all or do without their labors. The producers reluctantly gave in. It was a major victory for the American playwright, who had too often been treated as the poor relation at the feast.

Too, the director and the set designer were finally acknowledged in the twenties, with Broadway profoundly influenced by the off-Broadway rebels in these artistic concerns. Before this time, the director was seldom mentioned on Broadway or in the press, hiding behind the mask of producer, artistic manager, or some other title. He was to become—and rightly so—a dominant figure in this and succeeding decades. The set designer also came into his own, under the magnetic influence of explorers Robert Edmond Jones and Lee Simonson. These men became prestigious names on any playbill, along with such scenic artists as Boris Aronson, Donald Oenslager, Jo Mielziner, and Norman Bel Geddes.

Among the American playwrights who came forward on Broadway was Elmer Rice, who had already concocted, for the Washington Square Players in 1914, *On Trial*, a clever courtroom melodrama of flashbacks. This testy playwright, with a lively awareness of economics and politics, wrote an arresting expressionist drama in 1923, *The Adding Machine*, a passionate diatribe against American materialism. In *Street Scene* (1929), he created a sentimental yet withal honest study of the sleazy milieu of New York's poor.

Maxwell Anderson began his long career in the twenties, though his best work was to come later. With Laurence Stallings, a Marine who had lost a leg in France, pacifist Anderson co-authored *What Price Glory?* Though today it seems irritatingly feeble in its attack on war, the drama was a more forthright and less glamorized look at the battlefield than was customarily shown theatregoers. The play was one of the few American efforts to gain overseas fame, excepting, of course, O'Neill's work. The ribald dialogue was strong for its time, and I relish the oft-told tale of the impressionable dowager at a matinee, who was overheard at the end yelling in a distraught voice: "Where in the hell are my goddamned overshoes?"

Philip Barry and S. N. Behrman were Broadway's most suave practitioners of high comedy in the twenties. In their particular genre, they still have not been equaled. Offering something new under the Broadway neon—a sparkling erudition, a broad tolerance, an ironic stance, and a casually worn breeding—they did provide certain civilized values missing from American stages. Barry's *Paris Bound* and *Holiday* were his most charming contributions. S. N. Behrman was perhaps the more mature and full-bodied of the two, and his *The Second Man*, produced by the Theatre Guild in 1927 with the Lunts, was a work of considerable merit.

Sidney Howard, who with Barry was a graduate of Baker's famed Harvard Workshop, was a social critic in a more direct fashion. *They Knew What They Wanted* was a highly effective theatre piece, written with contagious verve. *Lucky Sam McCarver*, a vastly underrated play, examined our lack of values from both the top and the bottom. *The Silver Cord* dissected a castrating mother. In *The Torch-Bearers* (1922), George Kelly made Broadway audiences laugh at the intensity of the Little Theatre movement (Broadway always enjoys a laugh at the expense of the avant-garde). In 1924 he created a much deeper comedy, *The Show-Off*.

It was a study of a familiar American type—the brash and presumptuous wheeler-dealer. A year later, he presented *Craig's Wife*, a solid study of a compulsive, dominating female. Robert E. Sherwood had his first success in 1927 with *The Road to Rome*, a drama touched with the civilized comedy which was his forte. His best work, however, was to be in the thirties.

George S. Kaufman offered broad American banter at its best —laced with skeptical wit. Today, most of his work seems too full of tricks, but the dry, sly, disbelieving mood remains useful in a gray world of gray organization men. Kaufman's work is cheerful burlesque, not profound satire. He was basically a collaborator. His one solo, *The Butter and Egg Man*, does not hold up, as was witnessed by a 1966 off-Broadway revival. Kaufman's best work was written with Marc Connelly. Their *Beggar on Horseback* (1924) should be revived; it is still pertinent. Borrowed from a German expressionist piece, the play gleefully analyzed the conflict of art and business, spoofing along the way assembly lines, giant corporations, pompous executives, and our barren Success fetish. It included some unusually imaginative staging, with several delightful dream sequences and a charming ballet, "A Kiss in Xanadu." Few dramas equaled its skill and punch. Kaufman was to collaborate with many another, Edna Ferber, Morrie Ryskind, and Moss Hart, but *Beggar on Horseback* remained his most memorable effort.

There were a number of fast, breezy, robust shows that did not hold up as works of art, but they did introduce a certain peculiarly American pace and cheekiness to our stages. These included the Ben Hecht-Charles MacArthur *Front Page*, and such hard-boiled (all sticky sweet inside) melodramas as *Broadway, Burlesque*, and *Chicago*. Heaven forbid that all theatre should be art with a capital A. Mae West proved in *Diamond Lil* that she was the most endearing female impersonator in American history. Bela Lugosi frightened the populace with his *Dracula*, and Jeanne Eagels made a stunning triumph out of a routine play about the evils of sin, *Rain*. Some writers introduced in the twenties did better in subsequent years, including Thornton Wilder, Paul Green, Edwin Justin Mayer, Samson Raphaelson, and John van Druten.

Perhaps an event of 1927 had the most lasting effect on the

theatre, at least in the economic sense. In April, Samson Raphael-son's repulsively hearts-and-flowers *The Jazz Singer*, with George Jessel in the lead, ran only eighteen performances on the stage. Later in the same year, it became the first successful talkie, with Al Jolson in the Jessel role. Mr. Jolson broke the sound barrier by singing, in blackface, a tasteless tune titled "Mammy." That cinematic scoop forever changed the face of American theatre. Ever since, the stage has been threatened by the roving camera. Television later spelled even more trouble. The facts: in 1928 there were seventy first-class legitimate theatres in New York; by 1969 the number had dropped to thirty-three. In the 1927–28 season there were two hundred and eighty new productions on Broad-way; in the sixties, that figure often dipped to well under fifty.

4

BREADLINES
AND THE
NEW DEAL

HISTORIANS OFTEN DIVIDE the twenties and thirties too sharply and mechanically, for in perspective they fall together. Both were decades of revolt. In the twenties, the revolt was gay and personal and unprogrammatic. Against the thirties' stark and bitter panorama of the Depression and the rising threat of world fascism, it deepened into a political revolt with New Deal, quasi-socialist overtones. Though the two decades differed in tone and texture, they were intimately related in their profound sense of dissatisfaction with yesterday's rules and conventions. They were more akin to each other than to the succeeding decades of gloom and retreat, of atomic threats and counterthreats, of witch-hunts and cold wars and hot lines.

The thirties properly began in October of 1929 with the stock market crash. *Variety*, the Broadway trade paper, put it inelegantly: "Wall Street Lays An Egg." The crash began a period of harrowing poverty for millions of Americans. Breadlines, rent strikes, unemployment marches bloodied by police brutality—these were the signs of the times. The Land of Opportunity had suddenly collapsed. In the rest of the world, the news was equally ominous. Hitler came to power in Germany, and radicals, liberals, and Jews suffered torture and death in ingenious and most business-like camps set up to destroy all opposition to fascism; stating to the world that his final intention was the destruction of socialism and the Soviet Union, Hitler began his systematic annexation of powers to the East. Unhappily, several Dr. Frankensteins in the West gleefully approved the creation of a monster, applauding the plan to march to the East. In Spain, the republic was overthrown by native fascists, aided by planes and guns from Germany and Italy. It was a dress rehearsal for the war to come. The West stood by, meekly advocating "non-intervention." Mussolini contributed his Ethiopian adventures; the Japanese, allies of Hitler & Co., invaded Manchuria. Internationally and nationally, it was a time of dire but unheeded warnings and unbelievable suffering.

The intellectual climate of the country quickly changed from gay, impish, nose-thumbing revolt to a bitter, depressed mood a little left of center. The intellectuals were deeply affected by the dynamism and excitement of the New Deal. Some hard-nosed members of the radical right recall the thirties as the Red Decade. That is, of course, a gross exaggeration. The Communists were always a minuscule group who hoped to influence the country in a time of economic chaos. They failed spectacularly. However, there was a definite and important turn in national thinking toward economic planning, toward redistribution of wealth through more stringent taxation, and toward greater freedom for all. It was primarily a spiritual change, not at all a socialist takeover. Many intellectuals became committed New Dealers; some began to study Marxism. Certainly the nation's most balanced and learned critic, Edmund Wilson, began to take Marxism quite seriously. It was everywhere evident in his *The American Jitters* (1932), and underlay much of his literary criticism of the period. Even that charming gadfly of fashionable paganism, Carl Van Vechten, sensed a new temper in his *Parties* (1930). In the gayer twenties, Van Vechten had been New York's most celebrated party-giver, urbanely mixing royalty and penniless poets, Negro jazzmen and the curious rich. *Parties* suddenly took stock, and it was filled with confusion and misgivings. It was written with a painful, hangover nausea. The party was most definitely over, and *Parties* was the coda of the twenties. The boozy, disordered central characters were based partly on Zelda and F. Scott Fitzgerald, the flaming legends of the bootleg era. During the novel's alcoholic merry-go-round, someone casually capsuled the changing mood: "We're all a little tired." Fitzgerald himself obliquely caught the new spirit in his nostalgic, insecure, and moving *Tender Is the Night* (1934). The struggle for bread and rent became more vital than *Replenishing Jessica* (the title of an earlier Maxwell Bodenheim novel). In Greenwich Village, the see-the-artists-at-play commercialism prevailed, but tourists now visited the seedy Waldorf Cafeteria (later to become a bank) to watch the disheveled Trotskyists remake the world over bad coffee.

James T. Farrell, in his painstakingly literal Studs Lonigan trilogy, chronicled the Chicago proletariat, spattering his pages with four-letter words new to popular literature. Michael Gold, in an essay in *The New Republic* entitled "Wilder: Prophet of the Genteel Christ," attacked Thornton Wilder as a parlor Christian in the midst of child labor, strikes, and breadlines, branding him the "Emily Post of culture." Such savage literary broadsides were typical of the times. Gold himself completed his rousing, colorful, Messianic *Jews Without Money* in 1935. Ernest Hemingway, in a tentative, faltering style new to him, contributed his bit to the economic struggle with *To Have and Have Not*, and later limned the agony of Spain in *For Whom the Bell Tolls*. John Dos Passos was to join the parade to the left with his giant trilogy, *U.S.A.*, a panoramic look at an America gone mad. A hauntingly apt line from an Alfred Hayes poem, "In a Coffee Pot," summed up the attitude of the unemployed: "The agencies are filing cards of hate." Perhaps the tone of the thirties was best expressed in John Steinbeck's novel, *The Grapes of Wrath* (1939), a social document which poignantly captured the despair of the thirties—and the pleas for human solidarity. The harshest novelist of the thirties was Nathanael West, who, with his wife, the gay Eileen of Ruth McKenney's memoir, was killed in 1940 in an automobile accident at the age of thirty-six. West did not write in the prescribed leftist manner; his subtle work avoided clichés and easy propaganda. Yet two of his books, *Miss Lonelyhearts* and *The Day of the Locust*, cut deep in their caustic, horror-filled vision of the emptiness of American life. He will be read long after many a "proletarian" hack is forgotten.

The decade was rich in the contributions of artists in many areas. The American Scene painters, led by Grant Wood, Thomas Hart Benton, and John Steuart Curry, dominated the art world, with abstraction and non-objectivity temporarily bypassed. Under the subsidized Federal Arts Project, scores of murals, good, bad, and indifferent, adorned national, state, and local government buildings. A number of discerning painters, with sharp social comment coloring their work, emerged in this fecund period, including Ben Shahn, William Gropper, the Soyers, and Philip Evergood. The decade also saw several composers win international fame, including Virgil Thomson, Aaron Copland, Roy Harris, Walter Piston, and Roger Sessions. This was extraordinary, for America had heretofore lagged behind Europe in the creation of "serious" music.

Modern Dance, child of two mothers, Isadora Duncan and Ruth St. Denis, leaped into vivid activity in the thirties. Martha Graham, Helen Tamiris, and Doris Humphrey had all made their dance recital débuts in the mid-twenties. However, in the thirties, their immense talents deepened, influenced by the despair and hope of the times. They created powerful and lasting works of revolt. One of them, Helen Tamiris, introduced Negro spirituals and Gershwin melodies into dance as well as scores by Poulenc and Stravinsky. Someday the entire nation will properly honor the enormous contributions of these dancers to world culture, for they have pioneered in an art form as American as baseball, as indigenous as jazz. Photography as an art form elicited the attention of new groups of intellectuals in the thirties, and many flocked to galleries to admire camera viewpoints by Edward Weston, Dorothea Lange, Paul Strand, Ansel Adams, and Berenice Abbott, as well as work by pioneers Stieglitz and Steichen. A fresh and poignant social vision permeated much of their lens-work.

These dazzling developments stimulated the dramatic arts. There is in every period a profound interaction, sometimes on the surface, sometimes subterranean, among all the various arts. But, of course, it was the Depression itself that most obviously and radically altered the theatre. It was a matter of survival, for the theatre was seriously threatened by a partial loss of audience. During the early thirties, when Franklin D. Roosevelt was preparing his vast emergency measures to revive an ailing capitalism, half of New York's theatres were shuttered. In some showcases, tickets were reduced to twenty-five cents minimum and one dollar top. Some weeks, actors were paid; other weeks, they worked for nothing. Playwright Rachel Crothers helped organize the Stage Relief Fund so that actors might pay food, medicine, rent, and utilities bills. Actress Selena Royle helped found the Actors' Dinner Club, where meals were served for one dollar apiece to those who could pay and free to others. During one of the leanest seasons, more than 120,000 free meals were served.

It was a time when millions of Americans were poorest and when theatre was also at a low economic ebb. Paradoxically, it was also a time when our theatre was at its most exciting, when the nation's deepest spiritual values were revived and strengthened on stage. The most exhilarating experiments of the thirties were the Group Theatre and the Federal Theatre Project. In the arid sixties, these two groups were to become a golden albeit misty memory and an inspiration. They remind us of the theatre's limitless possibilities.

In certain ways, the Group was the rebellious child of the Theatre Guild. Many of the early members had appeared in Guild productions; many held minor production posts with the Guild. For these young theatre people, the Guild had lost its earlier glow. They detested the hit-or-flop psychology of the Broadway show-shops and the paltry definition of theatre art as merely something that is big at the box office; they despised the star system and flashy, exterior, rhetorical acting. They dreamed of a true theatre company, not just a marketing outfit—a permanent troupe of actors and directors and set designers, with a point of view and with a fresh ensemble style of acting derived from long and searching training *as a group*. In brief, they envisioned an American theatre which cynics have long held impossible. It was Harold Clurman, today a leading critic and director, who ignited the torch. During the winter of 1930–31, while he was engaged in reading plays for the Guild and appearing in bit parts, he fitfully outlined the idea of a permanent ensemble to some friends. In the summer of 1931, the newly formed group (average age: twenty-five), which included twenty-eight actors, seven husbands, two children, and three directors, spent the summer in a bungalow colony in Brookfield Center, Connecticut. Rehearsals were held in a barn. Their room and board was their only pay. The fervent band included

Cheryl Crawford, Lee Strasberg, Stella Adler, Art Smith, Franchot Tone, Morris Carnovsky, Sanford Meisner, J. Edward Bromberg, and Clifford Odets. Lee Strasberg, with the passion and single-mindedness of a revivalist camp-meeting savior, taught the group the fundamentals of the Stanislavsky System (Strasberg version, of course). With a wise innocence, they all deeply believed that with their own glowing commitment to theatre as art, they could somehow create something new. In its first summer sessions here and elsewhere, the Group entertained many distinguished observers, come to marvel at this strange breed of theatre fanatic. Novelist Waldo Frank and photographer Paul Strand came to praise; choreographer-dancer Helen Tamiris came to teach "body" classes, temporarily disabling Tone, Odets, and half the staff. Some members complained the dedication of the Group was too total and the zeal too puritanical, but they all stayed on—fascinated, hopeful.

The Theatre Guild, discovering these vigorous upstarts within its midst, was not altogether unsympathetic, and gave them a small capital fund. The Guild grandly donated to the insurgents the rights to Paul Green's *The House of Connelly* and presented it under Guild auspices. It was a good start. The play was a brooding tale of the decadent South, presented without *Gone With the Wind* illusions. The Group then tried Claire and Paul Sifton's blistering if rather crude indictment of capitalism, *1931—*, and it flopped resoundingly. With the smell of the Depression on every page, John Howard Lawson's 1932 *Success Story* was a sensitive if confused examination of moral choices in a sick society. It enjoyed a moderate run of sixteen weeks. A deserved failure was Maxwell Anderson's *Night Over Taos*, a pseudopoetic examination of the Mexican War, with settings and costumes by Robert Edmond Jones. In 1933, the Group had its first outright box-office success with Sidney Kingsley's *Men in White*, a rather pedestrian look at internes in a hospital. It was directed by Lee Strasberg.

With Clifford Odets, the Group found its voice, its own playwright. The Provincetown Players had nourished O'Neill; the Group Theatre nurtured Odets. At first, he was a Group actor. In 1935, fame came to both Odets and the Group with his first script, *Waiting for Lefty*, an urgent one-acter about a union meeting of striking taxi drivers. Whenever one young actor, Elia Kazan, prodded the audience directly with "Well, what's the answer?," the incited audience roared a rousing "Strike! Strike!" Coupled with another Odets one-acter, *Till the Day I Die*, a pioneering outcry against the Nazis, the short protest play had an intellectual influence far beyond its moderate run. *Waiting for Lefty* was performed in union halls and on labor stages all over the nation. When Will Geer produced it on the West Coast, he was severely beaten by Bundist hoodlums. In 1935 came *Awake and Sing*, Odets' best play. This strangely gentle tale of the struggle for dignity amid ugly poverty was directed by Harold Clurman, with Morris Carnovsky, Stella and Luther Adler, Art Smith, Phoebe Brand, and Sanford Meisner in the cast. Here Odets perfectly displayed his special talent for deftly combining ordinary speech and lofty moral lyricism into a personal idiom. One line remains unforgettable, the advice of an old man to his grandson: "Get out and fight so life shouldn't be printed on dollar bills." It expressed the essence of the Group's dream. The playwright's biggest financial hit was *Golden Boy* (1939), the somewhat too melodramatic saga of a violinist turned prize-fighter. *Rocket to the Moon, Night Music*, and *Clash by Night* were all done before the Group's dissolution in 1941.

Odets was not, as is sometimes supposed, a radical playwright on the barricades. Most of his plays were slightly Chekhovian tragicomedies of the American Dream gone sour. Both in his personal life and in his plays, Odets grappled with the true American tragedy, the widespread, highly contagious worship of a tawdry Success measured in terms of money and status. Odets' dramas constituted an open wrestling match with something seldom displayed on our stages, conscience. Odets, too, lusted after the wrong gods, and he never expressed this more bitterly than in his *The Big Knife* (1949), a sardonic, neurasthenic laugh at Hollywood. He never won his marathon wrestling match, and even his last play, *The Flowering Peach* (1954), a neo-primitive, Klee-like glance backward at the Old Testament, was strangely inconclusive. As for the rest of us, the whole subject embarrasses us in the Age of Affluence. We cover it by easy wit and nervous giggles. But Odets' theme was never more pertinent. His own death in 1963, while he was a fifty-seven-year-old Hollywood hack, was, in a sense, an obituary of the Broadway theatre.

The Group did promote other playwrights, of course. In 1936, the company produced Irwin Shaw's *Bury the Dead*, in which the author summoned six slain soldiers who could not rest in their graves until they warned the living that war is criminal as well as hell. Shaw also wrote *Siege*, a Spanish Civil War drama, and *The Gentle People*, pitting two old men against a racketeer. But he later turned to short stories, novels, and the films, never to regain his early theatre passion. Robert Ardrey was not introduced by the Group, but the company did present his *Casey Jones* and *Thunder Rock*. The latter was a good entry in the radical fight for world peace. Sweet anarchist William Saroyan was presented by the Group in 1939. The play was *My Heart's in the Highlands*, and it was directed by Robert Lewis. Here was a new writer of considerable charm, optimism, and fresh individuality. A few months later, the Theatre Guild produced his *The Time of Your Life*. Afterward Saroyan became mannered and stale. One recalls critic Van Wyck Brooks's great and true observation that America is a country of promising first acts.

Why did the Group Theatre die? One reason was that many of its people began to crave California gold. The first to leave for Hollywood was Franchot Tone, although he continued to aid the Group financially for many years. The disease of each-man-for-himself has always been the major threat to any cooperative theatre enterprise. And the Group's own leadership was severely divided in its later years. Furthermore, the Group did not establish a school or a theatre building or even a healthy subscription audience. But perhaps none of these provides the basic answers. The reasons can be found in American audiences and in American life. The mood of the nation changed after the thirties, and the New Deal passion for social change faded. The Depression and its lessons were easily forgotten by all too many. The search for values, for spiritual identity, was suddenly old hat. But for those who remember and retell the epic and for young off-off-Broadway idealists today, the Group Theatre symbolizes a special fervor and a sense of purpose. The Group members struggled for their goal. (At one perilous period in the early days, half the entire membership was sharing a ten-room, fifty-dollar-a-month apartment on the West Side, each taking turns cooking for Strasberg & Co.) The Group found—all too briefly—a rare and precious joy of community that will forever be above the squalid values of Broadway.

Today, one can clearly see that the Group Theatre enormously influenced the theatre of the next generation. Many former Group members are now leading producers, directors, teachers, and actors in the theatre, still gadflies trying to sting a sluggish theatre into art. Some, including Lee Strasberg, Cheryl Crawford, and Elia Kazan, formed the Actors Studio, both a school and a home where serious actors, always waifs in a society indifferent to the dramatic arts, could grow and discover new directions. In an artistic sense, such superior actresses as Maureen Stapleton and Geraldine Page are grandchildren of the Group.

America's most exciting experiment in Federal support of the theatre arts came in the thirties. Nothing of its astonishing scope has happened here before or since. It is a theatre phenomenon to be studied carefully by future stage seers, for government subsidy will come again. (Indeed, it already has, in various timid and tentative forms.) The Federal Theatre Project came into being October 1, 1935, as an activity of the Works Progress Administration, through which agency Harold Ickes and Harry Hopkins sought jobs for the unemployed. Hallie Flanagan, who had been production assistant to George Pierce Baker at the 47 Workshop and later director of Vassar's Experimental Theatre, was in command of the Project during its entire existence. Mrs. Flanagan had first been invited to the White House, where she discussed the theatre at great length with Mrs. Eleanor Roosevelt. They both touched on our heritage of Puritanism in relation to the stage and the sad fact that theatre was not accepted in America as a normal part of our education in the manner of European culture. Mrs. Flanagan was eager to do her duty, and she started the enormous task with unbounded enthusiasm for theatre and for the New Deal. She later copiously documented that stupendous experiment in her joyous and sad tome, *Arena*.

More than eight thousand jobs were created, with an audience of millions in forty states. Many of the theatregoers were seeing live theatre for the first time. The top admission price was one dollar. Sixty-five per cent of all productions were free. Over a thousand works were presented—Shakespeare, Marlowe, Gilbert and Sullivan, modern plays from Lady Gregory to Thornton Wilder, tent shows, puppets, ballets, circuses, special shows for children, and productions in French, German, Yiddish, and Spanish. New York was given six production units, since the theatre capital naturally had the largest reservoir of unemployed talent.

Many leading playwrights saw the benefits of this spectacular experiment, this unparalleled widening of the audience. George Bernard Shaw, in a rare gesture of generosity, allowed his plays to be done by the Project for a mere fifty-dollar weekly fee. Eugene O'Neill enthusiastically offered the same extraordinary arrangement. The Project presented nine Shaw plays, fourteen by O'Neill. America's noblest playwright presented the case admirably: "The theatre is becoming a great force in the life of American writers and in the history of our stage. It has been a tonic effect on me to think of my plays being done in places where, without Federal Theatre, they would most certainly never have been produced."

The most novel of all the Federal Theatre ventures was the Living Newspaper, which employed a staff set up much like a metropolitan daily (editor, reporters, copy desk, etc.). Playwright Elmer Rice, with his vast knowledge of world-wide theatre techniques, first handled this project of the New York wing, but he was soon to quit because of censorship from Washington. In the Living Newspaper, such pressing national problems as farm poverty, the harnessing of water power, and even syphilis were dramatized. The Living Newspaper editorialized, but it never expressed anything more radical than the familiar New Deal panaceas, contrary to some outraged conservatives. The best included *Triple-A Plowed Under*, *Power*, and *One-Third of a Nation*.

Some of the finest productions in the Project were under the leadership of Orson Welles and John Houseman. They had flair, and they presented a daring, original version of Marlowe's *Dr. Faustus* and an all-Negro *Macbeth*. They ran into great trouble, however, with Marc Blitzstein's *The Cradle Will Rock*, a brilliant cartoon-musical about unionization in the steel companies and an early American example of the Brechtian style. (For off-stage cross references, study the newspaper reports of the bloody Memorial Day Massacre at Chicago's Republic Steel, and the emergence of the dynamic Congress of Industrial Organizations.) The wire from Washington authorizing the premiere of *The Cradle Will Rock* at the Maxine Elliott Theatre in New York failed to come, so the performers marched a number of blocks north to the empty Venice Theatre. The audience marched uptown with them. Author-composer Marc Blitzstein played a piano on the bare stage. Some actors were onstage; others were in the boxes and the orchestra. Abe Feder, today one of America's top theatrical and industrial lighting men, bathed each performer in a circle of light. It was an intoxicating union of theatre and life. The insurgents who disobeyed orders were, of course, fired from the Project and deprived of their precious pay. But they created one of the theatre's great legends. Welles and Houseman then formed the Mercury Theatre, which continued to present *The Cradle Will Rock* and later a *Julius Caesar* in modern dress. Both enjoyed good runs.

The Project's incredibly varied productions included Obey's *Noah,* the world premiere of T. S. Eliot's *Murder in the Cathedral,* Aristophanes' *Lysistrata,* dramas by Lynn Riggs, Theodore Ward, and Virgil Geddes, dance works by Doris Humphrey, Charles Weidman, Katherine Dunham, and Helen Tamiris, and the musical *Sing for Your Supper* (out of which came Earl Robinson's "Ballad for Americans"). Elmer Rice's *Judgment Day* clearly depicted the Nazi menace long before such exposures became fashionable.

The Jewish Theatre unit created a chilling production of *Professor Mamlock,* by Friedrich Wolf, an exiled German doctor who also warned of fascism. Negro units in every major city presented both contemporary and classic dramas to new and excited audiences. Under Project auspices, Paul Green presented *The Lost Colony* in North Carolina, and started a trend toward historical drama produced as spectacle in outdoor amphitheatres. *Battle Hymn,* by Michael Gold and Michael Blankfort, told the epic story of John Brown, with inspired settings by Howard Bay. A Sinclair Lewis–J. C. Moffett dramatization of Lewis' novel, *It Can't Happen*

Here, another warning to Americans about the meanings of fascism, was perhaps the Project's most popular effort, and it was produced simultaneously by twenty-one companies in seventeen states—each production staged in a style all its own.

By late 1938 the Project was being undermined by Congress. Martin Dies, an illiterate Texan who headed the Committee on Un-American Activities, called Mrs. Flanagan to task and darkly intimated she was under the influence of the Reds. After all, had she not gone to Moscow more than a decade ago to study Russian theatre? The tactics were all too familiar: innuendo, guilt by association, headline hunting, intellectual terrorism. The entire Project, the committee apparently had decided, was under the wing of atheistic, depraved Communists. Individuals and committees in both houses of Congress grossly misrepresented the Project. The Congressional records are full of such tragicomedy. One industrious senator included *Up in Mabel's Room* (a Project production) in a list of plays "spewed forth from the gutters of the Kremlin." Witch-hunting of this nature was—and remains—a national sickness, perhaps an offshoot of our fanatical Puritan roots. Nonetheless, the Federal Theatre showed that the stage still retains tremendous power to stir up controversy and to provoke the strongest emotions, a power today unused and anemic.

One episode remains to perhaps amuse but surely shame the nation. A congressman by the name of Joseph Starnes asked Mrs. Flanagan about a Mr. Marlowe she had mentioned in an article for *Theatre Arts* magazine. "You are quoting from this Marlowe," observed Mr. Starnes. "Is he a Communist? . . . Tell us who Marlowe is, so we can get the proper references, because that is all we want to do." "Put it in the record," Hallie Flanagan replied, "that he was the greatest dramatist of the period of Shakespeare, immediately preceding Shakespeare." Later she recalled the bizarre Washington episode: "The room rocked with laughter, but I did not laugh. Eight thousand people might lose their jobs because a congressional committee had so prejudged us that the classics were 'communist'."

Let it be said, however, that practically every reputable theatre critic in America rallied to Mrs. Flanagan and the Project and sent telegrams to Congress to that effect, from Brooks Atkinson of *The New York Times* to Mrs. Euphemia Van Rensselaer Wyatt of *The Catholic World*. But it was to no avail. The Project was voted out of existence June 30, 1939.

The Project will not be forgotten. Many of its personnel have since and often contributed richly to the theatre. And it proved that millions of Americans are hungry for live theatre, if it is accessible and inexpensive. The oft-told inspirational tales of the Project performing before the Joads of Oklahoma, rednecks and share-croppers in the South, and blacks in the northern ghettos are now part of theatre legend. These and other millions are still there; many have seen only the most rudimentary forms of theatre. The audience awaits—today, now.

Of the vigorously and clearly left-wing groups in the theatre in the thirties, most deplored both the Group Theatre as too involved with psychology and the Federal Theatre Project as too eclectic and unprogrammatic. The most articulate and potent leftist group was the Theatre Union, which flourished for a few years of sharp social protest in the Fourteenth Street theatre abandoned by Eva Le Gallienne and her gallant company. Like most such groups, the Theatre Union did not get the vast support from labor it so earnestly solicited. It tried. The best seat in the house was never more than one dollar and a half. Perhaps its worst enemy was its doctrinaire and sectarian approach, an infantile plague that infested much of the radical politics of the thirties. For the Union, George Sklar and Paul Peters wrote a drama, *Stevedore*, about the unionization of Negroes in the South. Paul Peters adapted Brecht's dramatic version of Gorky's *Mother*. It was not a great success. The play remains an important one, but the company did not find the proper style and nuance for Brecht. They offered a vast number of thesis scripts—John Wexley's *They Shall Not Die*, about the Scottsboro boys; Albert Maltz's study of coal miners, *Black Pit*; Albert Bein's look at Southern mill workers, *Let Freedom Ring*. Some of these scripts were dramatically awkward and philosophically simplistic, but they did introduce material too long missing from our stages.

One union, the International Ladies' Garment Workers Union, plunged into the theatre business with a vengeance. In 1937, Harold

Rome's musical revue, *Pins and Needles*, opened at the Labor Stage, its cast composed entirely of I.L.G.W.U. members. The revue was sprightly and pert and full of lighthearted social comment. "Sing Me a Song of Social Significance" was a new kind of insouciant love song. No critics attended the opening, but they soon discovered it was a hit and hurried to the Labor Stage. The show ran for four years. Rehearing it today, only a madman would call it dangerous or subversive. Now, it seems just a touch too bland, a bit too sweet. Political cabaret sprang up, too, in nightclubs, social halls, and union auditoriums. Perhaps the best of the political cabarets (an old and well-established custom in Europe) was T.A.C., or more accurately, the Theatre Arts Committee for Democracy. This hard-hitting, talented, politically sophisticated group offered social satire on a level unfamiliar to Americans. They often gave benefit performances for the Spanish Loyalists and the International Brigades. The industrious artists even edited a bulletin of theatre news and gossip.

The optimism for some better if vague future affected everyone in the theatre. Even the more conservative playwrights felt the change in the climate, and they all began to tilt slightly left of center. Never before or since has there been such commitment in the theatre. Some of it was mere sloganeering; a lot of it was immature. Most of it was exciting and, at times, inspiring, as men realized how drama could influence other men's minds and emotions. A Broadway musical, *Americana*, provided the theme song of the period, the Depression ditty plaintively titled "Brother, Can You Spare a Dime?" Sidney Howard offered a number of dramas in the thirties. Perhaps his best were *Yellow Jack*, with Paul de Kruif, and his tender, thoughtful *Alien Corn*. In the unconventional spirit of the times, Howard startled his friends in 1932 by announcing that he was voting for Communist William Z. Foster for President. S. N. Behrman continued his graceful comedies from the twenties with superb craftsmanship, taste, worldly tolerance, and a sense of decent values. He was gentlemanly, quizzical, not too keen on joining the new causes but sympathetic to both the old and new worlds. In *End of Summer*, a 1936 Theatre Guild production, he unexpectedly presented a cast of characters who discovered the Depression, radicalism, fascism, and psychoanalysis. He treated all these subjects with his customary calm and balance. Urbane Philip Barry created a number of high-style dramas throughout the thirties, including *The Animal Kingdom* and *The Philadelphia Story*. He was ingratiating and trivial. In *Hotel Universe* and *Here Come The Clowns*, he tried philosophy. Here he proved sophomorically mystical. He was better at comedy without preachment.

In *Waterloo Bridge*, Robert E. Sherwood, a most civilized wit, fashioned a feeble love story with antiwar overtones. He somewhat resembled Behrman in that he was a man deeply concerned with the preservation of values. In retrospect, Sherwood lacked sharpness of attack, a firm grasp of global politics, and an unswerving commitment to change. *Reunion in Vienna* and *The Petrified Forest* appear excessively melodramatic and sentimental now. In the Theatre Guild production of *Idiot's Delight* (1936), Sherwood tried to come to grips with the coming World War. His touching *Abe Lincoln in Illinois* did provide the success and the force to rally a new theatre team, The Playwrights Company, with Sherwood, Elmer Rice, S. N. Behrman, Maxwell Anderson, and Sidney Howard as their own producers. The arrangement gave these playwrights a new freedom for awhile to produce as they pleased. But eventually the group fizzled out.

Maxwell Anderson poured out a large number of plays in the thirties, a steady flow of Broadway dramas good, bad, and routine. Once upon a time, it was thought that Anderson, who died in 1959, had a touch of genius. In retrospect, he seems mediocre. However, he employed themes of grandeur: he courted beauty. For that we must be grateful. "If we are to have great theatre in this country, somebody has to write verse, even if it is written badly," he once stated. "It is at least a beginning." He was right on all counts, including his own bad verse. But Anderson did seek dimension, the large gesture. In *Winterset, Mary of Scotland, Elizabeth the Queen, Valley Forge, Key Largo, High Tor*, and a number of others, he made an admirable and unsuccessful attempt at something beyond dull naturalism; however, he seemed to be shallowly in love with the stars of history, and he offered few pertinent insights into history's meaning. It was too often surface, albeit a surface glittering with theatricality. Somehow we must recapture the theatre of dimension to which Anderson clumsily aspired and which we have lost since O'Neill first pointed the way.

O'Neill continued writing in the early thirties. His *Mourning Becomes Electra*, a massive trilogy about a New England family, offered Alice Brady in the Electra role and Alla Nazimova as the modern Clytemnestra in an epic retelling of the Greek myth. His 1933 *Ah, Wilderness* presented O'Neill in a startling new guise, a writer of winning, sentimental, nostalgic comedy. *Days Without End* (1934) was a resounding flop, and he was silent for the rest of the decade. Thornton Wilder won enormous success with his insipid *Our Town* (1938). It may be remembered more for the dazzlingly inventive use of Oriental stage techniques than for the rather too pretty a portrait of a small town. Wilder is a felicitous and deft arranger of cut flowers. But his work lacks robustness and *merde*.

Such minor pleasantries as *Once in a Lifetime, Merrily We Roll Along, You Can't Take It With You,* and *The Man Who Came to Dinner* were concocted by George S. Kaufman and his bright new collaborator Moss Hart. Early in the decade, Kaufman created, with Edna Ferber, *Dinner at Eight*. It took a sidelong glance at the Depression, but it cut about as deep as a pinprick. George Abbott wrote and directed and play-doctored reams of scripts, most of them forgettable. But he did establish a Broadway style still celebrated around the world—fast, furious pacing. The only trouble was that everybody began to believe that nothing was good unless it was fast.

In 1939, Paul Osborn offered a charming and vastly underrated folk drama, *Morning's at Seven*. Cartoonist and savant James Thurber, one of the great satirists of the period, co-authored with Elliott Nugent a most witty comedy devoted to questioning the false values of a university. *The Male Animal* was also notable for its inclusion of a profound letter written by the anarchist Vanzetti.

Two scripts, neither of them at all important as dramatic literature, were destined to run on and on. Indeed, they remain the longest-running dramas in the history of the Broadway stage. First place goes to Howard Lindsay's *Life With Father* (1939), co-authored with Russell Crouse and based on Clarence Day's stories of a not-very-attractive father. It ran for seven-and-a-half years. Jack Kirkland's rather routine dramatization in 1933 of Erskine Caldwell's novel, *Tobacco Road*, offered titillation and shock as well as a few keen observations about the debasement of the Deep South. This one continued for seven years.

Other than Odets, the best playwright to emerge in the thirties was Lillian Hellman. Her first play, *The Children's Hour* (1934), was a good if somewhat contrived study of guilt by slander, a theme pertinent in all periods. A child accuses a couple of schoolteachers of lesbianism—and ruins lives. Her second work, a 1936 strike drama entitled *Days to Come*, opened and closed abruptly. In 1939, Miss Hellman created her masterpiece *The Little Foxes*, an uncompromising attack on an acquisitive society, without sentimentality or illusion. The Louisiana-born playwright specifically placed her vicious Hubbard clan in the American South, but she created a universal and timeless study of greed worthy of an honorable position near Jonson's *Volpone*.

The decade was to end with a razzle-dazzle World's Fair in New York, in which Eleanor Holm swam and Sally Rand waved her fans. On a sadder and more savage note, the decade ended with the start of a devastating world war. The road to war had been inexorable, a Greek epic in its foredoomed tragedy. Madrid fell to the fascists in March of 1939. In the same month, Hitler moved into Prague. After a period of the "phony war" and diplomatic maneuverings, Paris fell in June of 1940. Russia was invaded in June of 1941, and the attack on Pearl Harbor came on December 7, 1941. The Cassandras of the thirties, the "premature" anti-fascists, had lost. Their earlier and eloquent pleas to stop fascism in its infancy had gone unheeded; bloody war was here. There was little solace for those American playwrights who could say, quite correctly: If you had only listened.

CHAPTER 5

THE BOMB IS DROPPED

AFTER THE PASSIONATE and promising years of the twenties and thirties, the Broadway theatre went slowly and sadly into a long stupor. Unhappily, it has not yet regathered its energies. In the early forties, however, the decline was not so noticeable, for there were still happy reminders of the recent past and a certain continuity. To this was added a wartime élan. In addition, a suddenly prosperous public, eager for amusement, piled into the Broadway theatres.

As during all wars, the mood of the Second World War was mixed. The "premature" anti-fascists of the thirties fought side by side with men who had not the remotest idea of what fascism really meant. Many wily diplomats and statesmen maneuvered to turn the war from a truly anti-fascist battle into just another struggle for position among the powerful. With the bombs raining down on the great cities of Europe, the savage destruction reached a degree of wantonness new to mankind. Commitment and greed, nobility and butchery—they were hopelessly intermingled. At home there were black markets and rationing, profiteering and sacrifice. At home, too, 110,000 Americans were shamelessly herded into concentration camps, their only crime their Japanese ancestry. In a happier circumstance, many American women found new opportunities in a wartime economy which was desperately in need of all the workers it could get. For them (and most especially for Negro women), the war provided a giant step forward in industrial democracy.

The year 1945 ushered in another phase. In that year Franklin

Delano Roosevelt, the nation's father image, died, and the rest of the decade became the Time of Truman. The awesome weapon of destruction, the A-Bomb, was dropped by the American government on Japan's Hiroshima and Nagasaki in August, 1945. In Hiroshima, the Bomb razed four square miles of the city, killed altogether 80,000 men, women, and children, and maimed and disfigured thousands of others. The second bomb, which exploded over Nagasaki, slaughtered 40,000 more persons. To modern man's consciousness was added another burden. Belsen and Buchenwald had forever changed the modern world for many of us; now Hiroshima and Nagasaki taught us that world destruction was easily possible. To the screams and shrieks of organized murder was added a somewhat comforting note: the World War ended in 1945 and in that same year the United Nations was born in a San Francisco conference of fifty nations. But the peace quickly turned into the Cold War, with its insane round of fabrications, recriminations, and a macabre, hysterical roulette with the Bomb. In 1947, that magnificent old imperialist, Winston Churchill, coined the phrase "iron curtain," in a speech in Fulton, Missouri. There followed a long, hallucinatory night of Bosch-like fear, a vicious circle of terror. The U.S. and the U.S.S.R. were playing with the possible destruction of a planet, and to add to the nightmarish tensions, China, an awakening giant, went Communist in 1949.

In American cultural life, the glamorous posturing, heroic war novels of the past were conspicuously absent. Norman Mailer's *The Naked and the Dead* was not published until 1948, and its stance was critical, tough, and anti-heroic. These soldiers were confused men, talking a brutal, four-letter-word English not found in other prettied-up war memoirs. James Jones's equally bitter and biting *From Here to Eternity* came in 1951. Both books enjoyed spectacular success. A quite different literary trend was the sumptuous, sometimes fruity, neo-Gothic Southern School of writing. The still feudal South, with its racial and economic tensions, its outmoded codes of chivalry, and an extreme violence just below the magnolia surface, was a rich lode already mined by William Faulkner in labyrinthine prose. In varying styles and attitudes, Truman Capote, Carson McCullers, and Eudora Welty led the quixotic, slightly odd Southern miners. They explored personal relations in a still exotic setting, stressing the ultimate loneliness and the ultimate mystery of life. A Southerner distantly related to them, William Goyen, with an atmospheric, mythic haze of brilliance all his own, emerged in 1950. Other notable writers in the forties included Jean Stafford, with her precise, evocative, and almost Proustian prose, and Saul Bellow, introspective, fantastic and wildly comic. Vance Bourjilay and Paul Bowles heralded the Beat School which was to multiply in the fifties. Most of these writers shared one quality: they explored the complex underground of man's mind, not his actions in social protest. They were altogether unlike the "social" writers of the thirties.

The same lack of interest in protest, thirties-style, was apparent in criticism. The New Criticism was the tune of the day. It was a term coined by John Crowe Ransom in 1941, and its practitioners concentrated on the literary opus at hand as an autonomous work of art rather than on the author's background or the age in which he lived or the social point of view he was expressing. It was a limited and sometimes pedantic approach, and it was more often than not a conservative trend. It was perhaps the literary parallel of the tightening of the social reins in the political arena. A valuable counterforce was Edmund Wilson. His book reviews and his occasional long critical essays, mostly in *The New Yorker*, were models of sanity, wit, and social bite in the somewhat out-of-focus forties. He was a man who invariably and clearly saw the sinuous interconnections between the arts and politics.

Other cultural forces were simmering. Robert Lowell's first volume of poems graced the forties, and he was later to emerge as the nation's leading twentieth-century poet, with a witty, extraordinarily compact, deeply resonant, and very personal style. Lowell was one of the Boston Lowells, cousin to the equally unconventional Amy Lowell. He declined to be drafted because he objected to the Allied bombing of civilians in World War II, and he was jailed for a year. He was to continue to talk back to Presidents and policy-makers in the sixties, most particularly on the undeclared American war in Vietnam. Certainly, the appearance of Leonard Bernstein, with his virtuoso command of music, helped speed the world-wide applause for American orchestras and composers. Bernstein was a brilliant conductor who could also write with distinction in both the symphonic and jazz idioms. But it was in the somewhat rarefied temple of ballet that Americans both pioneered and excelled in the forties. The earlier periods had been dominated by ballet as an exotic import from Russia, a kind of vodka-and-caviar affair. In the forties, ballet emerged as an American art, with local dancers, local composers, and local themes. Eugene Loring's *Billy the Kid* had started the trend in 1939, but it was Agnes de Mille and her *Rodeo* in 1942, with an ugly-duckling plot set in the American West and a buoyant score by Aaron Copland, that won the new day for American ballet. Of the companies to dance in this decade, the dominating force was Ballet Theatre, which made its first appearance in New York on January 11, 1940. The company created an unforgettable impact in 1944 with Jerome Robbins' *Fancy Free*, a ballet about three sailors on shore leave, danced to a jazz-flavored score by Bernstein. It was a revolution at the rococo, gold-and-red-plush Metropolitan Opera House. Ballet had discarded its kings and peasants and sylphs and gone modern and native. This dance revolt was soon to make itself felt in the Broadway musical, with both Agnes de Mille and Jerome Robbins preeminent in revitalizing Broadway choreography.

How did the theatre express the war years on the stage? There was a series of war plays, some good, some bad, none of them brilliant. Most were too contrived, with pat moralizing. The list included Robert E. Sherwood's *There Shall Be No Night*, James Gow–Arnaud d'Usseau's *Tomorrow the World*, and John Patrick's *The Hasty Heart*, which became a perennial in little theatre and summer stock circles. Lillian Hellman, after her earlier masterwork, *The Little Foxes*, disappointed with her somewhat preachy *Watch on the Rhine* and *The Searching Wind*. S. N. Behrman adapted Franz Werfel's *Jacobowsky and the Colonel*, and Paul Osborn dramatized John Hersey's novel, *A Bell for Adano*. In 1940, Ernest Hemingway created a very bad and belated play about Spain, *The Fifth Column*. It was his only attempt at theatre. Thornton Wilder's philosophical comedy of 1942, *The Skin of Our Teeth*, was not at all profound, but it did offer a kind of rocking-chair, platitudinous comfort in the war years. Critic Alexander Woollcott, that irritat-ingly gushy man who came to dinner, was absolutely certain it was the finest play ever written by an American.

Two playwrights dominated the forties—Arthur Miller and Ten-nessee Williams. Though they were later to prove disappointing in both productivity and quality, they were then the theatre's brightest hopes. Both playwrights first appeared on Broadway dur-ing the 1944–45 season, Miller with a box-office failure, Williams with a hit. Miller's *The Man Who Had All the Luck* ran only four performances, but it showed a man of virile and supple mind, a man capable of resistance to a world gone flabby and corrupt. It was a fascinating flop. Tennessee Williams found success with *The Glass Menagerie*, in which the incandescent Laurette Taylor offered one of the richest impersonations of the century as the genteelly impoverished mother living among her pathetic illusions of Southern Belle-dom. In a jocular and slightly alcoholic mood, Williams once confided to a reporter friend of mine: "If it weren't for the Southern belle, I'd be up the creek without a paddle." He was to have paddles for a long time ahead. The concept of the Southern lady was deeply American. These women were hope-lessly given to fantasizing their social position. Williams' class-con-scious women, whether mothers or whores, shared one trait: they all had delusions of social grandeur.

Throughout the decade, Miller's and Williams' dramas were major events. Miller offered *All My Sons* in the 1946–47 season. In the blunt tradition of the social-protest theatre of the thirties, this well-made but overly melodramatic play angrily attacked the chiseling manufacturers who lined their pockets in wartime, even if it meant endangering the lives of men overseas with inferior equipment. Miller's finest work came in 1949 with *Death of a Salesman*. His strikingly original portrait of Willy Loman, an aging salesman who spouted and believed the empty slogans of a materialist America, depicted a man who was defeated by his own gullibility. Rarely has an American theatre artist managed to com-bine a personal portrait with a larger social canvas, all painted with subtlety and proportion. Miller's deft drama was directed with un-common skill by one of the graduates of the Group Theatre, Elia

Kazan. Kazan also staged Tennessee Williams' *A Streetcar Named Desire* during the 1948-49 season. Here in another guise was Williams' familiar and tragic Southern belle. His has always been a hothouse world of problem females, sometime nymphomaniacal, sometimes inhibited (*Summer and Smoke*, a box-office failure of 1948). His preoccupation with sex, particularly in its more perverse forms, was apparent from the start. The sense of loneliness and the sex obsession tell us a good deal about our folkways. In many ways, the once-shocking sexual imagery of Williams' plays seems a bit old-fashioned in the light of the erotic revolution in the sixties, but he pioneered in areas few dramatists had probed. Sometimes, however, his pity and his compassion seem dangerously close to mere hearts-and-flowers sentimentality. An air of murky nineteenth-century romanticism mars some of his most poetic passages. His attack is indirect, somewhat passive and feminine. He has not the virility and the clarity of a Miller, but he is, nevertheless, an impassioned dissenter. He sometimes sings with a bitter eloquence, for behind the Southern façade lurks a genuine rebel-poet. Williams is more of a social critic than perhaps he himself knows, more akin to Miller than most chroniclers suggest. Just as O'Neill before them, Williams and Miller were produced in theatres around the world. Europeans quickly saw that these gifted men had something of value to say about America and that they said it in a new and arresting manner.

In earlier decades, special groups and companies had enriched the theatre—the Provincetown Players, the Neighborhood Playhouse, the Civic Repertory, the Theatre Guild, the Group Theatre. In the forties, this was less so. Theatre Incorporated began in 1945 as a nonprofit group set up to encourage new playwrights and the "ultimate development of a true people's theatre." The company financed a tour of London's Old Vic, with Laurence Olivier, Ralph Richardson, Joyce Redman, and Margaret Leighton on the roster. Theatre Incorporated also presented Gertrude Lawrence in Shaw's *Pygmalion*, and it ran for months. But the original idea of a "true people's theatre" was forgotten, and the project folded. (Might this be a capsule history of the American theatre?) Eva Le Gallienne, ever constant to a dream not yet realized in this country, organized the American Repertory Theatre with actress-director Margaret Webster and producer Cheryl Crawford. The three ladies offered Shakespeare, Barrie, Wilde, Ibsen, and others in a big barn of a theatre on Columbus Circle. But the dream soon faded, the causes including union hassles, public indifference, insufficient rehearsal time, and a dozen other problems in a nation hostile to the drama as art. The Equity Library Theatre came into existence during the war, but it has seldom been much more than an occasional showcase for unemployed Equity members.

Late in 1943, New York City, with the blessings of Mayor Fiorello LaGuardia, took over the mosque-like Mecca Temple, a former Shriners' headquarters in the Broadway area, in lieu of tax arrears and offered it to the nonprofit City Center Corporation. The City Center of Music and Drama became a temple of the arts, with ticket prices always considerably lower than those of Broadway. It was not at all like the great subsidized art centers of Europe, but it was a step in the right direction. A superb opera company established itself here quite early, and in 1946 the New York City Ballet Company, the stunning, priceless creation of Lincoln Kirstein and George Balanchine, moved into the temple. A drama company took shape in 1948, but it has been an intermittent experiment. Under the leadership of Jean Dalrymple, it served as a source of sturdy revivals of both dramas and musicals, with, out of economic necessity, inadequate rehearsal time. Both the opera and the ballet companies moved in the sixties to the multi-million-dollar Lincoln Center complex. The drama company remains—on that precarious, what-next basis peculiar to American theatre projects. It has never become a resident troupe of actors and is in no sense a repertory company. Whether City Center will ever become a center of consequence to drama is dubious.

The American National Theatre and Academy, chartered by an act of Congress, is one of those institutions with noble talk and visions—and little else. Will it flare into activity in the sixties or the seventies? Perhaps its greatest contribution has been in keeping alive the idea that theatre could be art and that government should care about its national drama with the same zeal and respect found in European countries. In the forties, the Experimental Theatre

[68]

grew out of ANTA and there were a couple of seasons of distinction, most notably with the Charles Laughton version of Bertolt Brecht's immense *Galileo*. But the experiment soon languished. In 1950, ANTA purchased the Guild Theatre, scene of many earlier triumphs, and renamed it for ANTA. It meant very little, really. A sad tale of large, lofty unrealized dreams. In the 1948–49 season, the young Actors Studio, led by alumni of the Group Theatre and, most especially, Lee Strasberg, produced Bessie Breuer's *Sundown Beach*, an inconsequential play about fliers in a veterans' hospital. The play flopped, but it did introduce talented Julie Harris to Broadway. The history of Actors Studio as a producing company has been another irritating and erratic case. As a workshop for actors, it has given us some of the most fascinating performers of our time, witness Kim Stanley, Marlon Brando, Geraldine Page, and Maureen Stapleton. But the Studio has no stability as a company or an integrated ensemble of actors with a purpose.

A major event was the return of Eugene O'Neill to Broadway in a Theatre Guild production of *The Iceman Cometh* in 1946. The script was harsh and disillusioned and powerful. However, the production was an indifferent one, staged as a series of arias for actors rather than as a totality of mood. An off-Broadway edition in the next decade was much better. It was O'Neill's first play in eleven years. By this time the dramatist was a bitter man, bitter about the quality of American life as well as the low estate of the theatre. In an interview at Guild headquarters which I attended with a couple of dozen others, O'Neill, hands shaking painfully with the wracking pain of Parkinson's disease, pronounced: "If the entire human race were flushed down the john, it would be a good thing."

After the war, Lillian Hellman regained some of her earlier fire with *Another Part of the Forest*. With ruthless clarity and classic economy, she went back twenty years into the lives of the predatory Hubbard clan and showed them in the inexorable process of becoming the little foxes. In a sturdy adaptation of Emmanuel Roblès' heroic Latin drama, *Montserrat*, Miss Hellman celebrated hostages who chose the firing squad rather than divulge Bolivar's whereabouts. Arthur Laurents in *The Home of the Brave* and Gow and d'Usseau in *Deep Are the Roots* offered intelligent if surface sermons against prejudice. Maxwell Anderson flopped spectacularly with his pretentious *Anne of a Thousand Days* and *Joan of Lorraine*, the latter impersonated by Ingrid Bergman. Robinson Jeffers' stirring, beautifully chiseled *Medea* starred Judith Anderson, who was impressive despite her desperate need for more subtle direction. Garson Kanin created the best comedy of his career with *Born Yesterday*, which laughed knowingly about the wicked state of the union; it was a rare and effective American example of social satire, a genre in which Broadway was usually at the bottom of the class. Judy Holliday brought a very special political sophistication to the dumb-blonde role.

There were, of course, many notable imports on Broadway. More often than not it was the foreign playwrights who made the seasons glow. Surrounded by a glittering London company, John Gielgud made a deserved splash in Oscar Wilde's *The Importance of Being Earnest*. These visitors showed their plainer American cousins how to do high-style comedy. Jean Giraudoux' *The Madwoman of Chaillot*, with England's Martita Hunt in the title role, displayed the irony, paradox, and skeptical intelligence of a French playwright unfamiliar to Broadway audiences. Jean-Paul Sartre's *No Exit*, with Claude Dauphin, Annabella, and Ruth Ford, presented an existentialist hell as human beings make it. Jean Anouilh's black-comedy version of Sophocles' *Antigone* marked the Broadway début of a playwright long familiar to Parisians. Barry Fitzgerald, Sara Allgood, and other stars of the Abbey Theatre gave America a practically perfect revival of Sean O'Casey's *Juno and the Paycock*. Britishers J. B. Priestley and Terence Rattigan entertained us. At decade's end, T. S. Eliot's *The Cocktail Party* spotlighted a brilliant conservative author at work, and enjoyed a questionable kind of snobbish cocktail-party-chatter éclat.

In the late forties, there were a few stirrings and a few hopes for reviving the old off-Broadway movement of the glorious Provincetown days. It centered mostly around the New Stages group in Greenwich Village, which offered, among other things, Jean-Paul Sartre's *The Respectful Prostitute* and Barrie Stavis' compelling play about Galileo, *Lamp at Midnight*. But it was only a fleeting flicker of hope.

The economy of the theatre sagged dramatically near the end of the decade. During the war years, Broadway did surprisingly well for its impresarios. With lots of war-prosperity money, legal and illegal, in ostentatious evidence, people gaily flocked to Broadway. The actors not only spent happy hours at the Stage Door Canteen and other soldier haunts to keep the spirits high, they were also employed in the theatre—a novel state of affairs for many members of Actors' Equity. However, after the war, the number of productions dropped drastically, and many theatres were transformed into television studios. Though television was still young, the influence of the eight-inch home screen was beginning to be felt. In the 1947–48 season, there were eighty productions on Broadway; by the 1949–50 season, there were sixty-two.

But a far more sinister menace than television began to show its un-American face in the late forties and was to come out in full and blatant regalia in the fifties. It was an obsessive hunt for witches. The House Un-American Activities Committee, under the leadership of J. Parnell Thomas, began its deplorable and ridiculous investigation of Reds in and under Hollywood beds. Everybody from George Murphy to Ronald Reagan testified on communism in Hollywood. Ten men refused to testify on the grounds that the questions were unconstitutional. They went to jail despite the cries of protest from such distinguished men as Van Wyck Brooks, Thomas Mann, Albert Einstein, and Professor Thomas I. Emerson of the Yale Law School. One scene in particular deserves to be remembered. It was the appearance under subpoena of Bertolt Brecht before the committee in October of 1947. Brecht had been in Hollywood, an exile from German fascism. He had had quite a few hassles with un-German activities committees, and he knew what was happening here. The committee, however, did not understand that before them was the most significant world playwright of our times. The testimony, now available on a Folkways recording, is a tragicomedy. The investigators knew practically nothing of Brecht's work. They mangled or misquoted his writings. Brecht, sensing this appalling ignorance of dramatic literature, led them such a merry and bewildering chase that they thanked him as a cooperative witness. But it was America and the theatre who suffered at this carnival of unreason. Brecht had his airline reservation in his pocket when he appeared before the committee; he immediately departed for Europe after the inquisition, never to return. In a few years, his Berliner Ensemble was celebrated throughout Europe as the finest repertory theatre company on the continent. The incredible tragicomedy was merely a foretaste of what was to come in the fifties with McCarthyism. There were many other portents. In 1949, Arthur Miller was denied a passport by the State Department. The playwright had wished to view a production of his prize-winning *All My Sons* in Belgium. This passport refusal was a peevish and childish effort both to punish Miller for his political stance and to hamper the play's production abroad. A startling edict was in effect being promulgated: foreigners must be shown an America always in her Sunday best, in a false, ever-smiling guise. Another disastrous notion logically and inevitably followed. Americans were not to be allowed to tell the whole truth at home, either.

CHAPTER 6

A
WITCH-HUNT

IN THE FIFTIES, the theatre decline became more painfully apparent than in the preceding decade. In fact, there is a good deal of ironic and sardonic contrast between the forties and the fifties. After the glow of another war to end all wars and of a long overdue commitment against world fascism, America was devastated by the most tragic witch-hunt, the most inglorious spree of anti-intellectualism in our history. A war followed by a witch-hunt! It is typical of our anemic theatre that few playwrights wished or dared to put this powerful theme on stage. No American Brecht was forthcoming.

The dispirited fifties were variously called the Age of Eisenhower, the Age of McCarthy, the Age of Anxiety. Our President, bland and pleasant, mumbled his mangled, incomplete sentences in the same manner as did a flock of Actors Studio mummers. In the colleges, the youngsters were publicized as the Silent Generation, much more interested in getting ahead than in changing the world. But it was Senator Joseph McCarthy of Wisconsin who put his special stamp on the unhappy decade. The Korean War came in 1950, and the debate raged over whether we should or we should not invade China. Senator McCarthy, sensing a springboard to fame hidden under our "containment" policy, inaugurated his spectacular campaign of demagoguery, playing with inflammable words like "treason" and "conspiracy" and making no secret of his dislike for liberals, Harvard intellectuals, and Boston Welches who cherished the Bill of Rights. As the head of the Senate Internal Security Committee, McCarthy was cruel and vicious and won

[73]

battle after battle with innuendo and half-truths. Before he was stopped, he had frightened a large part of the liberal community, to their shame, into disgraceful submission. McCarthyism came to mean all governmental and industrial snooping into citizens' private beliefs, not just the work of a particular Senate committee. It will be many decades before the nation will completely recover from the indignities and the illegalities of the fifties. To translate the decade into McCarthy's own superpatriotic language, it was a blot on our flag. Too many stood silent as McCarthy and others like him raved on maniacally with their transparent lies. Most intellectuals saw through the witch-hunt, but few spoke up. A disheartening number of leaders, from college presidents to television executives, were strangely silent. The blacklist was evident in many industries, and indeed it became a way of life. It was, in Dalton Trumbo's vivid phrase, the Time of the Toad.

For a full decade the hunt raged at blood heat. Hundreds of persons in every area of cultural life—the films, television, radio, dance, concert stage, the press, and the theatre—were hounded, humiliated, bankrupted, and driven from their jobs. The diverse list included radio soap-opera stars, Broadway choreographers, tap dancers, movie queens, and folksong idols. It was a decade that lost its mind, a period when our cherished idea of an open society suddenly dissolved into nothingness, a time of loyalty oaths and other curious tribal incantations. The extreme right wing, armed with a hysterical devil theory of history, had persuaded Americans that the Reds were coming. The scene was something out of Goya. Books were burned and banned. Neighbors named neighbors. It was, of course, all a fraud, a trick to capture power and to scatter the liberal community. The Reds in American life had never been more than a handful and were about as much a threat as the Prohibition party.

A few men did speak out. Television-radio personality John Henry Faulk, blacklisted by the Columbia Broadcasting System and *Red Channels*, an erratic compilation of gossip and malice, went to court and, years later, won a whopping settlement of $3,500,000. Mark DeWolf Howe, professor of law at Harvard and biographer of the great libertarian, Oliver Wendell Holmes, warned the liberals that they must unite against the "perversion of political decency for which the word McCarthyism stands." A few brave men chose prison rather than to defile themselves. The residue of the decade is still with us. However, a few victims now speak candidly about the past. Henry Morgan, theatre, film, and television wit, has commented openly and sharply on television shows about his own blacklisting. Millard Lampell, author of dramas for films, television, and the stage, startled a nationwide television audience during the 1966 Emmy Awards (awards for excellence in television) with his not-so-casual remark as he picked up his trophy: "I think I ought to mention that I was blacklisted for ten years."

McCarthyism affected the arts and our general cultural life in complex and often indirect ways. During this timorous, confused, and apathetic decade, the arts took a sharp turn away from content to an inwardness, a preoccupation with self, a frenzied interest in form for its own sake. It was a full-scale retreat from the political struggle and social commitment. The tranquilized fifties, poet Robert Lowell neatly labeled them. These trends could be discerned in music through the experiments of John Cage and other composers profoundly interested in the heartbeat of Eastern mysticism, in dance through the "spontaneous" movement of Merce Cunningham and a few imitators, in painting through slashes and dribbles of abstract expressionism, and in countless other new directions. Many artists created magnificent experimental work during this period, work unmistakably of a time and place and a special mood.

In *The Town and the City*, his first novel, onetime Columbia University football player Jack Kerouac defined in depth "the beat generation," a phrase he himself had coined. The 1950 novel influenced a flurry of imitators. Beatniks, as the phrase became in the typewriters of pressmen, were youngsters self-consciously Out of Society, youngsters with a kind of semi-anarchist revulsion against those who joined the rat race for Money and Status. To these beats, politics was a game for squares, a meaningless game pocked with meaningless words. With remarkable intensity, the youngsters practiced the fine art of disaffiliation, disengagement, or alienation. To both old-school Americans, trained on a philosophical diet of thrift, hard work, subordination, and rewards (in heaven if not on earth), and new-style Americans, nursed on grab-the-loot attitudes, the beats were shocking. The beats were saying No to the whole system, to the American Way of Life! The long hair of both the boys and the girls, the self-conscious agonizing, the preoccupation with Zen and drugs, the studied lack of interest in social matters, the peculiarly joyless quest for sincerity and purity—these signs of the beatified were evident not only in Greenwich Village but in ever-increasing numbers around the nation. The beats' ikons included saxophonist Charlie Parker and poet Dylan Thomas, both men who destroyed themselves in a frenzied horror of modern industrial life. Or so the legend goes. With the publication in 1956 of Allen Ginsberg's long poem, "Howl," a hysterical, obscene, and sometimes stirring wail at America's gross materialism and its crude money values, the beats at last found their high priest. There was a good deal of sexual and pseudoreligious mumbo-jumbo mixed with this copping out. The liberals and leftists of another generation looked on in perplexed alarm. What had happened to the young? To these battle-scarred oldtimers, taking the line of no resistance made no sense at all.

The beats dominated the feature pages of the magazines and were a perfect reflection of social retreat in the fifties. But, there were other important literary portents. J. D. Salinger's *Catcher in the Rye* caught precisely the reactions of a prep school lad to the moral ambiguities around him. Though the book could be vastly enjoyed as a wryly comic tale about Holden Caulfield, schoolboy, it could also be read as a portrait of a period: inchoate, amoral, unformulated in its uneasy, vague revulsion against society. Novels by Jewish intellectuals were on the rise, novels urban and sophisticated, with a dash of bittersweet and with a subtle "I've-been-there-before" flavor regarding the decade's hysterical persecutions.

Naturally enough, the immoral climate of the times was reflected in the theatre in labyrinthine ways. The theatre was not so easily frightened as the mass media, but playwrights and producers and backers proceeded with unusual caution. They did not go against the prevailing dogma. Controversy was avoided with special care, and the plays on Broadway gave little evidence of the fires raging outside.

There were many striking examples of theatre hysteria. In Peoria, Illinois, the American Legion attempted to prevent the showing of Arthur Miller's *Death of a Salesman*, for the reason that the author was listed in *Red Channels*. In Pasadena, the Legion campaigned upon the same grounds against *Legend of Sarah*, a wholly non-political farce by James Gow and Arnaud d'Usseau. The Pasadena Playhouse (which years before had bravely produced O'Neill's *Lazarus Laughed* when Broadway would not touch it) went through with its presentation of *Legend of Sarah*, but omitted the names of the authors from the program. These incidents of national silliness were multiplied many times. Broadway itself was not immune. Shows with actors listed in *Red Channels* were picketed. Protests by veterans' groups resulted in the cancellation of a performance of *Wonderful Town* because a block of three hundred tickets—out of fifteen hundred—had been purchased by an alleged left-wing group. Investigators from Washington held hearings in New York, hearings carefully staged to scare Broadway into submission. And I recall one poignant letter I received from two dedicated actors, Fredric March and Florence Eldridge, thanking me for an entirely non-political article I had written about them during the time they were shamelessly hounded by *Red Channels*. A score of theatre folk were summoned before Washington committees. Elia Kazan, Judy Holliday, Jerome Robbins, Arthur Miller, and Lillian Hellman were among the many commanded to testify. Some named names. A shockingly large number groveled in the most abject ways. A few refused to dignify the inquisitors with answers. Miss Hellman in particular came out splendidly. When she was summoned in 1952 to answer questions about her past associations, she refused. "I cannot and will not cut my conscience to fit this year's fashions," she wrote the Un-American Activities Committee chairman. "To hurt innocent people whom I knew many years ago in order to save myself is to me inhuman and indecent and dishonorable." For this, she risked jail but, luckier than many, she merely became unemployable. She was blacklisted in Hollywood, on radio, and on television. She recalls today: "It was the black comedy period of our time. . . . I used to wake up at least once a week and read in the paper something totally untrue that somebody had confessed to. There was a lot of confession of sins that nobody had committed." Happily, Miss Hellman was joined in her courage by several theatre people. Playwright Elmer Rice and critic Brooks Atkinson were among those who spoke out passionately against the blacklist and illegal snooping.

In retrospect, the salient feature of Broadway in the fifties was the dismal quality of its productions. It was the worst decade of theatre since the birth of the American dramatic arts back in the teens. I recall in horror the mountainous amount of trash I endured in that long, ugly decade. Mercifully, many of the efforts died after two or three performances. With the rising costs of theatre production and the growing caution of producers, it was instant success or instant failure. Perhaps worst of all were the items billed as "comedies," factory-made products which had nothing to do with laughter or reality and which revolved more often than not around the vital question of whether the sappy heroine was virginal. More and more, the audiences were dominated by the expense-account trade looking for a "good time." More and more, theatre parties became outrageously decisive in what was produced. The ladies who ran the theatre benefits (theatre-party-goers paid more than the actual ticket cost and often came reluctantly, only to help a worthy charity) demanded safe and conventional hits, with star names and lots of "entertainment." The theatre served up pallid pulp, and it had virtually nothing to do with the world outside or with art. The beats may have been taking drugs, but the older, prosperous generation who still taxied to the theatre were on their own drug—the Broadway stage. And it was a drug with no kick at all, a soporific.

Economically, the theatre was in unmistakable decline. Of course, there were flashy hits, mostly musicals, which made a few investors millions. But in overall terms, the industry was in grave trouble, not only on Broadway but around the nation. There were only thirty-six theatres on Broadway, and many of these remained in constant jeopardy. Theatres in other big cities were disappearing, too. The touring companies hit a new low. In 1950, a committee of press agents and theatre managers reported that less than 2 per cent of the country's population attended the living theatre and fewer than 1 per cent of this public was under twenty-five. A study by Dr. O. Glenn Saxon, professor of economics at Yale, pointed out in 1954 that total attendance at Broadway productions had dropped 27 per cent since 1944, that the annual number of Broadway shows had declined by 68 per cent since 1931–32, that the number of commercial theatres available for professional productions throughout the United States had declined by 64 per cent since 1921, and that in New York, the drop had been more than 50 per cent since 1931. Professional boosters angrily questioned the figures, but could not in all honesty question the general decline. In an Age of Affluence, the theatre skidded downhill. Television, on the other hand, prospered spectacularly in the fifties. Many practical people decided it was better to view the wasteland at home than go out to the theatre for a considerably more expensive version of the same desert.

Despite these dour notes, Broadway did offer a few works of merit. Art sometimes breaks through the most formidable of obstacles. Hellman, Miller, and Williams remained our best hopes in the bleak fifties, though there was the uncomfortable and uneasy feeling that theirs was not a sustained and dependable brilliance. Our playwrights wrote fitfully and went in for long silences. Miller did summon up enough strength to offer *The Crucible*, a curiously oblique comment on McCarthyism, in the 1952–53 season. In retrospect, this examination of the witch-hunts in Salem in 1692 contains considerable power and penetration in its blast against those who would cut man down to pygmy size. Since the fifties, this drama has been given far better productions both on and off Broadway. In 1955, Miller created *A View From the Bridge*, which in its wrongheaded, overproduced, and miscast Broadway version, was pretentious mumbo-jumbo about informing, spiced with hints of incest and homosexuality. Miller's own inflated comments likening his play to Greek tragedy were unfortunate. (In an off-Broadway production in the sixties, with sensitive direction by Ulu

Grosbard, with the highfalutin asides by a narrator excised, and
with other judicious cuts by the author, the work proved to be a
good, taut melodrama.) Aside from a sturdy off-Broadway adaptation of Ibsen's *An Enemy of the People*, Miller did not write
another play for ten years. Though he was silent, he was still
labeled *the* great American playwright. Compulsively, we need to
pretend greatness even when it is not evident. A prideful nation,
we give our theatre an aura of magnificence it does not really
possess.

Tennessee Williams started the decade well with *The Rose
Tattoo*, a gay salute to sensuality in a style more playful than usual
for the Lawrentian Romantic. It was not a significant offering, but
it was pleasant and workmanlike. *Camino Real*, produced on Broadway in 1953, was more ambitious, nothing less than a surrealist
phantasmagoria on the state of the nation, a poet's dark-hued
romantic rebellion against a materialistic society. It was, in quite
different tones and textures, the same "Howl" found in Allen
Ginsberg's historic poem. *Camino Real* failed with both critics and
audiences. True, it was clumsily and heavily directed by Elia
Kazan. But the work had merit, and it was eventually given a more
supple, subtle, *simpatico* staging by José Quintero in a 1960 off-
Broadway production. *Cat on a Hot Tin Roof*, with vigorous
performances by Burl Ives, Pat Hingle, and Madeleine Sherwood,
was directed by Kazan with a sure hand, stirring both realism and
expressionism into theatre fire. But underneath the play is a fatal
evasion. Williams coyly skirts around the subject of homosexuality
as though it were one of those nineteenth-century unmentionables.
He tried to deal directly with the subject of homosexuality in his
next play, *Garden District*, a disaster presented in an off-Broadway
showcase in 1958. However, it was not really a serious treatment
of the subject: it was merely second-rate Grand Guignol. Certainly
a subsequent script, *Sweet Bird of Youth* (1959), did little to
bolster his faltering artistic reputation, though it was a popular
success. Aside from the virtuoso performance by Geraldine Page
as the fading, insecure nymphomaniac of a movie star, the play was
trashy and wooden.

Williams is, unsteadily, one of the most important playwrights

America has produced. He is our poet of the misfit and the psychically wounded, and that alone is vital in our self-glorifying, smugly affluent society, usually painted solely in reds, whites and blues. By dipping deeply into the barrel, he gives us another valid and less eulogized America. From the angle of the dispossessed, he offers invaluable illuminations on the state of the union. It is a pity he is so soft and undisciplined.

The other member of The Big Three, Lillian Hellman, created one of her finest works, *The Autumn Garden*, in 1951. With her familiar astringent wit mixed with a new compassion, she dissected ten lives, commenting quietly and precisely on their moral choices, the lies they told themselves and each other, and the enormous gap between theory and practice. The playwright looked at middle age and an upper middle class with a maturity rare in American drama. At the decade's end, Miss Hellman produced what is undoubtedly the flimsiest of her dramatic efforts, *Toys in the Attic*. Paradoxically, it was far more successful at the box office than *The Autumn Garden*. In *Toys in the Attic*, a jarring effort, Miss Hellman seemed almost absentmindedly to have joined the tattered Williams band of Southern revivalists, with their showy violence, intimations of sexual abberrations, and the other baggage of magnolia-scented melodrama. It was a very uncharacteristic work for Lillian Hellman.

In the fifties, a great deal of hope was placed in a new writer, William Inge. He first appeared in 1950 with *Come Back, Little Sheba*, a quiet drama of a small-town couple impoverished in spirit and inarticulate in finding ways toward love. There was quality in it, and Inge seemed a fascinating mixture of Thornton Wilder and Sherwood Anderson. The play's enormous success was helped by a beautifully polished performance by Shirley Booth. With *Picnic* in 1952, Inge widened his portraits of sexual frustration in small-town settings to include a variety of types, but his original script was vulgarized by the flashy, coarse direction of Joshua Logan. *Bus Stop* continued his success at the box office, and it contained shrewd performances by Elaine Stritch, Albert Salmi, and Kim Stanley. However, Inge was obsessed with sex to the exclusion of other elements, and he became a pale parody of Tennessee Williams.

The lack of social vision and passion began to be painfully apparent. Was Inge as bloodless as Broadway itself? *The Dark at the Top of the Stairs* was a bit more vigorous, for it contained a number of complex social questions. But with his *A Loss of Roses* in 1959, Inge seemed to have fallen apart, with the standard hint of incest and a little titillation about pornographic movies. His is the sad story of so many of our promising playwrights, and it remains most doubtful that he is to be considered a serious candidate for theatre greatness.

Other dramatists represented in the fifties included familiar Thornton Wilder and newcomer Robert Anderson. Wilder offered in 1955 his successful *The Matchmaker*, an adaptation of the nineteenth-century Austrian drama; it was rather amusing and very forgettable. It was a little sad to see so expert a comedienne as Ruth Gordon camping it up outrageously. Anderson made a promising debut in 1953 with *Tea and Sympathy*, a sensitive drama of a boy accused of homosexuality at a prep school and of a very special sympathy offered him by a professor's wife. Directed by Elia Kazan in one of his quieter moods, it was better-than-average fare. Two later plays, both in 1959, *All Summer Long* and *Silent Night, Lonely Night*, again exhibited the playwright's delicate, ruminative, and restrained style, but both were mishandled on stage. His sharply observant humor was gentle, his intentions were modest. Broadway had little room for such qualities in its wham-bang, instant-hit-or-flop world of showbiz hysteria, where art is a bothersome word employed by those incorrigibles who just can't be Rotarian members of the gang.

Gore Vidal, a young man who had enjoyed success with novels and television writing (many Broadway writers were to arrive via television in this decade), came up with a light satire, a field rarely explored by our native dramatists. In *A Visit From a Small Planet*, he proved to be a young man who saw Americans and their politics with a clear, cold, and distantly amused eye. If he lacked passion, he was at least free of the cloying sentimentality that spoiled most native satire. Jerome Lawrence and Robert E. Lee collaborated on *Inherit the Wind*, a skillful semi-documentary on the Scopes monkey trial, with Paul Muni as Darrow and Ed Begley as Bryan.

There were attempts at drama by veterans Philip Barry, Sidney Kingsley, Robert Sherwood, Elmer Rice, William Saroyan, John Steinbeck, and Maxwell Anderson, but their efforts were not at their best level. The decade's most disappointing event was the premiere during the 1958–59 season of Archibald MacLeish's *J.B.* It was widely heralded and ridiculously over-praised. *J. B.* was a pretentious bit of pseudoreligious, middlebrow verse about the trials of Job, the kind of windy drama that gives culture a bad name. This high-flying flatulence was made almost bearable by one of Boris Aronson's imaginative sets (a circus-like effect) and an exceptional turn by a young Canadian, Christopher Plummer.

Paddy Chayefsky, graduate of television, wrought a soap opera called *Middle of the Night*, a lugubrious Broadway drama improved by the acting of Anne Jackson and Martin Balsam. At decade's end, Chayefsky presented *The Tenth Man*, a pallid reminder of *The Dybbuk*, this time set on suburban Long Island. Charter member of the Southern School, Carson McCullers dramatized her own novel, *The Member of the Wedding*, in 1950. Under the poetic but firm direction of Harold Clurman, it proved to be a sensitive, warming study of adolescence, and it brought deserved stardom to intense Julie Harris. The play was also an engrossing portrait of a motherly Negro cook. She symbolized the play's blues quality much more poignantly than did the twelve-year-old-heroine. Ethel Waters' portrayal was monumental in its insight into the blight of prejudice. *The Diary of Anne Frank*, co-authored by Frances Goodrich and Albert Hackett, was *kitsch* rather than art. This sentimental tearjerker with the very best of intentions did not do justice to its subject. I recall weeping over Anne's fate, but being equally annoyed that the writers had not given it the force and dimension the theme demanded. The funniest, wittiest work of the fifties was James Thurber's *A Thurber Carnival*. Based on his own earlier material, it offered a free-swinging, zany irreverence long missing from Broadway. Thurber himself pronounced that comedy had died in the fifties and blamed it on McCarthyism.

America's leading playwright died in 1953, but even after his death he dominated the fifties. Eugene O'Neill's *Long Day's Journey into Night*, which had its world premiere on Broadway

[83]

in 1956, was unquestionably the highlight of the decade. O'Neill had wished it to be produced twenty-five years after his death; his widow wisely allowed it to be done sooner. The long drama dissected a complex and tortured family, obviously the O'Neill clan, bared their separate guilts and private hells, and filled the theatre with their monumental rage and remorse. O'Neill was still showing Americans how to write for the stage. The work was masterfully directed by José Quintero and strikingly performed by Jason Robards, Fredric March, Florence Eldridge, and Bradford Dillman. Two lesser but distinguished O'Neill works, *A Moon for the Misbegotten* and *A Touch of the Poet*, were also given their Broadway premieres in this decade.

Many foreign writers were represented on Broadway, too. Where would a declining Broadway be without them? England's Graham Greene, a Catholic with a serpentine style, showed that a religious playwright could write plays that breathed life, not dogma. Though *The Living Room* and *The Potting Shed* did not enjoy long runs, they were works of an artist. Paul Shyre came up with deftly staged readings of the magnificent Sean O'Casey autobiographies, *Pictures in the Hallway* and *I Knock at the Door*. English playwrights Terence Rattigan, Noel Coward, Enid Bagnold, Peter Shaffer, Christopher Fry, and Peter Ustinov entertained with craftsmanlike, literate, pleasantly witty, and insubstantial works.

Three plays by John Osborne, London's angry young man, exposed a new England, a bitter, uneasy anti-Establishment England heretofore missing from the beautifully lacquered imports dear to the hearts of cultivated Anglophiles. It was a major revolt against the conventional drawing-room charades. Broadway had already experienced this revolt in the social drama of the thirties; now it was sweeping the London stage. *Look Back in Anger*, which was produced on Broadway in 1957, set the tone. The anti-hero, Jimmy Porter, was both fascinating and repugnant. His father had fought in Spain on the Republican side, but Jimmy Porter himself was a rebel without a cause. Neurasthenic, narcissistic, bitter, self-consciously vulgar, he represented the despair of a generation which felt itself betrayed and which had no loyalty to the old virtues of God and country. In 1958 came *Epitaph for George Dillon*, co-authored with Anthony Creighton, and it was a scathing, scalding lament for a writer who winds up a hack, in sick submission to less than his dreams. *The Entertainer,* in the same year, painted a fading British Empire through the person of a seedy vaudeville entertainer spouting all the cheap and leering comedy lines of yesterday. Laurence Olivier, richly inventive in the title role, hereby informed the theatre Establishment that he was a remarkably pliable actor willing—and eager—to join the young in their revolt. Yet one felt a persistent dissatisfaction with these plays and these angry young men. Could the callow lads change the face of England? They seemed, essentially, cry-babies. Given a few pounds and a place in the sun, would these vague rebels be tomorrow's placid fat-cats?

France found representation on our stages, too. Several Jean Giraudoux plays were produced, although his peculiarly French brand of ironic wit did not find easy acceptance in our essentially sentimental theatre milieu. The most distinguished was his *Tiger at the Gates.* Though it had been written in the thirties, it did not reach Broadway until 1955. This alternately cynical and hopeful antiwar play, a fresh look at the Trojan War, was directed by Harold Clurman with verve and care. I recall particularly one vivid scene in which Michael Redgrave conjures a deep, from-the-soul sob of despair over man's condition. The audience was magically hushed in this rare communal moment of great theatre. In 1958, Friedrich Dürrenmatt's *The Visit* came to New York, and it was a timely and bitter parable of how money and greed can control an entire community. It introduced to Broadway one of Europe's finest contemporary dramatists. The stars were Alfred Lunt and Lynn Fontanne, and for once they had a play of substance, not just a *Quadrille* or a *The Great Sebastians* created merely to show off their prodigious skills.

The Theatre of the Absurd (a convenient if inaccurate label for various experimental approaches in the European theatre) came briefly to Broadway in 1956, with the production of Samuel Beckett's *Waiting for Godot.* Inspired clown Bert Lahr and E. G. Marshall were the wandering tramps. The Absurdist writers, led by Beckett, Eugène Ionesco, and Arthur Adamov, were already the talk of Paris. They were not in revolt against the dispirited fifties; in fact, they were reflections of the Cold War and the general retreat among artists. To a degree, they were symbols of a society in decay. The Absurdists were not, of course, entirely new—what movement is? Beckett had his sources in the work of his friend, James Joyce; Adamov in a flirtation with surrealism; Ionesco in anarchism. Beckett's *Waiting for Godot* seemed, at first glance, to be a play by a tortured man who had lost his religion and was making too much of a fuss about it. Upon closer examination, it was a brilliantly dramatic version of Sartre's postwar existentialism, particularly his celebrated nausea. It represented the earlier Sartrean weariness before the incomprehensibility of the universe; it did not at all represent Sartre's later phase of social commitment. Beckett is a poet of the stage, with a masterly economy of language. His landscape is a joyless one, however, for in his metaphysical ennui he somehow misses the sensuality and élan of everyday living. But he is vastly important in both his faithful reflections of a period and in his impatience with the old theatre conventions. The poetic play was lost on its Broadway audience, an audience conditioned to both the earlier straightforward problem plays and the current trivia. Revived on Broadway the following year with an all-Negro cast, *Waiting for Godot* failed a second time. But Beckett did influence our younger experimenters, and their imitative work was to turn up in subsequent seasons in the off-Broadway theatre.

Aside from a few highlights, the fifties were a sad time on Broadway. The marquees, the neon, the opening-night ritual— it all seemed to symbolize a grinning, leering moron with nothing to say and no art at all. For the most part, it was a theatre littered with such trash as *Harbor Lights, Time Out for Ginger, Buttrio Square,* and *Portofino*. My chief pleasures in the fifties were found in the off-Broadway theatres. In this fallow Broadway period, the rebel movement was revived with brio. It was as inevitable as the morning sun. It was revolt against the dreary commercial theatre. The playwright revolted against the predictable, factory-made dramas. The actor wanted to stretch his talents. But it was primarily a rebellion by the consumer, who wanted quality, not formulas. This off-Broadway revolt was the decade's single most encouraging feature.

The Phoenix dominated off-Broadway theatre in the fifties. Founded by T. Edward Hambleton and Norris Houghton, it began life in 1953 in a large, 1,186-seat house on lower Second Avenue, the former home of Maurice Schwartz' Yiddish theatre. It contained within itself all the familiar problems—casual pick-up companies, with little continuity in personnel; low salaries; too brief rehearsals; an eclectic philosophy. Because the company attempted classics that would never make money on Broadway, it attracted a number of stars who yearned to flex unused acting muscles. Montgomery Clift, Robert Ryan, Judith Evelyn, Roddy McDowall, and a score of other stars worked eagerly for little money. The Phoenix mangled many classics during its history, including Ibsen's *The Master Builder* and *Peer Gynt*, Chekhov's *The Sea Gull*, Pirandello's *Six Characters in Search of an Author*, Aristophanes' *Lysistrata*, and Brecht's *The Good Woman of Setzuan*. However, the Phoenix succeeded with glory-be brilliance when Ivan Turgenev's *A Month in the Country* was produced in 1956. Directed by England's Michael Redgrave, it was a beautifully orchestrated piece on the different ways of love. Uta Hagen gave the finest performance of her career. A success, artistically, was Ionesco's *The Chairs*, directed by another Londoner, Tony Richardson, and starring Joan Plowright and Eli Wallach. However, the Phoenix fell in disarray by the end of the decade: without enormous transfusions of money, it could not escape the crippling and pervasive hit-or-flop economy.

Another worthy project was the Circle-in-the-Square, under the artistic direction of a young, intense Panamanian, José Quintero. In the 1951–52 season, at their Greenwich Village theatre-in-the-round, Quintero directed Geraldine Page in Tennessee Williams' *Summer and Smoke*, in a production far superior to that of Broadway in 1947. Quintero directed like a poet or a conductor of symphonies. His pauses and his silences were his hallmark. Other artistic successes of the group included Wilder's *Our Town*, Behan's *The Quare Fellow*, and Edwin Justus Mayer's too-little-known *Children of Darkness*. The group's greatest triumph came with a revival of O'Neill's *The Iceman Cometh*, starring newcomer Jason Robards. It was on the strength of that production that Carlotta

Monterey, O'Neill's widow, allowed Quintero to direct *Long Day's Journey into Night* on Broadway. By decade's end, Quintero was a director of world significance. But the Circle-in-the-Square had lost a good deal of its original impetus and power.

There were other groups. The Shakespearewrights produced a number of the bard's works in off-Broadway houses with a vitality and freshness missing from the rather declamatory, potted-palm productions of the visiting Old Vic. The Fourth Street Theatre, under the crusading aegis of David Ross, offered Ibsen, Strindberg, and Chekhov revivals. Most of them were good rather than great, but the production of *The Three Sisters* was outstanding, with a notably subtle performance by Peggy Mauer as Irina. Two productions at the Rooftop Theatre on Second Avenue were memorable for any decade. Stefan Zweig's adaptation of Ben Jonson's *Volpone* was staged by Gene Frankel, and he emerged, along with Quintero, as an impressive new director. The gaily inventive choreography (really movement for dancing stagehands) was by modern dancer Daniel Nagrin. *Ulysses in Nighttown*, a free-form dramatic adaptation of James Joyce by Marjorie Barkentin, under the guidance of Padraic Colum, was directed by Burgess Meredith. Broadway efforts seemed puny and unimaginative in comparison.

William Ball proved himself a significant newcomer with his staging of Chekhov's *Ivanov* in 1958. This Bleecker Street *Ivanov* (its first performance in English in New York) was premium vodka. Other excellent exhibits included Congreve's *The Way of the World*, with the remarkably resourceful Nancy Wickwire; David Garrick's *The Clandestine Marriage*, with Frederic Warriner fashioning an acting gem as the aging amoralist; and *The World of Sholom Aleichem*, a funny, sad, and compassionate amalgam staged by Howard Da Silva. The European Absurdists were given many off-Broadway productions, and these included Beckett's *Endgame*, Ionesco's *The Bald Soprano* and *Jack*, and Genet's *The Maids* and *Deathwatch*, if one places this Black Mass original with the Absurdists. In some instances, off-Broadway theatre was proving it could do earlier Broadway shows much better than the originals. Tennessee Williams' 1940 *Battle of Angels* never got beyond Boston; it was presented in a revised edition on Broadway in 1957, this time titled *Orpheus Descending*. Both productions were inept. Directed by Adrian Hall, an off-Broadway production in 1959 proved the play possessed social bite and a fierce urgency in its description of the lynch-law underworld of the South.

The off-Broadway stage, however, was by no means perfect. It was correctly criticized as too much a museum, a place for revivals; it was seldom an innovator; it produced many plays from Broadway that were not worthy of resurrection. Often it seemed merely a copycat, imitating the coarsest features of Broadway. Sometimes, it was merely a talent showcase for Broadway-bound actors and directors. Worst of all, off-Broadway produced precious few new playwrights. An exception was Jack Richardson, who presented a fresh view of a classic theme in *The Prodigal*. Here was a new-comer with a felicitous gift for language.

The finest achievement of the decade was the establishment of free Shakespeare in New York's parks. It remains one of New York's glories. Back in the early fifties, lean, handsome Joseph Papp was possessed by the idea of free Shakespeare in New York. He started presenting Shakespeare in 1954 in a downtown Presbyterian church, and I recall a fine *Titus Andronicus*. Finally in the summer of 1956, he put on productions of *The Taming of the Shrew* and *Julius Caesar* in an East River Park amphitheatre, with a backdrop of beer signs and bridges. Dribbles of money came from everywhere. Ilka Chase, Richard Rodgers, and Doris Duke (via her Foundation) were among the early contributors. Julie Andrews gave Papp a pair of house seats to *My Fair Lady*, which he managed to sell for two hundred dollars. Even city officials began to take interest in this extraordinary young man. By the summer of 1957, the Shakespeare Festival opened in Central Park, and it was an instantaneous success. It was—and is—shown on a first-come, first-served basis, with the audience an exciting mixture of middle- and lower-class viewers never encountered in the Broadway theaters. In the midst of this experiment, Papp had his own political troubles. An employee of the Columbia Broadcasting System, he worked as a minor executive on a television quiz show, *I've Got a Secret*. When he refused to give the House Un-American Committee information on his past associations, he was promptly fired by CBS in a fanfare of publicity. Happily, it only temporarily endangered his dream. Today, the alfresco Shakespeare Festival is ensconced in a gala, permanent, two-thousand-seat home in Central Park, and is cautiously supported by city government funds, foundations, and the donations of private citizens. The Papp productions are direct, vigorous, clear, bawdy, and relevant. There is not only an annual season in Central Park, but the company also plays in various other parks and in the public schools. The Shakespeare Festival constitutes one of the few success stories in our dismal theatre history.

Certainly the most relentlessly irreverent group to emerge in the fifties was the openly anarchistic Living Theatre. Here, in a dingy off-Broadway walkup, was a sense of joy and nose-thumbing that was contagious, and it was a powerful influence on experimenters across the nation. Julian Beck and Judith Malina were original, audacious theatre spirits who bowed to no one—government, foundation, or box office. They were, perhaps, premature hippies. Their professionalism, according to the standards of Broadway, was sometimes wanting, but they made up for it in intelligence, imagination, and daring. William Carlos Williams' witty, wild *Many Loves* remains a highspot of my own theatregoing. In 1959 the Becks offered Jack Gelber's *The Connection*, which gave viewers a tantalizing glimpse of what a new kind of theatre might offer. Here was, on stage, America's Lower Depths, the sleazy alleys of drug addiction. On stage, too, was a splendid jazz group complementing the action. In an unusual program note, director Judith Malina dedicated the production "to the memory of Thelma Gadsden, dead of an overdose of heroin, at the Salvation Army, November 1957, and to all other junkies dead and alive in the Women's House of Detention." *The Connection* was a sardonic comment in reverse on fat-cat America, and it helped create the New Wave which was to come off-Broadway in the sixties. The Living Theatre was a portent—and a hope—that we might be, at last, emerging from the Time of the Toad.

CHAPTER 7

BLIGHT
ON
BROADWAY

COULD THE BROADWAY theatre get any worse than it was in the faceless, fear-ridden fifties? It could—and did. It is now a dull, creaking entertainment factory, selling hastily made, shoddy and overpriced goods; it is a factory especially designed for the expense-account trade, the out-of-town buyer, the client, the huckster, and the outrageously important theatre-party ladies. Most cultivated men and women have simply stopped attending with any regularity. Defection among the educated is high. Intellectuals scoff bitterly at any innocent who has the temerity to praise anything on Broadway. Some extremely sensitive souls even hesitate to speak unkindly of Broadway, since it is too much like beating up a little old blind lady. Of all the arts, the theatre is widely known as a diversion for squares. The dissenting young, of course, do not go to Broadway at all. To them, Broadway seems like some ancient, useless, irrelevant Establishment monolith. It is beneath contempt.

Broadway has become a confectioner's theatre. Now, there is nothing wrong with sweets and only dour, cloistered pedants would outlaw them. But one longs now and then for a more substantial and palate-stimulating diet. Routine musicals and fluffy, forgettable comedies with no wit and little laughter are the steady bill of fare. When a drama attempts to be serious, it is hopelessly sentimental and soggy; when it tries to be funny, it is appallingly stale. The days of intellectual dramas by American playwrights, plays of commitment, controversy, wit, and irreverence, plays about our specific time and place, are seemingly lost forever. Original and challenging native playwrights are as scarce as clean air. For entertainment of the mind, bland Broadway is the least likely place to visit.

Once upon a time, it was seriously expounded that the theatre aimed at a higher level of intellect than the mass media of films and television, that it offered adult themes in an adult manner without the usual commercial nightmare of pleasing everybody. If that thesis were ever true, it has certainly lost all validity in the 1960's. There is much more interest in films. Broadway and Hollywood, in fact, have reversed roles; nowadays Broadway is more culturally disreputable than Hollywood, even replacing television as a target of cocktail-party jests and jabs. It is ineffably sad for anyone who has ever enjoyed a love affair with Broadway. As the decade nears its end, there is no sign of change and little hope.

It is both funny and annoying to watch the Broadway business-as-usual crowd (producers, directors, theatre owners, ticket brokers, play doctors, and even some critics) during this crisis. Practically everybody denies with vehemence that a crisis exists. In their panic, they are angry at anyone who dares blurt out the truth. They insist that all hands play their familiar game: one must pretend that everything is just wonderful, simply wonderful. To point out that Broadway is gravely ill is somehow un-American. When veteran *New York Times* reporter Sam Zolotow figured that the 1966–67 season (only forty-seven productions) was the worst, in numerical terms, since the season of 1899–1900, the Broadway experts at first disagreed with the figures, then suggested that Zolotow should not be digging up such unpleasant facts. Concentrate, sir, on the smiling aspects of Broadway. And when some ungracious critics, not willing to be hucksters for Broadway, pointed out that the quality of productions was dismal, the showbiz imbeciles retorted that certain critics should take a rest—or be tried for treason. What a comedy it would make—way off Broadway, of course.

The decade started off with great expectations for both politics and culture. John F. Kennedy, young, handsome, vigorous, a man of grace and style, made his particular adulation of Thomas Jefferson most clear, and Jefferson had been, of course, our most cultivated leader. Kennedy invited poets, actors, playwrights, dancers, painters, and musicians to White House dinners and created a new ambience for the arts at the seat of power. For a precious moment, a President heralded a new day for culture. True, Kennedy's own cultural tastes were not always prepossessing. A favorite quote was a line from a song in the uninspiring musical, *Camelot*. But everyone sensed promise in this young man, a promise of a flowering of culture and a peaceful planet. Though the Cold War continued, Kennedy seemed genuinely interested in constructive diplomatic maneuvers for peaceful solutions to world problems. We shall never know, of course, how well he would have developed and matured.

A Texan of the old school of politics became President, a man with little concern for the arts and even less regard for intellectuals. Lyndon Baines Johnson was neither better nor worse than a long line of similar politicians who had preceded him—just more of the same. He dutifully continued the Kennedy campaign for the arts, but the degree and the concern were strikingly low-keyed. One would expect little more from Johnson's successor, Richard Milhous Nixon.

The undeclared war on tiny Vietnam has dominated the 1960's. Americans have rained bombs on Communist North Vietnam and on the insurgents in the South. New chemical warfare techniques have been developed. Jellied gasoline has turned the Vietnamese into the living dead. This has been America's most unpopular war, and it has alienated the artists and intellectuals whom Kennedy had carefully wooed.

Playwright Arthur Miller joined dozens of other cultural leaders in signing a full-page protest against the war in the august London *Times*. On national television, another playwright, Gore Vidal, dubbed Lyndon Johnson "a cornpone Genghis Khan." Other artists have publicly refused White House invitations. Many have agreed with Senator J. William Fulbright that the decade has spelled arrogance of power, an alarming self-righteousness, a Puritanism that led us to see ourselves as "God's avenging angels, whose sacred duty it is to combat evil philosophies." Too many Americans, he has eloquently argued, transform every war into a holy crusade, dehumanize their opponents, and "see principles where there are only interests and conspiracy where there is only misfortune." Vast numbers of other thoughtful Americans have feared a return of McCarthyism, as the fragile right to dissent on the issue of war and peace has become imperiled.

Increasingly on the home front, the bribe and the fix have become our native way of life, in both organized business and organized crime. Assassination threatened to become a way of political life, as the Reverend Martin Luther King, Jr., and Senator Robert F. Kennedy were both gunned down. Poverty, bigotry, and appalling politics-as-usual attitudes have turned our major cities into nightmarish jungles. To both Vietnam and the mounting urban crises, Broadway's response has been predictably escapist. The stage reflects little of the nation's turmoil except by a cautious neutrality. Broadway is safe in a sanitary, synthetic never-never land. The dramas of our times are, in the main, factory-made. One feels most scripts are selected by a computer hidden in some midtown hotel. *Under the Yum Yum Tree, Love in E Flat, The Paisley Convertible, The Mating Dance, Those That Play the Clowns*, and *Invitation to a March* (this last masquerading as a satire on conformity) are a few titles I vaguely recall in this parade of futility.

One new dramatist, however, has offered more vivid colors. He has become the talk of the nation, and he is, in several ways, symptomatic of Broadway. Although Edward Albee has created a sizable number of plays in the sixties, he remains—so far as greatness is concerned—a question mark. His work displays the same intensity without clarity, the same ambivalence, and the same shriveled fashionableness from which the period itself suffers. It is difficult to find the man under the verbiage. Albee was discovered off Broadway. First done in Berlin in 1959, his lurid *The Zoo Story* had its American premiere in an off-Broadway theatre (the old Provincetown Playhouse) in early 1960, on a double bill with Samuel Beckett's *Krapp's Last Tape*. It immediately established Albee as an important new voice, and he was pigeonholed by some over-industrious critics as an American member of the Theatre of the Absurd. *The Zoo Story*, however, was vastly overrated. It described a deadly encounter in the park between a cautious, well-dressed, smug publishing executive and an impoverished psychotic babbling about his sexual failures with men and women and a

strange love-hate encounter with a dog. Presumably Albee was trying to say something about our stuffy false values and about alienation. But it came out rather juvenile and Rimbaud-Genet romantic;
in its masochistic-sadistic interplay, it created (and reflected) a
murky, homosexual milieu. The psychotic was basically uninterest-
ing, and thus no true image of revolt emerged. But the short drama
appeared at a propitious moment, when the theatre desperately
needed a New Hero, when dramatic values were confused and
changing, and when the European Theatre of the Absurd was just
becoming intermission chatter. Other short (and better) plays followed in off-Broadway showcases, including *The Sand Box*, a
sardonic look at our attitudes toward the aged, and *The American Dream*, a dark comedy about psychological castration. *The
Death of Bessie Smith* was a particularly interesting realistic drama
obliquely attacking race prejudice. Based on a harrowing true story
(the great blues singer bled to death after a car accident in Mem-
phis, Tennessee, because she was denied medical assistance in all
the city's white hospitals), this brief script sharply concentrated
not on Miss Smith but on the burning fears and frustrations of
the white hospital personnel.

Albee became table-talk with his first Broadway drama, *Who's
Afraid of Virginia Woolf?* In this 1962 hit, he showed a striking
gift for crisp, crackling, ferocious dialogue. The mood of rage and
despair was about—what? And the non-existent child that became
the crux of the play—what did that mean? Was critic Tom F.
Driver correct when he explained that it was really a homosexual
play and that the imaginary son was merely the child the corrosive
couple could never have? Were George and Martha both men?
If the couple is homosexual, then the child makes dramatic sense.
Albee's next Broadway effort was a dramatization of Carson Mc-
Cullers' novella, *The Ballad of the Sad Café*, and it was stylized
and lifeless, a triangular love affair between an invert dwarf and
a muscular chittlings-and-gravy couple. A perfumed decadence
pervaded the adaptation. This was followed by *Tiny Alice*, a
windy sexual-religious fantasy, and it provided a pseudo-intellec-
tual puzzle for audiences with time on their hands. It was effective
only in its opening scenes, in which a pompous cardinal and a dis-

believer are given some livid lines of bitter banter. The 1966 *Malcolm*, an overripe, ultra-chic dramatization of James Purdy's bizarre novel about an adolescent's voyage into the adult world of sex and compromise, was a sorry mess, and it closed immediately. Perhaps *A Delicate Balance* in the same year was his most mature play, but it too was plagued with a glossy chic. Albee wrote about people of quiet understatement: passionless people surrounded by utter good taste. In his portrait of these wealthy, frightened, and impotent suburbanites, he wrote with a grace and compassion almost Chekhovian. Was he exposing his own dilemma on stage? For the lack of moral fervor, of robust humor, and of commitment is painfully apparent in his work. Perhaps he is the representative playwright for an age of fuzzy, ambiguous politics, national and international; perhaps he is apolitical or conservative at heart, with little to offer other than waspish dialogue.

Albee is our most produced playwright both abroad and in the university theatres. He is a celebrity. He has won his exalted position by default, for the landscape of new and important playwrights is unpromising and barren. When will the truly great voices emerge? Must we wait hopefully for the seventies? Are our Broadway playwrights all myopic?

The theatre gods of the past have faltered in the sixties. Tennessee Williams has continued his unhappy slide downhill, with *The Milk Train Doesn't Stop Here Anymore* (two versions), *Period of Adjustment, The Night of the Iguana, Slapstick Tragedy,* and *The Seven Descents of Myrtle.* Of these, *The Night of the Iguana* was his best, but it was erratic and it only occasionally recaptured some of his earlier poetic magic. *Slapstick Tragedy,* presented on Broadway in 1966, heavily underlined his steady deterioration. Williams was obviously seeking new ways to express his own special life-view; he experimented with grotesquerie and parable. He had done his homework and apparently read Brecht, Dürrenmatt, Beckett, and Weiss. But he was awkward and old-fashioned in his experimentation. Too, a new mysticism seemed more and more apparent, a confused mystical-sexual mumbo-jumbo pulled out of an old trunk from a cobwebby Southern attic. Was this the very personal mysticism of a middle-aged poet, or was he moving toward one of the organized religions, Catholicism, perhaps? Of the two short plays comprising *Slapstick Tragedy*, *The Mutilated* was an ode to the lonely, the deformed, and the queer, as a pretentious Greek-style chorus informed the audience. The two aging winos (whores when anybody wanted them) quarreled in New Orleans' Latin Quarter; after various tribulations, they happily patched up their differences and drank Tokay and ate Nabiscos (the wine and wafer of Christianity?) and miraculously saw a vision of Our Lady. *The Gnädiges Fräulein* was Bosch (or bosh) on the Florida Keys, with a vaudeville Irish landlady, an American Indian in a loincloth, and a German lady who caught fish in her mouth. Eventually, birds plucked out the versatile German's eyes. Was this a comment on our ailing society? If so, it was without clarity and bite. His *The Seven Descents of Myrtle* (1968) was sad beyond words, an out-of-focus, funereal parody of everything he has even written about the South. I found myself averting my eyes.

William Inge was at his banal worst in *Natural Affection* in 1963, an incredible mishmash of sex run amok, including a dash of incest. It was an hysterical amalgam of box-office sex, but this time the cash register did not ring. He gamely returned to Broadway in 1966 with *Where's Daddy?* There was a new quiet in this one, and a welcome degree of wit and charm and mellowed humor. In a look at the younger and older generations in conflict, he had compassion for both. But Inge did not really probe, and he obviously did not understand the issues underlying today's revolt of the young. Paddy Chayefsky came up with two samples of middle-brow supermarket *kitsch*, *Gideon* (The Book of Judges) and a turgid, jumbled epic about Stalin, *The Passion of Josef D.* The message in each was Love. Chayefsky was not content to settle for the small-sized television soap operas he seemed best suited for.

Early in the decade, a number of other established playwrights failed both artistically and at the box office, Sidney Kingsley with *Night Life*, S. N. Behrman with *Lord Pengo*, and Irwin Shaw with *Children From Their Games*. Kingsley's drama seemed an awkward effort to catch up with the sexual revolution. Behrman's drama was a craftsmanlike look at an old pirate of an art dealer, but it was tired and empty. Shaw came off merely as a middle-aged nag.

One middle-aged dramatist seemed to find his voice again in 1968. Arthur Miller's *The Price* was an affirmative and virile, if somewhat obvious, drama about lies and illusions, values and responsibilities. Two brothers meet in a Manhattan brownstone where they proceed to sell their late parents' stored furniture to an ancient, philosophical dealer. The brothers have not seen each other for sixteen years, and they probe their tortured relationship with a *Brothers Karamazov* relentlessness. There were happy echoes of the early Miller in *The Price*. The man many had filed under "Lost" might still surprise us in the next decade.

Another familiar name also reversed the downward trend. Robert Anderson admirably succeeded with his 1967 *You Know I Can't Hear You When The Water's Running,* three vaudeville sketches about the sex comedy that underlies everyday American life. He succeeded in an area which eludes most Broadway writers: he captured the earthy, zany, wry humor of sex. Here was a sharp-eyed, uninhibited, and compassionate look at the American male at sexplay. If it was, in truth, a little disappointing in its totality, the work did offer moments of originality and wit—no small achievement in our theatre.

Two Eugene O'Neill premieres have illumined Broadway in the dim sixties, even though the playwright died a decade earlier. O'Neill has persisted as the father figure of American drama. *Hughie* was a minor but absorbing portrait of a seedy, second-rate con man living on illusions, and the title role was magnificently impersonated by Jason Robards. Erratic, clumsy *More Stately Mansions,* drastically cut for Broadway production, was not O'Neill in top form, but it towered over the Broadway enclave, and it provided Ingrid Bergman, Arthur Hill, and Colleen Dewhurst with roles of stature. O'Neill himself had been unsatisfied with his ten-hour script, and he left a note explaining that it was unfinished and should be destroyed at his death.

A new playwright who first found success in the off-Broadway theatres was promoted—or demoted—to Broadway. For many a young writer, the leap to Broadway sometimes resulted in economic benefits but seldom in artistic ones. Frank D. Gilroy, a product of the Yale Drama School and television, found favor at the off-Broadway Phoenix with a gritty, honest, shatteringly beautiful work, *Who'll Save the Plowboy?* This clear-eyed, unsentimental, and unsensationalized view of a New York lower-middle-class family was presented with an uncanny economy and grace. None of his three Broadway plays was so thoughtful and intense. *The Subject Was Roses* was a luminous but extremely limited domestic drama. With *That Summer—That Fall* in 1967, Gilroy ambitiously tried for a larger dimension, transforming domestic-comedy realism into epic tragedy. Employing the classic myth of Phaedra and her passion for her stepson Hippolytus, he now set the legend in New York's Little Italy. The results were ludicrous, embarrassing, tawdry, and excessively melodramatic. *The Only Game in Town* (1968) was a flagrantly surface look at bittersweet love in Las Vegas. It mercifully closed with dispatch. Predictably, it was sold to Twentieth Century-Fox for half a million dollars.

Amid the debris of a decade, a number of playwrights rose above mediocrity and thus courted disaster at the box office. James Goldman, in a noble failure of 1966, *The Lion in Winter*, showed a lively talent for invective. The repartee between Henry II, a twelfth-century ruffian monarch, and his vicious but ever-loving wife, made Albee's dialogue seem tame. Robert Preston, wearing a Hemingway beard and strutting like a prize racehorse, and Rosemary Harris, her red hair in a knot and her face puckered up like a dried fig, snarled and raged at each other with singular skill. Novelist Saul Bellow tried Broadway twice, and failed spectacularly at the box office. However, neither *The Last Analysis* nor *Under the Weather* was a complete dud, artistically. In fact, Bellows' delicious wit and wild, fantastic, Rabelaisian ribaldry was, in a sense, too good for Broadway, accustomed to Joe Miller synthetics. The complex allusions and free-wheeling musings on the state of the union offered too much Bellows to fit comfortably on any stage. He must try again. It is a welcome sign when a major American novelist is attracted to our puny theatre.

Some comedies seemed a bit better than earlier examples of the genre, primarily because they were directed by a young wizard name of Mike Nichols. He and Elaine May had been a remarkable nightclub and television team who slaughtered our mindless pieties with a devastating instrument—a very urban humor, tough, know-ing, and on target. In 1960, the team offered a welcome *Evening of Nichols and May* on Broadway, providing a wickedly subversive wit seldom displayed there. After the breakup of the team, Nichols tried Broadway directing, "improving" comedies. One kept won-dering whether he was wasting his time. Before Nichols was on hand to improve matters, Neil Simon had written a very routine commercial comedy called *Come Blow Your Horn*. But three of Simon's later efforts, *Barefoot in the Park*, *The Odd Couple*, and *Plaza Suite*, were staged by the boy wonder, and they brought instant Broadway glory to both playwright and director. *Barefoot in the Park* became one of the longest-running plays in the history of the American theatre. Dissect it and it will crumble into the dust of butterfly wings. Done decades later without a Mike Nichols in charge, it will seem incredibly banal. The director performed the same invaluable box-office service for *Luv*, written by Murray Schisgal, a graduate of off-Broadway. *Luv* is a bright little satire on American sentimentality, self-pity, and self-delusion in affairs of the heart. Astutely directing Alan Arkin, Eli Wallach, and Anne Jackson, Nichols blew up this very minor effort into a deli-cious piece of raillery.

Two farces gave the theatregoer more solid laughter than he was used to getting for his money. S. J. Perelman's *The Beauty Part* was a worthy parody on the biggest sell of them all, the U.S. culture business. Perelman delivered neat jabs at the culture-vul-tures, the Hollywoodians, the advertising pundits, pompous mag-azine publishers, pretentious painters, and a colorful bag of oppor-tunists. I remember the inspired performance by clown Bert Lahr and my own astonishment that real rather than assembly-line wit was being offered on the Broadway stage. *The Beauty Part* folded almost immediately. Ronald Alexander, who had created some distressingly formula adolescents in a dull comedy hit of 1952, *Time Out for Ginger*, came up with a surprisingly honest satire in the sixties. *Nobody Loves an Albatross* was an acid, accurate blast at stupidity in the television zoo, replete with moronic agents, writers, producers, packagers, and even a man who created canned laughter. Had his earlier charade been written merely to fit a safe and lucrative formula?

The miracle on Broadway in the sixties is not a new playwright or a new actor or a new director. It is the emergence of a good, sturdy repertory company. The troupe is, of course, the APA or more properly, the Association of Producing Artists, with Ellis Rabb at the artistic helm. His company is not yet a great one, but it has an unmistakable feeling for quality. Beginning its precarious existence on the campuses of the University of Michigan and Princeton, the group made a visit or so to off-Broadway showcases early in the decade, then joined forces with the dormant Phoenix management, which had lost its way. They practiced true repertory, not some bargain-basement version. Off Broadway, they presented Pirandello, Gorky, Molière, Cohan, Shaw, and Giraudoux with a shining intelligence. During the 1966–67 season, they firmly established themselves at the Lyceum on Broadway, and announced a five-year program for that distinguished house. It was the decade's best news. The Lyceum, incidently, was a perfect choice. The city's oldest legitimate theatre, it had been built expressly for repertory by Daniel Frohman.

The APA's Broadway offerings have been uneven, but even their failures have a certain éclat. Among the most notable productions have been a brooding, panoramic, bravura adaptation of Tolstoy's *War and Peace* and a glistening revival of Ibsen's 1884 masterpiece, *The Wild Duck*. The APA has whetted a new interest in repertory in a country where the dramatic arts are still relatively unknown. By keeping its ticket prices at a modest level and reserving $2 seats for students, this non-profit troupe has partially subsidized audiences, too. Well-wishers hope the company will succeed in its ambitious Five-Year Plan on Broadway, but the social climate of the theatre and the nation does not augur well. A belated grant of $900,000 from the Ford Foundation, in mid-1967, has proved a temporary lifesaver. However, this grant, to be awarded over a three-year period, was based on matching funds to be raised by the APA. The company relied on the government arts program for a large part of these matching monies. During the 1968–69 season, the Federal funds were not forthcoming. War-minded Washington was busy economizing on the home front, and the APA's future was most uncertain.

Repertory is no magic word that automatically spells artistic perfection. Under the sponsorship of ANTA, the National Repertory Company has toured the nation a number of times in the sixties. The troupe seemed at its best when Farley Granger, Denholm Elliott, Anne Meacham, and Eva Le Gallienne headed the company, and they presented a memorable revival of Arthur Miller's *The Crucible*. But the company constantly changed casts, and the quality varied from season to season. In 1967, the troupe came to Broadway on a Federal grant from the National Council on the Arts. This was a faint sign that perhaps the government was coming to see the importance of the dramatic arts. The company of fourteen was disappointing, however, and they simply did not yet have the style to offer satisfactory productions of Molière's *The Imaginary Invalid*, O'Neill's *A Touch of the Poet*, and Coward's *Tonight at 8:30*. Perhaps the chief attractions of the company were the tasteful settings by young Will Steven Armstrong. Clearly, repertory is not enough: it must also be good.

Fiasco is the only word to describe the Lincoln Center Repertory Company, a grievously split outfit which cannot decide whether its heart belongs to Broadway or off-Broadway. Financed by wealthy citizens, corporations, and foundations, the company began with a good deal of excitement in 1964, in a handsome temporary home in Greenwich Village, the ANTA Washington Square. Its first directors were Robert Whitehead and Elia Kazan, both successful Broadway men. They opened with an advance of forty-seven thousand season subscribers. With the proper dramatic flourish, Whitehead and Kazan, aided by playwright Arthur Miller, were busy with hammers and screwdrivers almost up to the opening-night curtain, installing seats in the amphitheatre. The initial offering was a new play by Miller, *After the Fall*. With this strangely offensive, meandering play, Miller broke a seven-year stage silence. The script took place in the middle-aged hero's head, and the turgid outpouring represented a stream-of-consciousness total recall. Once he had a simple leftist faith, but he had lost his way. He tried to understand his three marriages. The vulgar hero mirrored perhaps the uncertainty, the impotence, and the moral void of the urban intellectual in the sixties. Many in the audience were appalled by what seemed a kiss-and-tell technique. Were the three women onstage Miller's actual wives—Mary Slattery, Marilyn Monroe, and Inge Morath? Probably not: he employed the poetic license that is the right of all artists. But the play did have the clammy, disturbing air of an onstage psychoanalysis. It was of especial interest to only one man—Arthur Miller himself. It lacked distinction.

A series of other artistic disasters followed. *The Changeling*, a bawdy, brutal tragedy penned by Thomas Middleton and William Rowley in 1622, was outrageously misdirected by Kazan and inexpertly acted, most notably by young Barbara Loden. Could a commercial Broadway director handle the classics? Certainly Kazan wrecked this one. *Marco Millions* was second-rate O'Neill performed in a decidely second-rate manner; S. N. Behrman's *But for Whom Charlie* was third-rate Behrman, presented without grace or invention. Only once did the company succeed, and that was with Molière's *Tartuffe*. An imaginative young director, William Ball, was imported from the off-Broadway stages, and Michael O'Sullivan was dazzlingly daft in the title role. The trustees of the new repertory company were in turmoil. There was a bungled attempt to blame Whitehead and Kazan for everything. Before the end of the second season, Whitehead and Kazan—and their followers—were gone.

The worried trustees called in Herbert Blau and Jules Irving, a duo who had put San Francisco on the theatre map with their venturesome, challenging Actor's Workshop. Blau and Irving knew what they wanted; they had a philosophy of theatre; they were perceptive about the theatre's high aims. In the fall of 1965, they presented their first season in the $9,500,000 Vivian Beaumont Theatre in Lincoln Center. The new glass showcase represented all that money could buy, including a handsome Henry Moore sculpture in the reflecting pool at the theatre's entrance. The choice of productions presumed an audience of highly literate, discerning theatregoers familiar with the world's dramatic literature. It was perhaps a foolhardy assumption. Buechner's *Danton's Death*,

Wycherly's *The Country Wife*, Sartre's *The Condemned of Altona*
—did these have a chance of success with an audience conditioned
to Broadway's trifles? The company offered, too, a middling production of Bertolt Brecht's *The Caucasian Chalk Circle*. Broadway
had never seen fit to present this great play at all, although it had
had its world premiere twenty years earlier. However, the public
was divided on the Blau-Irving directorship. The fashionables
wanted light diversions. After all, they came to be seen, not to
sit through dramas of ideas. The intellectuals admired the bill of
fare but rightly complained of the low level of the acting and the
direction. The trustees were not impervious to box-office pressures:
they wanted hits. And so, in mid-year 1967, Herbert Blau was let
go and Jules Irving reigned uneasily and alone.

The future of Lincoln Center repertory remains in doubt. In the
summer of 1967, Peter Ustinov's antiwar *The Unknown Soldier
and His Wife*, was produced here—a tryout for Broadway. It was
an Alexander Cohen production, and Lincoln Center was a heavy
investor. The public response was favorable to the British playwright's latest philosophical jest, and it moved to a regular Broadway house in the fall. This could be one ironic solution to the
crumbling repertory idea—a multi-million-dollar tryout house! The
first play of the regular season of 1967–68 was a revival of Lillian
Hellman's *The Little Foxes*. Anne Bancroft, Margaret Leighton,
E. G. Marshall, and George C. Scott were called in to play stellar
roles. The drama was staged by Mike Nichols, and it was presented
by Lincoln Center by arrangement and under the supervision of
Saint Subber, a Broadway producer. It, too, moved to Broadway.
It was an admirable choice of a play, but what happened to the
original idea of a permanent company acting in repertory? Will
Lincoln Center become merely a producing adjunct of Broadway,
run by cautious trustees demanding hits? Was the original plan for
an exciting temple of art just so much public-relations hogwash?

Another disappointment in the sixties is the Actors Studio. These
players chatter about becoming a producing unit, a repertory company, a pertinent force in the theatre. Occasionally waking from
their psychoanalytical chores, they have managed to get onto
Broadway an uneven *Strange Interlude*, perhaps O'Neill's worst

effort; *Marathon '33*, a pointless documentary about dance contests in the thirties; a dull, chic *Baby Want a Kiss*, with Paul Newman and Joanne Woodward taking time out from moviedom; a flickering if not consistently glowing production of *The Three Sisters*, and a revivalist *Blues for Mister Charlie* by James Baldwin. Few of them were successful, artistically or at the box office. What has happened at the Studio, once the fond hope of American theatre? Will it ever become a significant producing company or remain a psychiatrically oriented gym for actors? Another dream of the past, the Theatre Guild, had best be mentioned with merciful brevity. What a splash this organization had made in the joyous twenties! In the present decade, its occasional attempts to wake up are sadly feeble.

How will future drama chronicles remember the sixties? Will the decade be remembered primarily for three Equity strikes in which actors shut down all Broadway? Or will it be noted as the decade when some theatres introduced bars and sold refreshing liquor rather than the usual pallid orange drink? Certainly the patrons needed stronger brew than ever to sit through Broadway's banalities.

Perhaps Lillian Hellman's succinct summary of Broadway aridity will be the final word. With her expected trenchancy, she commented in 1966: "I have been telling myself for a long time that theatre will get better. Good people will appear again. Good audiences will appear again. I have seen interesting things, things I respect, in England and Europe and around the country here. But here, Broadway-here, it's getting late. I don't believe in the fabulous invalid theory. We forget that invalids can stay invalids. They don't always die and they don't always recover."

CHAPTER 8

FOREIGN AID

ARTISTICALLY, BROADWAY IS now an underdeveloped country. A once-proud citadel of promise after the glorious 1915 birth, Broadway is, in the sixties, a provincial and desolate outpost. Luckily for the underprivileged theatregoers, there has been vital aid from abroad. The best things in American theatre life are foreign. Without this welcome aid, Broadway would offer little of distinction, for most made-in-America dramatic fare is reminiscent of a trip to a nightclub or an evening of television-viewing. Though the foreign aid does nothing to advance the cause of American dramatic literature, it does provide audiences with entertainment of the mind. It gives art to a starved nation. And perhaps by example it will stimulate creativity in our own native theatre.

The most provocative dramas from abroad have come from three men who write in German—Peter Weiss, Rolf Hochhuth, and Friedrich Dürrenmatt. Of the trio, Weiss, a German forced to leave his homeland in 1934 and now a Swedish citizen, has enjoyed the greatest American success with his *The Persecution and Assassination of Marat as Performed by the Inmates of the Asylum of Charenton Under the Direction of the Marquis de Sade*, a hit not only on Broadway but on college campuses and in community theatres and, oddly enough, in summer stock. The lengthy title perfectly describes the action. The stage is peopled by inmates of an eighteenth-century insane asylum who perform, intermittently, a play; the audience in the theater becomes the group of fashionable Parisians who viewed such pioneering psychodramas. Under harsh lights and an almost bare stage set in tones of white and gray, an

impeccable cast from the Royal Shakespeare Company was mar-
shaled in 1966 by inventive British director Peter Brook. Here was
a taut, haunting production obviously influenced by Antonin
Artaud's Theatre of Cruelty. The economical, almost-Oriental use
of space, the stylization of movement, and the occasional inter-
ruption of the action by music and song also suggested Brechtian
techniques. The drama itself is an argument between Sade, the unswerving individualist and sensualist, and Marat, the dedicated,
disciplined revolutionary; within this framework, the author explo-
sively presents a debate raging within his own mind. The great
theme centers around how to create plenty for all and still nurture
individualism, how to establish a truly cooperative society and yet
guarantee personal liberty. It is a central theme of our time, but
it is seldom tackled in our theatres.

Weiss's work does not altogether succeed. The clarity and the
sting of Brecht are absent. Making all the world a madhouse (in
Genet, a whorehouse) insures vivid, shocking theatre, but it also
opens the way for ambiguity and weakens Weiss's inflammatory
call. Many in the Broadway audience viewed it as juicy voyeurism and ignored the great debate. Weiss himself later observed that
his play had been variously interpreted: in western Europe, the
play extolled Sade; in eastern Europe, the accent was on Marat.
Declaring himself a Marxist on the side of Marat, Weiss vowed to
write sharper, more partisan drama in the future. Nonetheless,
Marat/Sade is heady theatre—and very un-Broadway.

With *The Investigation*, Weiss put Auschwitz on Broadway.
Using a condensed but unadorned transcript, he recreates on stage
the trials of the Auschwitz concentration camp officials. He does
not, however, use the words *Jew* or *Nazi*, thus making it unmistakably clear that he is depicting events that could happen almost
anywhere in our Ice Age. The setting of unfinished lumber, with
large wooden gates serving as a curtain, reminds one of a camp.
Oversized lights glare out with Brechtian sharpness, warning the
audience not to attempt escape. In the dock sit the accused, who in
their bland, well-dressed prosperity and slightly overweight jollity
startlingly resemble Gropper cartoons of our own congressmen at
work. The trial details a system in which everything is filed, proc-

essed, indexed, and carried out according to standard operating procedure (this army phrase occurs frequently), a system of enormous efficiency that provides for the murder, with businesslike dispatch, of four million men, women, and children. It is a brutal, shocking, shattering play. Weiss brings power and dimension into our theatre. Yet without didacticism and without raising his voice, he miraculously transmutes his gory material into a testament to man's hope.

However, the script is a kind of open-ended documentary which can be staged and played in a dozen different ways. On Broadway in 1966, unfortunately, it was ineptly performed by a soggy, soap-operatic American cast, wallowing in an emotional, overwrought manner out of Actors Studio. *The Investigation* needs a brassier, colder, neo-Brechtian style, for Weiss wishes to avoid sentimentality and to provoke thought.

Rolf Hochhuth's *The Deputy*—the most controversial play of our time—opened on Broadway in 1964. It was both drama and public event; above all, it was a moral event. This remarkable first play had been given its world premiere at the Freie Volksbühne in Berlin, under the aegis of dynamic director Erwin Piscator, ardent advocate of drama as propaganda; it had already been produced in London, Paris, Vienna, Stockholm, and Athens before coming to Broadway. The eight-hour drama relentlessly examines men's varying attitudes—from indifference to horror to delight—over the recent massacres of millions of European Jews.

The author's own background was a confused one. He had once been a member of a Hitler youth organization. His wife's mother had been decapitated by the Nazis. He knew fascism's spiritual terrors from within the structure. His rambling, ponderous document-stuffed drama is a kind of confession for the sins of the world. Oddly enough, its clumsiness and bulk are part of its power. This grim, grave, idealistic Protestant writer is in a rage over the world's moral obtuseness, and his play is an unrelenting assault on the indifference and inaction in high places everywhere. Of the disturbing questions he poses, the most controversial are directed at Rome. Why was Pope Pius XII silent during the supreme tragic event of modern times? What was the role of the Catholic Church in World

War II? Many conservative Catholics see the play as anti-Catholic, many liberals within the church disagree. After all, the hero is a young Jesuit priest who chooses the gas chamber rather than stand aside with callous indifference.

In New York, the painstakingly detailed script was horribly mutilated, cut to one-third its original length. The plot bones were there, but the outsized agony of the spirit was missing. The Broadway staging, too, was much too literal and flat. Director Herman Shumlin might have profited by studying the Paris production of Peter Brook, who, for example, dressed all his actors in identical blue cotton suits over which, when any special identification was needed, were placed a cardinal's scarlet vestment, a Nazi's armband, etc. Still, Hochhuth's overedited, poorly staged drama displayed a power and a courage rare on bloodless Broadway. And it created controversy (when was the last time anyone argued about an American play?).

Perhaps *The Deputy* is not a masterpiece, but it does bring the world into the theatre. On Broadway, this alone is a major achievement. Opening night, young uniformed neo-Nazis on the sidewalk shouted slogans and imprecations at theatregoers. During intermission, the doors were locked and the audience not allowed outside. As I rode home, I listened to a taxi radio announcing that police dogs and water hoses were being directed against Negro college students in a lovely Southern town. The theatre and life were joined.

In mid-1968, Hochhuth's *The Soldiers*, which inexplicably has been banned in London, opened and closed on Broadway with unseemly haste. Far from debunking Winston Churchill, the play made him warmly human, less a toy soldier and more a man trapped in the paradoxes of war. It was even more misunderstood, however, for the grave drama was only partly about Churchill. Its central concern was the Allies' ugly saturation bombing of German cities in World War II, the carefully planned murder of millions of German children in densely residential areas. It was a stubborn and insistent probing of man's conscience.

Created in the shadow of the atomic mushroom, Friedrich Dürrenmatt's *The Physicists* is one of the most boldly theatrical parables of our time, a towering work of scope and imagination. Dürren-matt's sinuous, subtle script involves a trio of physicists who are patients in a mental institution. Deeply involved in the theories of nuclear destruction, they are men burdened with enormous guilt. With rival powers demanding their precious knowledge for mili-tary uses, the physicists have decided to be "mad but wise," "prisoners but free," "physicists but innocent."

Under Peter Brook's vaudeville-flavored direction, the play flopped spectacularly on Broadway, lasting only a few weeks. Foreign aid was not always appreciated by the culturally starved natives. Perhaps the critics and the audiences, long dulled by a routine naturalistic theatre, could not appreciate poetic stylization. Perhaps *The Physicists* needed glamour names; the stars, Hume Cronyn and Jessica Tandy, were merely dedicated theatre artists who consistently sought quality. Dürrenmatt—with his disturbing, raw provocations, his bitter ironies, his intellectual love of oppo-sites, his intense concern with greed, power, individual conscience and, in this instance, world suicide—is unappetizing fare for the expense-account trade and the buzzing theatre parties.

One of the finer imports of the sixties was Robert Bolt's *A Man for All Seasons*. The martyrdom of Sir Thomas More has a special relevance for many Americans, for More would not compromise in matters of conscience—even if state policy were overwhelmingly against him. The play introduced to Broadway an English actor of unusual quality, Paul Scofield. Here was an artist who used his voice as an instrument of power and beauty, avoiding both dull naturalism and oratory. He has much to teach our American mum-mers, who diligently employ the Method (Strasberg's version of Stanislavsky) to achieve a deeper realism but scandalously neglect the dramatic nuances of the human voice. A couple of seasons later, Scofield appeared with the Royal Shakespeare Company in a fasci-nating, Beckett-like, existential *King Lear*. The star of this eerie, frozen production was not Scofield or any other actor but the director Peter Brook. In the light of today's horrors and urgent metaphysical quests for answers, Brook tried to recapture the awe and the poetry lost in the Victorian emasculation of a fierce Renais-sance seer. Unfortunately, the English company was presented at

Lincoln Center's New York State Theatre, a cavernous hall ideally suited to ballet and opera and notoriously inhospitable to drama.

Harold Pinter, one of the most interesting of the new generation of British playwrights and a consumate craftsman, was first represented on Broadway by his engrossing, atmospheric, masterfully vague *The Caretaker*, with uncommon turns by three uncommon British actors, Alan Bates, Donald Pleasence, and Robert Shaw. Pinter's dark-hued *The Homecoming* was later exhibited in a luminous Royal Shakespeare Company production, with a notably skilled performance by Paul Rogers. However, the real star of the foreign troupe was John Bury, an English set designer extraordinarily attuned to nuance. His dilapidated living room was realistic at first glance, and yet it contained, in its subtle exaggerations, a hint of the secretly subconscious world existing behind conventional appearances. *The Birthday Party*, another of Pinter's evasive, out-of-focus parables of today, came to Broadway in late 1967. Everybody is busily reading all sorts of recondite meanings into these strange works, and they do make an oblique comment on the cruelties and insensitivities of our times. Pinter reduces man to a quivering mass in a senseless world. But to me, he seems primarily the last in a line of neo-Gothic spellbinders. He is to be savored, not interpreted.

London's cursing, flamboyant firebrand Joan Littlewood, engaged in a to-the-death battle with musty, frayed-velvet, tea-and-crumpets Culture, crossed the ocean with her Theatre Workshop disciples and presented Broadway with two productions. The first was Brendan Behan's *The Hostage*, a knockabout vaudeville that captured the cockeyed, surrealist quality of modern life. *Oh, What A Lovely War*, was a funny-sad cartoon about World War I. Borrowing newspaper headlines, snippets of speeches from the archives, film clips, advertising slogans, vintage songs and dances, this improvisational, irreverent, and disturbing montage of war was far removed from the mindless patriotism usually presented to any nation's citizenry.

John Osborne has been represented on Broadway stages in recent years by two plays: *Luther*, a strangely unsatisfying chronicle with an idiosyncratic concentration on the great protester's constipation, and *Inadmissible Evidence*, a 130-minute tantrum created by a stunning British actor, Nicol Williamson. The latter play is a portrait of a man in an undefined rage, a study in unrelenting hysteria, and in part a farewell to a decaying empire. The anti-hero, viewed in wavery focus in the manner of an amusement park's distorting mirror, is an obscenity-spewing Englishman who sees through the middle-class cant of his age and yet is lost in his own sick, backward-looking conservatism. He hates the committed young. In agonized spite, he cries out that his own daughter has lost her virginity to UNICEF. It is perhaps more a sermon or a non-stop monologue than a full-blown drama, but it is highly effective theatre.

Arnold Wesker, a young socialist celebrated in England for a series of impassioned scripts, was introduced here in 1963 via *Chips with Everything*, graced by the finely meshed ensemble playing of the English Stage Company and the dextrous direction of John Dexter. Wesker's script is a savage attack on the caste system in the British military. *Beyond the Fringe* spotlighted four young and sharp Oxonians on a delightful satirical spree, and one of them, a frighteningly erudite beanstalk named Jonathan Miller, stayed on to contribute discerning critical observations on American culture in the press and original staging in our theatre. Robert Shaw's *The Man in the Glass Booth* was imported from London in September of 1968. Mr. Shaw, who had earlier been acclaimed as both actor and novelist, now proved to be a playwright of distinction. From the fantastic angle of a paranoid New York financier on trial in Israel for atrocities he allegedly committed as a Nazi colonel in World War II, the taut, multi-layered drama probed innocence and guilt, illusion and reality. Shaw's drama of ideas was faultlessly staged by Harold Pinter, playwright temporarily turned director.

Not all these aid packages from abroad are of uniform quality. The playwrights vary in skills and insights. When the dramas are both directed and performed by foreign guests, they are usually startlingly superior to the American product. But some plays and productions from Europe are simply routine. The all-star Gielgud version of Chekhov's *Ivanov* was, in point of fact, not nearly so graceful and well-orchestrated as William Ball's production off-Broadway in the fifties. English playwright Peter Shaffer, a most competent artisan, gave us two one-acters, *The Private Ear* and *The Public Eye,* that were intelligent and minor. His *The Royal Hunt of the Sun* marked the first production (1965) of the British National Theatre on Broadway. Advertised as "total theatre," the play retold the bloody saga of the Spanish conquest of the Incas in the sixteenth century, and lavishly employed dance, mime, music, and pageantry. How desperately it needed the sweeping choreography of a José Limon or a Martha Graham! Though the script marked a welcome move away from frowsy naturalism, Shaffer's dialogue was empty and bombastic. *The Killing of Sister George,* a British import by Frank Marcus, was a tiresome domestic comedy reminiscent of *Life with Father.* There were differences: here the overbearing Father was a strident, tweedy lesbian; Mother was a retarded miss of thirty-four who wore Mod clothes; their children were Raggedy Ann dolls. English actress Beryl Reid strutted around the stage, cigar in hand, and gave a top-notch impersonation of pugnacious John Bull in drag. *Rosencrantz and Guildenstern Are Dead* by a welcome English newcomer, Tom Stoppard, was a superficial, rather collegiate, and damnably clever look at two minor characters in *Hamlet.*

France's Jean Anouilh has been represented by several plays in the sixties, including *Traveler Without Luggage* and *Poor Bitos.* Sir Laurence Olivier, in virtuoso turns, alternately impersonated the silken cleric and the coarse Henry in Anouilh's *Becket.* It was a Broadway box-office hit even though Sir Laurence did not seem at his best. A much superior Anouilh drama, *The Rehearsal,* failed, though graced by a British cast of unknowns who performed like a mellow and superior chamber music ensemble. Anouilh has never fared particularly well in America. His corrosive hatred of the middle class, his overripe disillusionment at once sentimental and cynical, and his worldly, disrespectful barbs directed at both church and state do not suit the Yankee temperament.

The celebrated Franco-Romanian Absurdist, Eugène Ionesco, came to Broadway in 1960 with his *Rhinoceros.* He seemed, however, to be a conservative in avant-garde clothing. The play is a

rather simple-minded attack on conformity, illustrated by a population willingly turned into rhinoceroses; it is essentially a one-act
cartoon, expanded far beyond its proper length. Zero Mostel, that
plump clown who somehow expresses all the sadness and absurdity
in life, did the impossible: he became a rhinoceros before one's
eyes—with not a change in costume or makeup. A hit in Paris,
Félicien Marceau's *The Egg* was a 1962 flop in New York. Its
theme is similar to that of *How to Succeed in Business Without
Really Trying*. The difference is that Marceau tells the truth, while
the American musical hedges. It is a hilarious, tough comedy about
an ambitious, petit-bourgeois scoundrel determined to make his
way into the Establishment, who succeeds beautifully by way of
seduction, adultery, theft, a smart marriage, and murder. An
American comic, Dick Shawn, was uncannily right as the anti-hero.
But alas, the natives as usual preferred a sugar-coated version of
life.

A number of permanent companies from many countries have
visited Broadway during recent years, and they have, of course,
enriched our stages beyond any mere recital of names and dates.
These secure companies have been nurtured with love and money
by their governments; they are recognized as national treasures.
The Moscow Art Theatre came to Broadway in 1965, its first visit
since the historic tours of 1923–24. Of the one hundred and fifty
actors in the permanent Moscow company, forty-nine came to
America. They displayed ensemble acting of an unusually high
order. There were no bit parts; each performer created a rounded
portrait, whether that of a faithful servant or an aristocrat with
an amused disdain for those in trade. One fact became startlingly
clear: these actors were not at all like the many celebrated American
practitioners of the Strasberg version of Stanislavsky's Method.
MAT artists did not overemphasize the actor at the expense of the
play. The actors were not hysterical or neurasthenic; they were
never lost in the characters they impersonated. They were always
in full command, and they listened to one another. They were not
stars; they were ensemble players, quite a different story. These
Soviet actors shone in productions of Chekhov's *The Cherry
Orchard* and *The Three Sisters* and in a dramatization of Gogol's

Dead Souls. A more contemporary work, *Kremlin Chimes,* written by Nikolai Pogodin during World War II, had charm and some truth in it, but it illustrated a danger of official, party-line Socialist Realism: there was a Rotarian air of forced good cheer and a one-dimensional optimism. Surprisingly and disappointingly, there was a musty, museum air hovering over the company's sets. Despite its accomplished performances, one felt that MAT, founded by Stanislavsky in 1898, had become frozen and had not moved with a changing world.

The Bavarian State Theatre also came to Broadway. Georg Buechner's *Woyzeck,* Goethe's *The Accomplices,* and Hauptmann's *The Rats* were presented at City Center (with its atrocious acoustics) in 1966. The Buechner work was particularly effective. Although he died at the age of twenty-four in 1837, Buechner uncannily foresaw the modern world and its horrors. Jürgen Rose's sparse, ominous set design had much to teach Americans about mood and style. From France came the Comédie-Française, with Robert Hirsch whirling and gesturing with the grace and abandon of a dancer, giving glorious acting lessons to our ill-trained realists. The Apparition Theatre of Prague, obviously influenced by Oriental stagecraft, created magical illusions by the use of special lighting, luminous paint, black-velvet, and miraculous timing: a boat seemed to float effortlessly in midair on the darkened stage; fish swam by and nibbled on a fisherman's line; a passing cloud produced a thundershower. For a brief moment, fresh, childlike wonder returned to the theatre. The chilling *Arena,* pitting man alone against threatening society, was marvelously danced by Jiří Srnec, the group's young founder, and it fleetingly indicated how dance and drama might again be united after centuries of false separation. The Hamburg State Opera, with its bold and contemporary staging, its non-star policy, and its versatile troupe of acting singers, showed us that opera need not be "grand" and ossified, that indeed it could be theatre. The Renaud-Barrault company, the Piccolo Teatro di Milano, Israel's Habimah Players, Roger Planchon's Théâtre de la Cité, Japan's venerable Grand Kabuki and the Bunaku Theatre puppets, Russia's Obratsov Puppets and its joyous Moiseyev dancers—all brought milk and honey to the desert

This does not imply that we in America see all the best and most provocative drama from abroad. To the contrary, the aid is much too limited. We need more, not less. There are several plays by Rolf Hochhuth and Peter Weiss Broadway has not exhibited. At this writing, there is no plan to present Weiss's *Discourse* (the actual title is forty-eight words long), which is a fierce blast at American policy in Vietnam. When will we see the Berliner Ensemble or the Peking Opera? Theatregoers in many other countries have been fortunate enough to view these troupes. On Broadway, Beckett has been represented by one play, *Waiting for Godot*—and that in the fifties. Ionesco, Frisch, and Dürrenmatt have been skimpily sampled. Jean Genet, John Arden, Günter Grass, Arthur Adamov, and Fernando Arrabal are entirely unknown to Broadway audiences. Arnold Wesker's richly textured, intensely exciting trilogy (*Chicken Soup with Barley*, *Roots*, and *I'm Talking About Jerusalem*), which was staged in 1960 at the Royal Court by John Dexter, is not planned for Broadway viewing. Yet these Wesker works, which combine domestic and political themes in an almost classical unity, contain some of the most theatrically effective scenes in modern playwriting. Indeed, there are many excellent expressionist odes by the late Sean O'Casey never displayed on Broadway. One could easily fill the bills of several repertory companies with major twentieth-century dramas never produced in our impoverished theatre. Americans traveling abroad have returned in recent seasons with wondrous tales of theatre experiments in Eastern Europe. These intrepid explorers aver that the most exciting stages in the world can now be found in Poland, Russia, Czechoslovakia, Hungary, and Bulgaria. Here bold, uninhibited young pioneers, in open rebellion against the elderly fuddy-duddy curators of Socialist Realism, are creating new stage techniques and even new forms of drama. When will Broadway see productions by the Taganka and Contemporary Theatres of Moscow, the Gorky Theatre in Leningrad, Jerzy Grotowski's Laboratory Theatre in Wroclaw, or the Comedy Theatre of Bucharest?

The most dramatic instance of Broadway's spiritual starvation is contained in the strange saga of Bertolt Brecht. The late German playwright is the most significant dramatist in our century. His works are central to our times, containing within their taut forms the tensions, dualities, and ambiguities of modern man in search of the Grail. No other writer has expressed so penetratingly the great issues of today—nihilism or discipline, chaos or planning, war or peace. His masterly plays (a legacy of forty-nine) have been performed around the globe as well as at the Berliner Ensemble in East Berlin, and his vigorous, invigorating ideas in stagecraft have influenced theatre artists in every nation. Yet when he lived in exile in this country, he was considered something of a security risk. Now he is considered a box-office risk. Why attempt Brecht when you can make a killing with a cute little sex comedy or a meaningless musical? Broadway has yet to see *The Rise and Fall of Mahagonny, The Days of the Commune, St. Joan of the Stockyards, The Measures Taken, The Visions of Simone Marchard*, or a number of other plays written by the German genius who died in 1956. In fact, Brecht has been rarely attempted at all in the strictly commercial showcases of Broadway. The first try was a disastrous production in 1933 of *The Threepenny Opera* which lasted only a few days. Its style was totally misinterpreted, and it was launched as a sort of gay, saucy Shubert operetta. Two other botched attempts came in 1963, and both *Mother Courage and Her Children* and *The Resistible Rise of Arturo Ui* closed quickly. Neither production was graced by style or intelligence. Instead, the performers seemed innocent and gay children at play, children who had missed the horrors and the key political issues of this century. *Mother Courage* lacked the grittiness of the original (which was not a sweet pacifist play but rather a violent indictment of an economic way of life). *Arturo Ui* turned out cute rather than sardonic or biting. After the playful shenanigans preceding it, the epilogue of *Arturo Ui* did not possess the grim and dark beauty it should: "The womb from which this beastly thing issued [read both Hitler *and* Chicago gangsters] is still fecund." To a market-oriented Broadway drugged by literal, naturalistic theatre, inimical to dramas of ideas and plagued by inadequate rehearsal time, Brecht is perhaps an impossibility.

The master has been attempted twice in the sixties by the non-profit Lincoln Center Repertory. The troupe fashioned a passable version of *The Caucasian Chalk Circle*, a dramatic gem Broadway had never offered theatregoers. The play had been given its world premiere in 1948 at a tiny theatre in the basement of the women's dormitory at Carleton College, Minnesota, and was then produced in university and resident theatres in most of the fifty states—but not in Manhattan. It came to Lincoln Center after the longest national tour on record. Lincoln Center Repertory also produced Brecht's *Galileo*, the title role astutely given to English actor Anthony Quayle. Within the unusually complex, intricately woven fabric of this masterly drama, Quayle impersonated a Galileo magnificently alive and sensuously aware of life's multiple choices. The scoundrel and the saint are always at work in fascinating combinations in the Brechtian dialectic. No play is more relevant to the U.S.A. in the sixties than this masterpiece about seventeenth-century Italy.

There is irony in the continuing foreign aid to Broadway. For this artistic bonanza, the intellectuals must thank two Broadway Barnums, David Merrick and Alexander H. Cohen. These brigands have produced most of the quality imports. Both are tough, practical businessmen who know how to use carnival publicity to make a buck. Both have produced junk as well as quality. Yet without these two colorful pirates, Broadway would be artistically worthless. These gentlemen have imported dramas by Osborne, Pinter, Anouilh, Delaney, Ustinov, Littlewood, Wesker, Friel, Weiss, and an impressive and lengthy list of others. Many of these have been brought over with director, set, and most of the cast intact; others were local productions. Merrick is a particularly fascinating study. Many connoisseurs regard him as the greatest s.o.b. since Jed Harris. He is supremely gifted at creating both publicity and enemies and invariably tries to browbeat the press. In a further irony, Merrick has created a kind of government subsidy of the arts, without bureaucratic control. The non-profit David Merrick Arts Foundation was set up in 1962. If Merrick makes money on a trifle like *Hello, Dolly!* or *Cactus Flower*, he can put some of the cash into his own tax-defying foundation in order to bring over an *Inadmis-*

sible Evidence or a *Marat/Sade*. He also uses profits to help finance a fine experimental university theatre at Brandeis. The current tax laws allow such indirect subsidies, and if a production loses money, Merrick figures that no harm is done—the money would have gone to the government anyway. One suspects these two tough showmen of the worst crime of all: that they have marshmallow hearts. Merrick and Cohen are artists disguised as businessmen. Secretly, they are hopelessly stagestruck, deeply aware of Broadway's lack of quality, and determined to improve the state of affairs. But don't call them artists to their faces.

There is another equally delicious bit of irony current on Broadway. The Theatre of the Absurd is present in life as well as on stage. In recent years, certain members of Actors' Equity have taken to picketing shows with English actors and suggesting the English go home. These Equity members believe the roles filled by the English actors should have gone to Americans. They have picketed Cohen's imports, Peter Shaffer's *Black Comedy* and Harold Pinter's *The Homecoming;* they have noisily opposed the casting of Anthony Quayle in *Galileo* and Margaret Leighton in *The Little Foxes.* The English variant of our Actors' Equity, we are told, discriminates against American actors abroad, and thus we are justified in reciprocating. I disagree. I am all for breaking down national barriers and making international art accessible to everyone everywhere. As a member of the audience, I find the picketing appalling—for the most selfish reasons. I have spent perhaps the best hours of my own Broadway theatregoing watching the work of British playwrights, directors, set designers, and actors, largely through the efforts of Merrick and Cohen. If these joys are taken away from me, Broadway will be a far dimmer place for one member of the audience. It is all too ridiculous. Certainly, Broadway needs all the foreign aid it can possibly get. Thank God and Queen for the British. They have temporarily saved us in time of peril.

The artistic situation in the off-Broadway theatres is, of course, vastly different. Foreign plays are always welcome in these smaller showcases, but they do not constitute a lifesaving action. For here the native playwright—experimental and unhampered by Broadway slickness—is coming into his own.

Brecht has been done in the off-Broadway theatre of the sixties with love and care and respect. His earliest works, *Baal, Drums in the Night, In the Jungle of Cities,* and *A Man's a Man,* have been especially fascinating as clues to his later thinking. *Baal,* his first play, was given its belated New York premiere in 1965. Though *Baal* was written in 1918, one can discover in it themes popular in the sixties: existential nausea, harsh rejection of bourgeois values, a strong interest in perverse sexuality, beatnik defiance, an over-wrought sense of the absurdity of life. Here sweaty sex is curiously mixed with a brooding, searching quality. *A Man's a Man* was given two concurrent productions off-Broadway, each valid. John Hancock used masks, presented a virile, social Brecht; the Living Theatre fashioned a more subtle, sensuous, psychological Brecht. George Tabori has compiled the ultimate tribute to any playwright —a dramatized pastiche of his life and works. However, *Brecht on Brecht* amounted to an emasculation of the great man. The arch-rebel was suitably Americanized, palatable for next week's church-social drama hour. Only the abrasive appearance of Lotte Lenya saved this "tribute" to Brecht from total disaster.

That sad-eyed clown Samuel Beckett has been garlanded with many productions in the Other Theatre, even though he has been ignored on Broadway. The most memorable in the sixties was the Cherry Lane production of *Happy Days,* a tender monologue with a harsh *No Exit* theme. Winnie, a garrulous woman in her fifties, is sunk up to her waist in a mound of sand (in the second act, she is up to her neck). Willie, her colorless husband of sixty, is lying nearby; he occasionally grunts a reply to her incessant chatter. Life is bleak and without meaning or aim. Yet Winnie is an optimist, forever looking on the bright side of everything. She endlessly opens and closes her handbag of possessions, examining comb, scent, mirror, handkerchief, etc. *Happy Days* is a strange, ironic, and profoundly lyric play about the absurdity of the human condition. One need not agree with Beckett's particular brand of *Weltschmerz* to enjoy and savor its wild and singing poetry. Madeleine Renaud, one of the most magnetic actresses in the international theatre today, came over from Paris to play Winnie in this converted stable. She alternated in the role with American actress Ruth White, and both of them were near-perfect. English playwright John Arden has been represented by two of his scripts, *Live Like Pigs* and *Serjeant Musgrave's Dance*. The first is a curious comment on the obtuseness of bureaucrats in a Welfare Society, with a touch of *Tobacco Road* sensationalism. His *Serjeant Musgrave's Dance* is a far sharper piece with a rough mixture of realism and outsized poetry, a dash of O'Casey, a pinch of Brecht, and a special stubborn quality all its own. The script examines the role of the military in a miners' strike in nineteenth-century England, and it becomes a relentless, brooding, bitter attack on militarism. Though there are awkward moments, Arden's fierce play burns with a hatred of colonialism and war that is exciting to dulled audiences long bereft of controversy and spiritual nourishment.

English socialist Arnold Wesker has been shown in tantalizing bits and pieces. *Roots,* a section of his celebrated trilogy, was presented briefly in 1964 in a converted nightclub. This luminous, affecting tale is of a simple Norfolk country girl returned from a long stay in the city. Deeply influenced by her absent Jewish-socialist lover, she learns painfully to find a voice of her own. *The Kitchen* is another Wesker drama in the English anti-Establishment tradition. Here, on stage, is rush hour in the kitchen of an enormous restaurant, as shrewdly and compassionately observed by a social dramatist who was once himself a pastrycook. The play was strikingly directed, with verve and relish, by Jack Gelber, the author of *The Connection.* Another off-Broadway import was *Hamp,* John Wilson's searching if somewhat conventionally structured drama about the horrors of war, a World War I tale of a naive, likable, honest, and inarticulate soldier of twenty-three shot for desertion. From an impoverished English mill town, the boy had enlisted and fought in a long series of bloody battles. He deserts his company at a moment of hysteria ("I couldn't stand it no more."). The case reminded me of a similar one, that of Pvt. Eddie Slovik in my own outfit, the 28th Infantry Division during World War II. An almost spiritual glow surrounded this off-Broadway production. Harold Pinter was represented by *The Lover,* a very observant and amusing playlet on role-playing in sex and marriage. A misty Pinter double bill, *The Room* and *A Slight Ache*, was distinguished by the presence of Frances Sternhagen, an amazingly versatile American actress seen too infrequently. An open-stage revival of Behan's *The Hostage* proved superior to the Broadway original. A 1963 mini-revue, *The Establishment*, clearly showed that the British could be much more savage than their American cousins in attacking religion. The British knew how to be sacrilegious with a wicked twinkle, how to offend and yet please.

Although he has been produced everywhere in Europe, France's Jean Genet has been exhibited in New York only in the off-Broadway theatre. His *The Balcony* and *The Blacks* are both genuinely subversive. Liberals are at a loss to define this perversely honest homosexual thief. He is an original, who does not write in the prescribed manner. Will our essentially stodgy liberals, often frozen in dogma, ever learn that art is not something that can be bought and sold by the yard, that drama is not the same as an editorial or a political speech, and that art has a special life and a form all its own? The greatest art is magically created out of form as well as content. *The Balcony*, which was directed by José Quintero at the Circle-in-the-Square in 1960, is a house of mirrors. It is a study of a whorehouse and of society: each, says Genet, is a reflection of the other. Each is based on fakery and sham. Genet is endlessly fascinated with role-playing, and his brothel customers play-act the roles of bishop, judge, general, etc., with a perverted grandeur. *The Blacks* (1961) is not a liberal tract for white-and-black integration. In fact, it rips apart the liberals' well-constructed façades of good will. It is a bitterly twisted play in which Genet's homosexual sado-masochism is given free rein, for he is more interested in the sinuously complex drama of the oppressed and the oppressors than in platitudinous freedom polemics. Here is a dark ritual of murder, an ironic slaughter of the white race beyond the tortured fantasies of a LeRoi Jones. It is scorching and elegant at the same time. Far from incidentally, the play became *The Green Pastures* of the sixties, and during its long run, practically every unemployed Negro actor in New York appeared in it, including

Godfrey Cambridge, Louis Gossett, Roscoe Lee Browne, Cicely Tyson, James Earl Jones, and Cynthia Belgrave.

Foreign aid, whether it came from an anti-American ex-German Swede or a bastard homosexual thief from France, was most welcome. America has sent Europe money and guns; they have sent us art.

CHAPTER 9

REVOLT
OFF
BROADWAY

THOUGH FOREIGN AID has provided temporary relief to grateful audiences, it does not offer any viable alternative to Broadway. Fortunately for the adventurous theatregoer and for the vigor of American drama, there is an alternative to the tired gags and familiar formulas of Broadway—a theatre committed to youth, boldness, and revolt. Broadway is like a used-up bejeweled old whore; the Other Theatre is saucy, fresh, and fervent. Broadway is a tiny, expensive enclave a dozen blocks long by two blocks wide; the Other Theatre is found off Broadway all over New York, in brownstone walkups, church sanctuaries, coffee houses, garages, lofts and basements, converted movie houses and nightclubs. Broadway is a soporific, a time-killer, and it carefully avoids any jarring references to the real world outside its walls. The Other Theatre is audacious and alive, and it reflects, with wit and irony and sometimes vulgarity, the social changes rocking the nation. The Other Theatre is, hopefully, our salvation.

One cannot understand the Other Theatre unless one understands the decade's young. All America is getting younger. The nation's businesses, armed with the latest statistical studies which indicate that soon the average age will be somewhere in the early twenties, are astutely aiming their fashions, furnishings, and leisure products at the dominant buyer—the young. And in the sixties, the young themselves are in unmistakable and refreshing rebellion against yesterday's clichés and platitudes. There is a reawakened sense of commitment, power, and joyousness among the young that was conspicuously absent in the fifties. This is not a collegiate

Silent Generation playing it safe. For the first time since the McCarthy plague of the fifties, youth seems to have found its voice again. It is exhilarating. Neither a full-dress revival of McCarthyism nor patronizing advice from scoffing elders can stop them: they have found something precious—the dream which had been lost in the postwar years.

Many of the nation's searching, intellectual young take their direction, consciously or unconsciously, from the New Left and, to a lesser degree, the hippies. Both groups overlap and often are found in the same person. Both have been bitterly critical of Lyndon Baines Johnson; both have opposed the undeclared war in Vietnam. Both are fascinated in varying degrees by the possibilities of drugs; both applaud the new free-and-easy, swinging, color-splashed styles in dress and in the arts. Both are unalterably opposed to the prevailing prejudices of White America against Black America. Indeed, it was the young, both black and white, who were most active in the civil rights movement and the great liberation marches in the first half of the decade. Many risked and some lost their lives in the crusade.

Perhaps the greatest bond which unites them is an unalterable opposition to censorship of any kind. Both groups are part of the sexual revolution which is sweeping America (and will, hopefully, sweep away the nation's Puritanism, both sexual and political, within the next few decades). Both groups approach heterosexuality, homosexuality, and bisexuality with a startling new tolerance. The young are opposed to hypocrisy about four-letter words in speech or in literature or in deed. They have been brought up in the literary climate of Burroughs, Selby, Miller, Southern, et al., where men's room graffiti has become the norm. They have expanded this freedom in novels to include their underground films, rock lyrics, poems, and even their magazines. The Fugs, one of the most ribald and respected of the electronic rock groups, sing bawdy songs not played on radio and television. Ed Sanders, bearded guru of the Fugs, sometimes operates a bookshop and sporadically publishes a magazine entitled *Fuck You*, which the stately *New York Times* cannot bring itself to mention by name, even though its contributors have included such elder-statesmen poets as W. H. Auden. In another irreverent magazine, Paul Krassner's *The Realist*, the four-letter word is an obsession. Provocative lapel buttons are seen everywhere (and they earn a tidy fortune for their manufacturers), buttons with such sentiments as "Jesus Wore Long Hair," "Pot, Peace, Pussy, Perversion," "Make Love Not War," "Love Is a Many Gendered Thing," and "Not With My Life You Don't." Even Soviet poet Andrei Voznesensky, on a 1967 American tour, was caught up in the button craze and sported one which read boldly, "Fuck Censorship." His delighted fans replied with a button reading "Voznesensky Glows in the Dark."

But there are significant differences between the New Left and the hippies. The New Left is convinced that America can be changed by organized social protest. The Students for a Democratic Society, one of the most articulate of the many Left groups, is vociferous on the campuses in the demand for better education. These activists want more democracy in the running of the mind-factories and in the choices of curriculum and faculty. The New Left is strongly anti-dogmatic, with little sympathy for the blind sectarianism of the earlier Left. These youngsters know that socialism does not necessarily mean democratic socialism: they are acutely aware that the extreme Left once deified Stalin, only to learn later that he was a fearfully sick man guilty of heinous crimes and untold murders. They cannot trust the old dogmatists, but they clearly recognize the cancer in American life and are determined to do something about it. They are tired of phony heroes and unresponsive politicians; they are horrified by the paranoid violence of those who oppose freedom of dissent. All the New Left organizations sympathize with the hippies as rebel brothers, but they detect an intellectual flabbiness in them. They do not copy the hippie costumes and hair styles with any fidelity, and they feel that frenzied concentration on drugs is a way of avoiding battle or, in essence, submitting to the enemy. To them, drugs in excess are essentially neo-romantic and reactionary.

In turn, the hippies (or whatever new label they might be given next week) find the New Left too tightly organized and unloving, too much like the cold middle-class America they despise—in other words, another form of tyranny. They look inward, not outward, for kicks. These intense, bearded young men and these soulful, dreamy-eyed girls, congregated in the urban slum-bohemias, are totally disorganized save for a gentle communal sharing. The hippies scorn the American rat race for Success, and, by choosing poverty, they make a society Outside Society. Though drugs and Hindu chants are still in, these hippies are not the same as the beats of the fifties. There is a new and subtle sense of revolt and power: they stage be-ins and pelt the police with flowers and join peace marches. The Flower Children are less withdrawn, less alienated than their predecessors in the fifties, for they vaguely sense they might change the world. Of course, their fashions and fancies are quickly commercialized (psychedelic disks, prayer beads, body painting, Indian necklaces) by a dulled majority in search of voguish kicks, but there is validity in the hippie distaste for a dehumanized society. In their curiously apolitical stance, there is an implied criticism of our highly advertised American Way of Life. In some ways, theirs is a positive nihilism.

What does this have to do with the Other Theatre? Absolutely everything. The influence of the young is everywhere evident to those who visit the off-Broadway showcases. The bracing gusts of change, in both content and style, are coming from here. Certainly these experimenters have provided me with the bulk of my theatre-going pleasures in the sixties. I'm counting on these young artists, most particularly the activists, with their cheek, imagination, and fresh vision, to show us again what *living* theatre can be. Within another decade, they might possibly change the look of American drama.

To be exact, the Other Theatre is composed of two related New York groups: off-Broadway proper and its exciting new sub-division, off-off-Broadway. These guerrilla bands control some fifty showcases far from the Broadway neon. *Succès scandaleux* and the Other Theatre's brightest bull's-eye is Barbara Garson's *MacBird*, which opened in a Greenwich Village cabaret in early 1967. It is an impressive political parody of the postwar world seen through the eyes of a member of the New Left. Miss Garson, a graduate of the University of California, was twenty-five when the production opened in New York. An activist in the Students for a Democratic Society and the Free Speech Movement at Berkeley, she had been one of the eight hundred students arrested in the massive freedom rallies in 1964. The paperback edition of her play enjoyed an enormous underground success long before the off-Broadway premiere. The book's cover carried the following straight-faced statement from Lyndon B. Johnson anent World Theatre Day in 1966: "To the artists of the stage, who give us all mankind in all its disguises and so give us ourselves as we truly are, I pay tribute . . ." The play's principal backer was Paul Krassner, editor-publisher of *The Realist.* Though many uptown newspaper and magazine critics were confused and appalled by the Garson caper, it won extravagant praise from gadfly critics Eric Bentley and Robert Brustein, veteran leftist don Dwight Macdonald, and leading poet Robert Lowell. The New Left drama was later presented in several editions around the nation and the world.

MacBird is a diabolically clever, outrageously hilarious version of the Johnson-Kennedy feud, using *Macbeth* as the model; it is also hellzapoppin far-out Pop Art, a nose-thumbing cartoon. It wonderfully catches the rhythms of Shakespeare, and it is flavored with wit sly and sardonic as well as brutal. In *MacBird* a vast spectrum of political leaders are all seen as calculating and power-hungry. Many members in the audience (particularly those past the age of disrespect) are deeply offended by the savage cartoon and the latrine language; some innocents falsely interpret the play as realism rather than as bigger-than-life grotesquerie. (America has little tradition of political satire in the theatre, and satire makes audiences uneasy.) In its totality, *MacBird* is about the shabby quality of American politics, the fading of the American dream. It is a cry of shame and anger from the younger generation; it is a round of wild laughter, with a certain sadness just below the surface. It would have lasted one night on Broadway—if by some miracle it had ever arrived there.

America Hurrah, another off-Broadway hit, is a blistering attack on the tone of American life, seen not from the political platform but from the employment office, the television studio, and the motel. Belgian-born Jean-Claude van Itallie does not write doctrinaire or simplistic political plays. Yet his scripts—and most particularly *America Hurrah*—express a deep discontent with our land. Though his credentials are impeccable (Deerfield Academy and Harvard), he is thoroughly at odds with the Establishment, describing modern American life as banal and mechanical and unfeeling. Of the three short plays which comprise *America Hurrah*, the dazzling tailpiece *Motel*, is the most spectacularly original—a fiercely funny, bitterly apocalyptic vision of America triumphant. Van Itallie uses electronics (deafeningly amplified rock and roll and psychedelic colored lights, madly swirling over the stage) and larger-than-life-size dolls. One doll is empty save for a recording of the droning, sticky-sweet, hypocritically pious voice of actress Ruth White, the voice of the eternal motel-keeper, selling her materialistic inanities about the best motel in the world. The smirkingly grotesque motel guests, a Don Juan and his per-oxided lady, are completely encased in papier-mâché-like material, including face masks. After knocking over the motel-keeper, the human puppets strip, wreck the motel room, and scribble crude four-letter words all over the walls to a wild rock beat. It is social commitment in a new way—impudent, bizarre, ironic.

Van Itallie, like so many of the best off-Broadway playwrights, is a graduate of the experimental off-off-Broadway workshops. He freely acknowledges his debt to them. He is typical, too, in that with many of the new playwrights, he places himself in deepest debt to Antonin Artaud, the late theoretician of the Theatre of Cruelty, and to Marshall McLuhan, the Canadian priest of the electronic age. Artaud, the French actor-director-playwright who died in 1948, was immersed in Oriental theatre ideas, particularly the Balinese. He sought "to break through language in order to touch life"; he destroyed all social proprieties in order to transform actors and audiences into "victims burnt at the stake, signaling through the flames." A man of unbearably intense vision, he spent nine tragic years near the end of this life in an asylum for the insane. In his radical break from photographic realism, Artaud has profoundly influenced modern European theatre (*Marat/Sade* is a choice example). Today he is a galvanic force among the young experimentalists of the workshops. Marshall McLuhan, director of the Center for Culture and Technology at the University of Toronto, is another god of the young—a dazzling erudite oracle. In a number of his books and essays (*The Gutenberg Galaxy* and *Understanding Media* are two of his most provocative works), he has demonstrated that through the centuries the means by which man communicates have determined his thoughts, his actions, and his way of life. Printing created the scholastic, alienated, typographic man; the electronic media of today are transforming man into a multi-sensory, intuitive, unified man, turning the planet into a village, catapulting man back to the communal values of the preliterate tribe. His provocative, ironic, playfully ambiguous ideas are, of course, much richer than this bald thesis suggests, and young theatre minds have discovered a fertile lode in McLuhanism, novel ways of total stagecraft, unifying sounds, colors, and motion, as well as language, in evolving a dramatic work of art. Van Itallie's *Motel* is an astonishingly deft use of the ideas of both Artaud and McLuhan.

Megan Terry's *Viet Rock*, which went from the off-off-Broadway workshops to off-Broadway production in 1966, is not entirely successful. It offers choreography, protest, improvisation, song, and scatology mixed together in a neo-Brechtian style. (Brecht continues to dominate serious theatre efforts in the twentieth century.) Miss Terry's ambitious attempt at total theatre is vehement and lusty, but it also seems vague and formless in its attack on war and on the Vietnam War in particular. There are some striking moments, most notably a mocking pictorial parody of Michelangelo's "Pietà." But *Viet Rock* is unfulfilled promise, its vaudeville form disguising more than it clarifies. Miss Terry, a prolific writer for the workshops, is a crusader for improvisation. Her plays are meant to be "reconstructed" rather than performed as written. Indeed, she describes one of them, *Comings and Goings*, as a "trampoline for actors and directors." Sometimes workshop improvisation provides brilliant results, sometimes slipshod amateurism.

A vast number of other off-Broadway productions originated in off-off-Broadway lofts, including Tom Sankey's *The Golden Screw*, which came to the Provincetown Playhouse in early 1967.

Author-performer Sankey, wearing boots and faded blue jeans and sporting a Noah Webster hairdo, illustrates at first glance the conformity of the New Bohemia in New York's East Village. A more penetrating look confirms that he is a poet, a genuine troubadour of the young, a prodigiously versatile musician who plays an autoharp and guitar and who writes his own tunes and lyrics. *The Golden Screw* is another example of total theatre, gentle, reflective, sometimes bawdy, sometimes defiant. "Jesus Come Down" is a remarkably touching, subtle antiwar song; "The Beautiful People" is *cante hondo*, a lyric cry of lives wasted, of innocence lost. Between songs, Sankey and a small cast tell the sad and very American tale of the cheap exploitation of folk music.

Lanford Wilson, one of the off-off-Broadway's most polished playwrights, came to off-Broadway and the Cherry Lane Theatre during the sixties. *The Rimers of Eldritch* is a powerful portrait of a small Midwestern town. On several levels of unpainted boards, a symphony of small-townness is orchestrated with enormous skill and beauty. One is reminded of Grant Wood and his stolid American Gothics or Sherwood Anderson and his spiritually starved rustics or Thornton Wilder with *Our Town*. However, in the Wilder instance, the likeness is mostly in the imaginative, Orient-inspired staging. Wilder's people are carefully censored and edited, artfully placed in pretty cut-flower arrangements. Wilson is more full-blooded and contemporary—more vinegar and less sugar. Here are glimpses of greed, intolerance, jealousy, status-seeking, self-righteousness, sex-repressions, blind conformity—in short, all those simple small-town virtues missing from *Our Town*. Wilson laces his rather grim study with delicate irony and sometimes unbuttoned hilarity. His cameo of four farmers laconically discussing crop and weather problems is a gem of absurd dialogue. His musical sense is everywhere evident in the way his actors repeat the themes of various movements before pushing forward to a new synthesis; and he has added a splendid touch by having the actors suddenly break into actual song now and then, repeating music from three standard Protestant hymns, "In the Garden," "When the Roll Is Called Up Yonder," and "Shall We Gather By the River?"

Night of the Dunce, by Frank Gagliano, a Brooklyn-born writer who has been playwright-in-residence with the Royal Shakespeare Company, bears the imprint of the New Left. *Night of the Dunce,* produced at the Cherry Lane in 1967, takes place in a decaying public library branch, where nobody borrows books any more. The frustrated library staff tries valiantly to encourage reading, but ends up in petty quarrels. A nameless fear pervades the library, the menace and tension subtly mounting. Then a sadistic gang of toughs calling themselves the Dunces attempt to destroy the library. Gagliano is writing not only about punks who plunder; he is warning us of the menace of fascism in America. Most important, he is a playwright who can combine almost unbearable tension with uncanny political insight. Would such chilling parables ever be produced on Broadway again?

Mississippi-born Mart Crowley may or may not write another play, but he has made stage history with his first, *The Boys in the Band,* which opened in a former church in the spring of 1968. This is the frankest and best play about homosexuality ever written by an American. Most efforts to dramatize this once-forbidden topic have been either stereotyped, sensational, embarrassed, or evasive. Crowley's unusual charade is thoughtful and adult, and his homosexuals are meticulously and honestly observed in all their rich variety. *The Boys in the Band* is both funny and ineffably sad; it marks a real breakthrough in uncompromising stage treatment of sexual deviation.

Pugnacious Norman Mailer, who miraculously avoids middle-age flabbiness of the spirit, remains staunchly with the young, half hippie, half New Left. In the sixties, he was represented off-Broadway by his dramatization of his novel, *The Deer Park.* Mailer paints a dazzlingly wicked picture of Hollywood and its neighboring desert playpen peopled by whores, pimps, slimy gossip columnists, half-educated studio executives, homosexual stars, and recanting victims of the political witch-hunts. They are a fascinating lot, ripe for the pen of another Ben Jonson or Nathanael West. However, Mailer's messianic strain ruins his good-bad script. Since he is a fervid preacher, his audience is treated to purple philosophical passages about hell, jellied gasoline, the bomb, the sex mystique, and the Apocalypse. During his sermon, Mailer uses more four-letter words than any literary effort since Henry Miller's reveries. The rough language is perfectly justified, however. How can you write dialogue about Hollywood without coarseness? Of the performances, one was a gem of mummery. Group Theatre veteran Will Lee, made up to look startlingly like Louis B. Mayer, limned a beautifully etched portrait of a hypocritical old pirate of a studio executive.

The classics are not neglected in the off-Broadway showcases. Indeed, were it not for this invaluable alternative to Broadway, the great plays of the past would never be seen in the New York professional theatre. One of the decade's top dramatic events was the production, at the Circle-in-the-Square in late 1963, of an antiwar play written twenty-four hundred years ago. Euripides' *The Trojan Women* is a scathing indictment of military murder, and in a clear, crisp, miraculous translation by Edith Hamilton, one could hear the echoes of Lidice and Hiroshima. Michael Cacoyannis came over from Greece to direct the work with sweep and scope. Ironically, four years later, when a modern tragedy overtook Greece (a vicious military dictatorship), certain dramas by those old subversives Euripides, Aeschylus, and Aristophanes were banned there. Nothing demonstrated more clearly the potential power of drama than this censorship. Luckily, the Greek colonels-turned-critics could not ban these classics from performance in other lands. Another delight of the sixties was the Sheridan Square Playhouse revival of Shaw's 1894 *Arms and the Man* (at what age does a classic become a classic?). This antiwar burlesque remains as fresh as today's television news, and proves once again that the bearded old British subversive is still a valuable security risk. Happily, too, by vigorous and suave direction, the excessive campiness and coyness of earlier revivals was avoided this time around.

Miracle worker Joseph Papp, who has taken Shakespeare out of the classroom and made him startlingly alive to millions of New Yorkers with his *free* productions in Central Park, is now masterminding another major endeavor. Shakespeare alfresco continues in the park in the summers, but for the theatre season proper, Papp has now gone indoors. He saved the Astor Library, a handsome

1854 landmark in danger of destruction (our architectural heritage is scandalously vanishing), and turned it into not one, but three theatres. The interior of the building is breathtakingly beautiful, with its early Victorian Classic balustrades and columns, chastely white with gold-leaf detail. Papp not only offers the classics, but presents the work of unknown experimentalists. The new Papp adventures began in late 1967 with *Hair*, a very un-Shakespearean rock musical about the pot-flavored pleasures and hang-ups of today's hippies. It was a lively beginning. Tickets to the 300-seat Public Theatre were priced at $4.75 or less. At all performances, 100 tickets at $1.75 apiece were set aside for those under twenty-five. Papp blandly stated that it cost him $6 to fill each of those seats. He was acutely aware that theatre must be subsidized, and he bravely went forward to underwrite the theatre, finding needed funds from millionaires, big business, the city, state, and federal governments, and such celebrated theatre partisans as Elizabeth Taylor and Richard Burton. He was determined to find and attract a new audience of the young and the poor. As for playwrights, he ridiculed the idea of a shortage: "I have no trouble in finding what I want." Indeed he has introduced a raft of works by unknown Americans and several Europeans new to New York. By the nineteen-seventies, Papp's projects may well prove to be the most bracing and influential in America.

Improvisation came to New York in the sixties. The Committee, which had started in San Francisco in 1963, invaded Broadway—and flopped. The Premise, which had begun in St. Louis, came to off-Broadway and prospered. But the wittiest group of improvisers came from Chicago. A parent group, the Compass Players, had bloomed near the University of Chicago, and produced Mike Nichols, Elaine May, and Shelley Berman. A fresh form of theatre by and for the well-educated, urban-wise young, it was the closest we have come since the 1930's to the European political cabaret. The successor company, the Second City, produced such uncommon talents as Barbara Harris and Alan Arkin. Here was a political sophistication new to the theatre, and here the young wits could hone their talents as actor-citizens and lustily prick a paunchy middle class. The accent was vaguely leftist and unmistakably irreverent: even those most sacred cows, J. Edgar Hoover and God, were not spared. The Second City, with sparkling, inventive turns by Harris and Arkin, came to Broadway in late 1961 and folded after a few weeks. It was predictable: the troupe was simply too good for Broadway. They wisely went off Broadway into a Greenwich Village cabaret (liquor, sandwiches) and lasted for a number of years, attracting all of New York's brightest citizens to their carnivals of unreason unmasked. In some of the later editions before its demise, Second City became too messily involved in the psyche, in personal fantasia. But it was a vitalizing force in New York, teaching the young that theatre could be contemporary and pertinent and fun. They clearly demonstrated, too, the value of improvisation, especially in rehearsals under the control of an inspired director. Many of the off-off-Broadway workshops were to develop those improvisational techniques even further.

Two established groups dominate the off-Broadway theatre today, one in a slum church, the other in exile. These are, of course, the American Place and the Living Theatre. The American Place is an experimental theatre housed in St. Clement's Episcopal Church in the slums of Hell's Kitchen. (Incidentally, Episcopal churches have for some reason or another been extraordinarily hospitable to theatre rebels.) Under the early leadership of idealistic clergyman Sidney Lanier, the American Place was first a private workshop and then, late in 1964, a public arena, a church sanctuary turned into a stage. The premise of the American Place, which took its name from photographer Alfred Stieglitz' legendary art gallery, is the most ambitious in the city: to create an aura of creativity similar to the ferment at Stieglitz' center. The promising rebels state their ambitions thus: "The American Place exists to foster good writing for the theatre. It hopes to accomplish this by providing a place, a staff, and a broad program of practical work to American writers of stature: our poets, novelists, and philosophers who wish to use the dramatic form, and to serious new playwrights."

The American Place has not, of course, achieved these noble aims. But the exciting potential is there. The group has produced a number of quality scripts, and even the flops have been fascinating. Most important, it has been a place to work without fear of failure. That is, every work need not be a box-office smash or an absolutely finished work. It is a place where the artist can grow. There is an intelligently conceived program of readings in progress to allow for revisions, and there is a loyal audience of subscribers who understand they are a part of an experiment in theatre. The American Place has received several grants from the Rockefeller Foundation. In the spring of 1967, help also came from the Ford Foundation in the form of a $475,000 gift so that the theatre could continue for the next three years.

At least two of the group's productions are lasting achievements, *The Old Glory* and *Hogan's Goat*. The first is an ironically titled historical trilogy by America's leading poet, Robert Lowell. *Benito Cerino*, the finest section of the trilogy, is a dark, brooding parable on the American ambivalence toward slavery, engrossing both as a drama of warring psychic tensions and as profound social comment. Though it is an adaptation of a Herman Melville novella, it is unmistakably first-rate Lowell. The other distinguished sections, *My Kinsman, Major Molineux* and *Endecott and the Red Cross*, have also been performed at the theatre. The towering poet is deeply committed to the American Place, and, hopefully, he will provide it with a number of dramatic works. It was Lowell who brought William Alfred, a professor of English literature at Harvard, to the attention of the American Place. A richly hued portrait of Brooklyn's Irish Catholics in the 1890's, with last hurrahs, deathbed revelations, and priestly rites, Alfred's *Hogan's Goat* details how persecution can twist a man's mind rather than make him more compassionate toward the suffering of others. Vicious prejudice ("No Irish Need Apply") and tenement poverty, the lot of so many Irish immigrants during the great American exodus, sometimes brutalized these newcomers. Without raising his voice, Alfred suggests that people ought to be more careful of one another.

All too often America neglects her most original artists, particularly if they cannot be tamed. Julian Beck and his wife, Judith Malina, are America's most valuable theatre experimentalists. Judith, dark, flaming, gay, and Julian, fair, bald, scholarly-looking, are also the theatre's most arresting and arrested (for a variety of ever-changing social causes) couple. They mix irrepressible laughter with thoroughgoing revolt. In the fifties, the Becks—as producers-directors-actors—wandered from rickety loft to loft, slowly gathering around them a dedicated band of rebels. Before decade's end, they finally settled into a second-floor walkup in Greenwich Village and made a deserved splash with Jack Gelber's *The Connection*. In the sixties, the Becks presented a harrowing documentary duplication of sadistic life in a Marine Corps prison, Kenneth H. Brown's *The Brig*. In the fall of 1963, during the run of this controversial drama of military inhumanity, the Internal Revenue Service closed the theatre without warning. The Becks reportedly owed $23,000 in back taxes. The actors exuberantly broke the government locks to stage a spectacular and unauthorized sit-in performance of *The Brig*. They were arrested, and the Becks were given jail terms. Many theatre people wondered openly if the Living Theatre was being persecuted for tax problems or for the politics of the Becks. After all, as proud anarchists, the Becks had been identified with many minority causes—peace, civil rights, Cuba, civil disobedience during air-raid drills, etc. It was ironic. The Living Theatre was the most celebrated group in sight. They were the talk of Europe. Earlier, the troupe had won the grand prize in an international theatre competition in Paris, a prize which went to the U.S. Government. The Living Theatre should have been heavily and gladly subsidized by both foundations and the federal government rather than penalized for a clandestine stage performance.

For most of the sixties, the Becks have chosen exile in Europe, and their rag-tag company of brave mummers has willingly followed. The wanderers have continued to present the scandalous *The Brig* and have introduced America's Other Theatre to startled Europeans under near-starvation conditions in London, Antwerp, Basel, and Berlin. In Paris in October of 1964, the company presented *Mysteries—And Smaller Pieces*, and it was an immediate hit with a select and vastly appreciative audience. The unusual work, based on the theories of Artaud, is a series of happenings created by the entire company. There is no playwright or director in the conventional sense. One sequence offers a military drill, precisely executed during a recital of a poem about the U.S. dollar bill. In another, a man sits on stage and shouts slogans, such as "Make Love Not War." The angry, anguished work ends with a plague in which the entire cast dies in a variety of patterns. The Paris performance of *Mysteries* was followed by similarly successful showings in Brussels, Rome, and Vienna. In Berlin in February of 1965, Malina directed a male cast in Genet's *The Maids*, and a second hit was in the repertory. In September of the same year, another communal spectacle was created, merely using Mary Shelley's novel, *Frankenstein*, as a starting point. Again there is neither playwright nor director. Improvisation, ritual, dream, myth, electronic sounds, free-form Artaud—all go into this *Frankenstein*, a surrealist musing about man's vain attempts to improve his own state and his constant creation of destructive monsters. Electrocutions, garrotings, hangings, and gas-chamber deaths are all part of the violent stage action. The last section of the play takes place *within* the monster's head. For the company's production of *Antigone*, Malina adapted Brecht's version of Sophocles' drama so that it was particularly relevant to today's acts of civil disobedience. In *Paradise Now*, the Becks departed even more radically from conventional theatre. In ten sections, based on Martin Buber's *Ten Rungs*, the lengthy work called for non-violent revolution then and there. Members of the audience were invited to come onto the stage to liberate themselves and later to participate in improvisations in the open street. The Beck's four-year exile has been anything but tame.

In September of 1968, the 34-member Living Theatre returned to the United States, performing works which had found favor among Europe's young dissenters. The crusading troupe first appeared at Yale and then New York's out-of-the-way Brooklyn Academy of Music. After a long national tour, they went back to Europe. Their American admirers hoped they would end their exile —for good.

In many ways the Becks are the spiritual parents of the off-off-Broadway movement, which is the most significant new force in American drama. Most of the young, fearless explorers start off with the radical premise that there is another America and another culture conveniently ignored by the mass media; they are in absolute revolt against the Establishment and those they regard as its brainwashed followers. Off-off-Broadway is vastly freer and more imaginative than the highly unionized, upholstered, and somewhat cautious off-Broadway stages it sometimes feeds with new dramas. (Off-Broadway is much too expensive for these rebels: in the fifties, a production there cost a few hundred dollars; in the sixties, $10,000 and up.) Most of the off-off-Broadway showcases are non-profit (any profits usually go into the next production) and strictly a labor of passion. Within a few short years, however, they have created a sizable and impressive group of playwrights, directors, and actors.

Off-off-Broadway started in 1960 with a production of Alfred Jarry's *Ubu Roi* at a Greenwich Village coffeehouse called Take 3. The term "off-off-Broadway" was coined by Jerry Tallmer, then critic for the small but influential Greenwich Village weekly newspaper, *The Village Voice*. Throughout the sixties, hope has flamed to life in these pioneering temples of drama (mostly cafés, churches, and lofts), despite spartan seats, sparse decor, and frequent lapses into production shoddiness. To a growing and devoted audience, this is the true theatre capital of America. Spokesmen for off-off-Broadway disdainfully refuse the secondary role of training-ground for Broadway. Instead, they aver, they are an answer to Broadway, a New Theatre. Most of the tiny theatres exist precariously on a pass-the-basket basis. They are often operated as "clubs" (one pays an admission fee in the form of club dues, usually amounting to a dollar), and they are constantly harassed by the License, Fire, and Buildings Departments of New York. It is all very reminiscent of the early days of the Provincetown Playhouse, also operated as a "club," also an angry, visionary answer to Broadway, and also perpetually in and out of police stations.

Some of these theatres might more properly be labeled workshops for dramas-in-progress. One of the most venturesome is Joseph Chaikin's Open Theatre. Chaikin is a former member of the Living Theatre tribe, and his workshop is, in a sense, an offshoot of its more publicized parent. Here playwrights, actors, directors, designers, and musicians can explore and improvise together. Megan Terry has been a part of the Open Theatre since its inception, and a number of her boisterous scripts, peppered with a ribald celebration of sex, were given birth here. Jean-Claude van Itallie has worked here since 1963, and his *America Hurrah* had its genesis in this New Drama incubator. In *America Hurrah*, both Chaikin and co-director Jacques Levy displayed their masterly skills at fluid staging. Another extraordinary honeycomb is the Playwrights' Unit, the joint enterprise of Edward Albee, who has made a fortune from his plays on Broadway, and his long-time associate Richard Barr. This workshop was started in the summer of 1963 with $25,000 out of the profits of Albee's Broadway hit, *Who's Afraid of Virginia Woolf?* No other American playwright has so practically encouraged fellow-writers. Whenever a promising newcomer emerges in the non-profit, tax-free workshop, he or she is given a professional off-Broadway production. Adrienne Kennedy, Frank Gagliano, LeRoi Jones, and Lanford Wilson immediately come to mind, but there have been many others. Albee may or may not be a playwright of the first rank, but he has firmly established himself in stage history as a dramatist who encouraged others.

Caffe Cino, a narrow storefront in Greenwich Village, opened in 1958 and in no time at all it was producing dramas while the *espresso* machine sputtered and frothed. Its impresario, the late Joe Cino, was a pioneer in combining food, non-alcoholic drinks, and iconoclastic drama; he was herculean in his long battles with city bureaucrats who deemed drama should be done only in conventional theatres. Lanford Wilson, the young playwright from Lebanon, Missouri, achieved his first success at Caffe Cino with several short scripts. His *The Madness of Lady Bright* is a minor sketch, but it is a carefully observed, classically cool portrait of an aging and pitifully deluded homosexual with varicose veins, a sort of male Blanche DuBois.

Some of New York's churches are hotbeds of theatre revolt. Theatre Genesis, located in St. Mark's-in-the-Bouwerie, one of the city's oldest and most historic houses of worship, has offered more than fifty original plays since 1964. Under the supervision of lay minister Ralph Cook, Genesis is a thriving workshop where actors read promising scripts. Selected dramas are given full production on three consecutive weekends. Tom Sankey's *The Golden Screw* was first presented here, as were the earliest plays of Sam Shepard, *Cowboys* and *The Rock Garden*. In such subsequent scripts as *Chicago* and *La Turista*, Shepard, a young playwright from Fort Sheridan, Illinois, has shown a remarkably felicitous gift for words, Joycean in their whirling stream-of-consciousness fecundity. Analyzed, word for word, they mean nothing; taken together, they create meanings within meanings, moods within moods. Admission at the Genesis is by contribution, as it is at the Poets' Theatre, another first-rate stage in a church. Under the leadership of the assistant minister, Al Carmines, who is also an excellent composer, dramas are produced in the choir loft of the Judson Memorial Church, a handsome Italianate, Stanford White-designed building on Washington Square. Playwrights Joel Oppenheimer, Rosalyn Drexler, and Maria Irene Fornes have shared this lively church with happenings, art shows, and avant-garde dance programs. What is truly remarkable about all these guerrilla groups within churches is that they are totally free and uncensored by their religious hosts, even though any given play might well be obscene, sacrilegious, socialistic—or all three.

Of the growing number of revolutionary centers, the most exciting and the most fecund is Cafe La Mama (or, more formally, La Mama Experimental Theatre Club). Since 1962, more than three hundred new plays (one a week or every two weeks) have been produced at La Mama. Most of the top off-off-Broadway playwrights, from Sam Shepard to Rochelle Owens, have been lovingly presented here at one time or another. Megan Terry's *Viet Rock*, van Itallie's *America Hurrah*, and Lanford Wilson's *The Rimers of Eldritch* were all shown at La Mama before their more publicized off-Broadway displays. In the fall of 1968, La Mama, after a precarious existence in a series of rather scruffy lofts, finally acquired its own building, a former sausage factory in the heart of the Lower East Side's hippie-land. There are two theatres in the building, both capturing La Mama's earlier cafe-like atmosphere, with low tables and coffee or hot chocolate for those who wish it. These new showcases feature movable, revolving seats that can be rearranged to suit whatever environment and staging style a particular play demands. In addition to these theatres, a smaller room, resembling a plant-filled greenhouse, is devoted solely to poetry. The fee is the usual dollar "club" dues. Nearly everyone who cares deeply about the current Broadway blight is, sooner or later, a "member." England's icon-smashing director Peter Brook is a member, as is *Marat/Sade* author Peter Weiss. There is an ambience here, a warm embrace between audience and company that I had forgotten could exist. La Mama is, first and last, *alive*.

Magnificent mother of this voltaic theatre is tireless Ellen Stewart, who by day earns a living as a fashion designer. With a shattering smile, a voice that is delicate melody, and the lithe movements of an impala, Ellen Stewart is one of America's most beautiful women. Flamboyant, generous, intuitive, completely unconventional, Miss Stewart, who likes to describe her theatre as "subliminal" rather than hortatory, is constantly on the search for new talent. She is total in her commitment to the New Drama. She gives all her own income to La Mama, and she is no stranger to pawnshops and the loan departments of banks. The budget for a new production is usually about $200. Miss Stewart herself brews coffee, takes reservations, and manages the minutest details of La Mama, from finding food and shelter for her actors to sweeping the stages. Her group of actors and directors, fifteen or so, somehow survives on nothing. Yet La Mama goes on, and Miss Stewart is the most active producer in New York City.

It all started in 1962, in a basement a few blocks from the present La Mama, with a stage the size of a bed. It was Miss Stewart's own apartment in an unintegrated building. Miss Stewart is black, and trouble came soon enough. Somebody called the Health Department and angrily reported they had counted sixteen white men visiting a Negro woman in the basement for five hours. Luckily, the investigator who arrived was a retired vaudevillian, and he was all for her theatre project.

The East Village success of La Mama has not been enough for the insatiable Miss Stewart. She has also established branches in Paris, Copenhagen, and Bogota, Colombia, and has mothered her itinerant troupe across several continents. They have appeared as welcome guests at drama festivals all over Europe. In the tradition of the Living Theatre, La Mama proudly exhibits the Other Theatre and the Other America to the world.

The quality of the La Mama productions varies, with unforgettable invention one week and embarrassing ineptness the next. But, all in all, its plays and productions are the most vivid in New York by any standards save those of a hopeless conservative. Leonard Melfi's *Niagara Falls* is typical of many productions. It needs vigorous editing and ruthless cutting, but it contains an original social stance. The symbolism is based on fact: the American side of Niagara Falls is crumbling, while the Canadian side holds fast. Against the setting, Melfi places a varied and spiritually crumbling group of young jilted Americans in a cheap motel. *Niagara Falls* was staged with careful attention to mood and nuance by Kevin O'Connor, also one of the most pliable and subtle of the new off-off-Broadway actors. Remarkable, too, is Rochelle Owens' *Futz*, the outrageous tale of a village sodomist in love with a pig and hounded to death by a bestial society suffering from its pervasive hypocrisies. Tom Eyen's *Court* is an imaginative recital of a seduction presented in the form of a basketball game, even borrowing the costumes of that sport.

Paul Foster, an experimenter from Penns Grove, New Jersey, is one of La Mama's most promising talents. His *Balls* is more creative play (or finger exercise) than achievement—a conceit in which the only stage action involves two Ping-Pong balls in constant motion. But his *Tom Paine* is a splendid work of sweeping power. It is La Mama at its finest. In this play there are two Tom Paines, one dirty, drunk, confused, the other elegant and well-groomed— and they talk back and forth to each other during the action. For the original La Mama production, Kevin O'Connor, with consummate skill, impersonated the unkempt Paine; John Barkos (earlier the pig-lover in *Futz*) was equally deft as the prettier, tidier "conscience" of Paine. The entire production, like all of La Mama's efforts, was a group affair, relying on suggestions, interpolations, and improvisations by all the artists involved. When the script called for an ocean voyage, a ship tossing at sea is merely suggested by the actors. The actors, in black tights, wore masks on occasion, and when wigs were needed, they donned stylized rather than actual curls. Too, all the performers danced and played musical instruments. At one point, the Bishop, the General, and the Governor danced a deliciously decadent gavotte.

Towering force behind this production and an omnipresent influence at La Mama is Tom O'Horgan, one of today's seminal directors. A former professional harpist and music teacher, he is committed to, among other ideas, more music in the theatre. The present divisions (straight play, musical, opera, Modern-Dance dramas) are, he proclaims, "a twentieth-century hoax." All actors should sing, play musical instruments, and dance in the theatre of the future. O'Horgan rightly feels that one cannot express the complexities of contemporary life through photographic realism; we need and must pursue total theatre.

It is too early to know what lasting impact the Other Theatre will make on Broadway and our national drama. Is it a secondary path or a major new direction? Perhaps this will not be clear until the seventies or eighties. There are many valid objections to the Other Theatre, riddled as it is with incestuous in-fighting, with petty feuds and jealousies, and with the sickly cultism of any minority culture. The writing and acting are often slipshod. All too often professionalism is foolishly derided as "uptown." All too often these youngsters' frenzied, formless experiments seem merely a perverse reflection of the impotence of their elders—equally directionless and puny. Are these young artists disciplined and dedicated pioneers or are they the sulking offspring of an exhausted upper-middle class, neurasthenic variants of Mom and Dad? Will today's fake rebel be tomorrow's square? To deify the young is dangerous nonsense. Some of the innovators are much more involved with their precious psyches than with the war-ravaged world around them. Too many of them retreat from history, from political reality. Yet I am stubbornly certain that the Other Theatre is making a radical breakthrough onto higher and choicer land. The evidence is piling up each season. It is primarily from the Other Theatre—and not from the new and costly temples of dead Culture with government, foundation, and private patronage—that a genuine renaissance (protesting, kicking, and screaming) may come.

10

BLACKFACE,
WHITEFACE

NEGROES—PLAYWRIGHTS, PERFORMERS, directors, and other collaborative artists—have mattered very little in the American theatre until quite recently. This has not been, of course, by their choice but by the brutal decision of White Power. Until this century, in fact, blacks were neither on stage nor in the audience. They were represented in plays, musicals, and the ubiquitous minstrel show by white men whose faces were smeared with burnt cork. Today, an enormously gifted and fiercely original black playwright, LeRoi Jones, composes defiant dramas with a taut, verge-of-hysteria hatred of white insensitivity, white stupidity, and white cruelty. He once urged blacks to "smash the jellywhite faces" of the enemy. Among those arrested in the 1967 riots in Newark was America's most militant playwright, the same Jones, with his scalp split (seven stitches were required) by someone's unidentified weapon. Is it an illogical journey from the savagely caricatured endman, Mister Bones of the minstrel show, to the vicious, bestial beating of LeRoi Jones? Is it really a far step from burnt cork to burning houses?

Nothing on our stages, however, compares in intensity and fervor (not even the dramatic implosions of Jones) to the new black militancy now answering the 350 years of White Power which have held the black man firmly in his white-appointed place. In the fifties, the colored peoples of the world presented long-delayed answers to the colonialists with the emergence of an astounding number of new Asian and African nations. This was not lost on Afro-Americans, and it found expression in many ways in the sixties. The first half of the decade was the time of the sit-in, the freedom march, and the registration drive for votes, an heroic effort largely concentrated in the Deep South. A surprisingly courageous battalion of Northern whites, including a disproportionate number of college students, joined this great crusade. In the second half of the sixties, the slogan has changed from "We Shall Overcome" to "Black Power." The revolt has dramatically deepened and spread throughout the entire nation. With a more defiant, hate-Whitey coloration, the struggle is now led largely by young, well-educated Negro theoreticians, no longer tolerant of white or black misleaders with their castrating sermons of moderation and gradualism. These proud young blacks are keenly aware of their new power, secure in the grim knowledge that one must fight for every gain every step of the way.

The fate of the Afro-Americans on and off stage is a most useful index of the nation's maturity. The ugly racism of America, which has practiced *apartheid* much longer and with more subtlety than South Africa, is mirrored by the history of blacks in our theatre. As early as 1821, a company of black actors performed in an improvised playhouse at the corner of Bleecker and Mercer Streets in New York; they offered the classics, chiefly Shakespeare, to an enthusiastic Negro neighborhood. Leading player James Hewlett was acclaimed as Othello and Richard the Third. But white hoodlums invaded the theatre and caused such irreparable damage that it had to be closed. Frequent visitor to this theatre had been a rapt, impressionable child, Ira Aldridge. Stagestruck, he later took a backstage job at the white Chatham Theatre so that he could observe the art of acting at closer range. His minister father then sent him to the University of Glasgow so that he could get a good education.

By 1833, Aldridge was playing leading roles in the London theatres. Handsome, graceful, with a melodious and commanding voice, he was engaged by Charles Kean to play Othello to his Iago, and they toured Europe. Ira Aldridge was the first black man to play what had been white roles, including Macbeth, Shylock, and King Lear. He received more honors and decorations than any

American actor before or since. Made a "Knight of Saxony" by the state of Saxe-Coburg-Gotha, he ever after called himself Chevalier Ira Aldridge, K.S. Invited to Stockholm by the King of Sweden, he became a member of many learned societies in that city. He was an intimate of Alexandre Dumas, himself half-Negro, and a cherished companion of Leo Tolstoy. He triumphed in St. Petersburg and on several long tours through the Russian provinces: in Moscow enthusiastic students unhitched the horses from the actor's carriage and pulled it themselves through the city. His realistic acting style, his freedom from stilted posturings, and the natural but impassioned way he spoke rather than declaimed had a profound effect on Russian drama. Actors came to his performances as if they were classes in dramatic art. Aldridge died in 1867 at the age of sixty, during a touring season in Poland, four years after Abraham Lincoln's Emancipation Proclamation.

American audiences never saw their great tragedian on the stage, and indeed knew nothing of his existence. Even today, most white Americans are shamefully ignorant of Ira Aldridge. In the Shakespeare Memorial Theatre at Stratford-on-Avon, tourists are surprised to learn that one of the thirty-three chairs in honor of the great actors of the world bears his name. The chair was given by American Negroes. The first authoritative book about Aldridge appeared in 1940—not in New York but in Moscow. His dramatic self-exile tells more about our stages than reams of detailed theatre history.

On southern plantations, slaves did devise the rudiments of the minstrel show, and the form spread through the theatres like crab grass but not with its originators on stage. The humorous monologues, the clogs and shuffles, and the songs, sometimes sardonic and sometimes lyrical, were stolen and cynically distorted by whites. From the 1840's to the 1890's, the minstrel show, with white men in blackface, was the most popular form of entertainment in America. A few cautious changes occurred near the end of the century, and in 1893, the first mixed troupe appeared, boldly labeled "The Forty Whites and the Thirty Blacks."

In drama as well as the minstrel show, the nineteenth-century story was the same. Since 1852, *Uncle Tom's Cabin* was the sentimental favorite on American stages in villages as well as cities; it was truly the "World's Greatest Hit." The cast, however, was always white. Black talent was barbarously neglected. It was not until century's end that a black man, Sam Lucas, was allowed to play Uncle Tom with a white company. The black roles were, of course, stereotypes tailored to tickle white supremacists' fancies. Topsy was perhaps the greatest libel of them all. (Even in the 1960's, brilliant theatre and nightclub clown Mae Barnes could get knowing chuckles with her mocking lament—"I Ain't Gonna Be No Topsy, I Wanna Be Little Eva.")

In the early years of the twentieth century, white Americans were slowly, imperfectly, and grudgingly beginning to appreciate, via the cakewalk, ragtime, the "coon songs," the spirituals, and the blues, the extraordinary musical range, expressiveness, and vitality of Afro-American music. Even today many whites prefer to ignore the fact that jazz, the country's greatest cultural export to an applauding world, is a precious cultural gift from a despised minority. This musical minority came into the theatre via the "Song-and-Dance-Man." It was a role assigned the "Negro" by "Whitey," who decided he was a natural-born dancer and singer. The black entertainer as a happy-go-lucky, shiftless, lovable, and not at all uppity fellow suited White Power. No smart-aleck, Shakespeare-spouting intellectuals for America. The minstrel black-face tradition had been broken by several all-Negro revues, most notably *The Creole Show*. With a chorus of sixteen girls, *The Creole Show* first toured the burlesque circuit, then captivated white audiences at the Chicago World's Fair in the 1890's. From then onward the all-black musical was standard procedure and box-office gold. The land was flooded with shows titled *The Octoroons, Oriental America, A Trip to Coontown, Shuffle Along, Chocolate Dandies, Runnin' Wild, Plantation Revue,* and *Blackbirds of 19—*. Many of these shows delighted Broadway, and, during the 1920's, Broadway often returned the call. White Americans went slumming in Harlem, dancing to jazz and watching exciting stars aborning in Harlem nightclubs. (Ironically, many of these nightclubs did not allow black patrons, only white downtowners.) Most of the musicals, nightclub revues, and vaudeville acts did not bear close scrutiny: they were gimcrack and inartistic and seldom worthy of the artists who appeared in them. The producers and managers, usually white, pandered to prejudiced white tastes in both overt and subtle ways. The performers understood this, but hell, they were at least working. And these shows did introduce a number of charismatic artists to White America—Florence Mills, Josephine Baker, Bill Robinson, Trixie Smith, Adelaide Hall, Abbie Mitchell, Ethel Waters, John W. Bubbles, and a long honor roll of others.

The man who made the greatest breakthrough into the theatre of White America and who best expressed the bittersweet of the period—was Egbert Austin Williams. His well-to-do grandfather had been the Danish consul in Antigua; his grandmother was of Spanish-African ancestry. When the family fortune disappeared, young Williams had to go to work. He went from honky-tonks in San Francisco to vaudeville (the team of Williams and Walker). A superb singer and flawless mimic, he could also play any musical instrument. In blackface, he was a slouching, lazy, careless, unlucky Negro for whom everything went wrong; offstage, he was a tall, straight, handsome man with impeccable diction. On tour, Bert Williams became the rage of London, taken up by the King and the best clubs. In 1910 he joined the *Follies*. David Belasco offered him a straight role in a drama, but he stayed faithful to the *Follies* for nearly ten years. The *Follies* was the first to give a black man a featured role in a white company. To his black critics who accused him of playing an Uncle Tom in the *Follies*, Williams answered with dignity: "We've got our foot in the door; we mustn't let it close again."

Bert Williams was a truly great artist, another example of wasted talent in a hate-infested society. A keen mind and a sensitive soul, he enjoyed most his own library, where he spent hours on end, learning by heart passages from such favorites as Paine, Confucius, Schopenhauer, Goethe, Voltaire, and Twain. Whites thought it liberal and daring to entertain him in their homes. How little they knew the man. Upon his return from triumph in London, he once revealed himself in a casual offhand remark about life in America: "It is not a disgrace to be a Negro but it is very inconvenient."

Perhaps W. C. Fields, another magnificent vaudevillian-turned-*Follies* star, described Williams best: "The funniest man I ever saw; the saddest man I ever knew." Bert Williams knew better than anyone how marginal and degrading was the position of the American theatre artist who happened to be black.

The way to the stage was made a bit easier for black performers by the song-and-dance artists. But in the vital arena of dramatic literature, the obstacles were formidable. America simply would not pay money to see blacks as they really were. Thus the Negro the white playwright created never existed: he was a concept, not a person. And this unreal figure degraded radio, the films, television, and the stage until very recently. Even now, the portrait is a hazy, inchoate sketch. The pre-Lorraine Hansberry theatre was overwhelmingly a hall of horrors, a Coney Island of distorting mirrors. In 1906, one could buy tickets to Broadway's *The Clansman*—if you were white; tradition still barred Negroes from the audience. This dramatized version of Thomas Dixon's spew of hate glorified the Ku Klux Klan and classified Negroes (played by white actors, of course) as brutes. Edward Sheldon's 1909 *The Nigger* was touted as a giant step forward. It was nothing of the kind: it was merely a rousing melodrama about a white man deeply distressed to find he had some Negro blood. The first white playwright who presented blacks with both artistry and truth was Ridgely Torrence with his *Three Plays for a Negro Theatre*. Deeply influenced by the Abbey Theatre's folk plays of the Irish, Torrence saw dignity and beauty in the lives of blacks in his one-acters. *Granny Maumee* was a harsh portrait of a proud American woman of royal African blood who bitterly recalls how a mob burned her son; *The Rider of Dreams* was a gentle portrait of a music-loving wastrel and his industrious wife; *Simon the Cyrenian* told of the black Simon who bore Christ's cross to Calvary. In these plays, black actors had a rare chance at major roles, and audiences were startled by the emotional range of Opal Cooper and Inez Clough. Critic Robert Benchley raved in the *Tribune*, and Randolph Bourne, the nation's most perceptive literary critic, rhapsodized to any little-magazine editor who would listen. Black poet James Weldon Johnson wrote in the New York *Age*, a Harlem newspaper: "(These plays) mark an epoch for the Negro on the stage... give the American Negro his first opportunity in serious drama." The plays opened on Broadway in April of 1917. Within a few weeks, the epoch-making production was closed. The United States had declared war the day after the opening, and Americans were busy with their war games and jingoism; they had no time for plays about oppressed people in their own land.

There were other partial exceptions to the general rule of white distortion in the theatre. Three plays by white playwrights at the Provincetown Playhouse were slight advances. Eugene O'Neill's 1920 *The Emperor Jones*, an important American excursion into expressionism, was a bolder-than-usual look at the Negro. But its throbbing tom-toms and exotic setting were far removed from black life in America, and Brutus Jones was a highly romanticized figure subtly distorted by a white man's prejudices. The star was Charles Gilpin, an ex-elevator operator who had acted at the Lafayette repertory theatre in Harlem. After the long run of *The Emperor Jones* off and on Broadway, Gilpin went back to running elevators. The yellow press fumed against O'Neill's 1924 *All God's Chillun Got Wings*, for it treated miscegenation with a new dignity if a conventional futility. Paul Robeson appeared in this one. Paul Green's *In Abraham's Bosom* in 1926, again at the Provincetown, contained good roles for Jules Bledsoe and Rose McClendon (a great talent obscenely wasted by prejudice), and it showed the ferocity of white hatred through Negro eyes to a degree not usually understood by white playwrights.

But in general it was a white man's theatre, and his sick view of the black man prevailed. Producers understood all too well that one must cater to white stereotypes if one wished to make money with dramas about Negroes. In 1927, Dubose and Dorothy Heyward dramatized *Porgy* from the former's novel. Here was a picturesque tale of primitive passion on Catfish Row in Charleston, South Carolina, with its "amusing" Negroes seen through the distorted lens of a white couple. This error was later compounded into *Porgy and Bess*, with book by Heyward, music by George Gershwin and lyrics by Ira Gershwin and Heyward. Touted as the first American folk opera, it was rather a tired, stereotyped musical of never-never-land natives, happy with "plenty of nuttin'." Someday there may well be a great American folk opera based on Southern Negro themes, but this 1935 monstrosity, strictly Broadway and Hollywood in inspiration, was definitely the wrong direction. The Gershwin score is lovely, but the book is best forgotten. Another example of racism was Marc Connelly's *The Green Pastures*, a hit of 1930. Into this dramatized evocation of Roark Bradford's condescending tales, *Ol' Man Adam and His Children*, Connelly injected a gentler note of endearing and sweet fantasy. But even with this doctoring, the work was patronizing and repellent. Subtle racist thinking had so permeated the entire American fabric that one could be a racist without conscious intent. Perhaps the best that can be said for *Porgy and Bess* and *The Green Pastures* is that they gave a lot of work to black actors. But hasn't the familiar work theory been used to justify many unworthy enterprises in many lands?

In the thirties, both the left-wing playwrights and the dynamic Federal Theatre Project gave new impetus to plays and musicals with roles for black performers. A vast number of leftist "thesis" plays were sympathetic to the Negro's plight, but all too often the white authors depicted these second-class citizens as mere symbols in class or race warfare, not as rich, complex, fullbodied human beings. *Stevedore*, a 1934 drama by George Sklar and Paul Peters, was the best of the radical protest plays. Concerned with the unionization of Southern workers, black and white, the tale spotlighted a frame-up of a black union organizer on a charge of rape. Its dockhands were flesh-and-blood men, and its blacks a militant breed far removed from the passive Porgys.

One rich vein of theatre was explored by a leading modern dancer, the late Helen Tamiris. For the Federal Theatre, she created *How Long Brethren*, a stunning, stirring evening of spirituals and protest songs, danced by her company and sung by black artists. Rarely has anyone so profoundly distilled various aspects of black life, without fakery and without condescension.

But a new form of racism crept into the Federal Theatre Project and, later, into the commercial theatre. It was the disturbing tendency to find classic dramas and operas rendered quaint when performed by black casts. All-black Macbeths and Lysistratas were followed by Swing Mikados and, on Broadway, Hot Mikados. *Swingin' the Dream*, a Negro version of *A Midsummer Night's Dream*, featured Louis Armstrong and Maxine Sullivan. Broadway's rousing, jazzy *Carmen Jones* was the great success of 1942. One wondered whether every opera on record would be given the all-Negro treatment (*de rigueur* were tight red dresses, dialect, saxophones, and something usually labeled animal vitality) by greedy producers who worshiped the buck and not the truth. Would a Harlem rent-party become the setting for a sepia *La Bohème?* Would an all-black Ring Cycle employ dusky Lorelei caressing wailing saxophones? The "fun" possibilities were limitless.

For the performing artists of the black community, Broadway in the forties and fifties was a series of ups and downs, of false starts and renewed hopes, of one step forward and two steps back. In 1944 the hit of Harlem's American Negro Theatre was its production of *Anna Lucasta*. The poor Polish-American family of Philip Yordan's melodrama easily became a poor Afro-American family. When the production moved to Broadway, it enjoyed a long run, introducing to downtown audiences such splendid actors as Hilda Simms and Frederick O'Neal (later to become the first black president of Actors' Equity). The cast also included Alice Childress, who imparted a fiery depth to a standard prostitute role. (Miss Childress was later to become an important playwright.) The Yordan drama concerned a girl who returns home after being tossed out; falling in love with an innocent, she nobly leaves again before he learns of her lurid past. The actors, however, gave the routine script a glowing intensity and beauty rare on Broadway. And for once, a modern drama showed black people as persons and not as stereotypes. It was simple: the playwright had white characters in mind when he wrote it. Along with a rare *Anna Lucasta* were the well-intentioned but often boring white sermons on tolerance. These uplifting dramas seldom showed the searing violence black people lived with daily in White America; they were tailored instead for the vaguely liberal members of the audience who went away in a glow of fuzzy goodwill, smugly happy that God and country were dissolving silly little prejudices.

One longed to hear an authentic cry, a poet-prophet shouting obscenities at the top of his voice, yelling the vivid and ugly truth about racism somehow obscured in these neat and blunted problem plays. Or a slyer, sinuous Brechtian voice, mocking the white man's sick fantasies. Or a Balzacian storyteller, placing his detailed black characters in the middle of life's tragicomedies, displaying them in all their multi-faceted humanity. In other words, where was the black playwright? For he remains the nitty-gritty of the matter. Black performers must zigzag in every direction for their place under the Broadway neon, but the black playwright can wield the most effective and satisfying of all weapons. He knows the power of the word. To him falls the greatest burden—and the greatest challenge. Will his plays get produced in a white-dominated society? Will anybody listen to him? In general, the history of the American theatre indicates that the answer is a thundering no.

However, since the Depression days, there has been a small but growing audience of theatregoers genuinely interested in works by black playwrights, an audience which sees culture not as tiresome stereotyped patterns or as lifeless sermons on tolerance but as unstuffy and honest expression. Broadway's first commercially successful play of black authorship was Hall Johnson's *Run, Little Chillun* in 1933. Based on a conflict between Christianity and a pagan cult, the unusual production made sensual, elemental use of spectacle, dance, and music. It was a far better drama than *The Green Pastures*. Whereas *The Green Pastures* was essentially a white man's play about the Negro's docile acceptance of his lot, *Run, Little Chillun* was more realistic, peopled with passionate, power-conscious blacks. It was later revived in several cities by the Federal Theatre.

No American drama project had as much meaning and hope for black people as the Federal Theatre Project of the thirties, and there were black units in New York, Philadelphia, Boston, Los Angeles, Seattle, and other cities. The Federal Theatre produced several startling scripts by black authors, including Theodore Ward's 1938 *Big White Fog*, a powerful Depression drama with keen insights into the Marcus Garvey back-to-Africa movement. Incidentally, this Federal Theatre discovery was to suffer artistic mutilation on Broadway in later years. In the 1940's, Ward's *Our Lan'*, a beautifully constructed, searing, semi-documentary of white betrayal after the Emancipation, was first performed to critics' cheers in an off-Broadway showcase, but it folded after a few performances on Broadway under Theatre Guild auspices. The playwright was justifiably angered, for old Broadway hands tried to turn his revolutionary play into another *The Green Pastures*.

In the forties, Mississippi-plantation-born Richard Wright, who had been nurtured by the Federal Writers' Projects in Chicago and New York, dramatized with Paul Green his own ironically titled novel, *Native Son*. Though it was excessively mechanical and coarse-textured, the play bared the fury and despair of a scorned and rebuked black man in more powerful images than Broadway was accustomed to. In 1955, Alice Childress' bitter and beautiful *Trouble in Mind* opened in an off-Broadway church basement. Here was black humor in both meanings of the phrase. A brilliantly mordant inside look at black people in theatre, it had a disappointingly brief run (it was too sharp, too uncomfortably true, and ahead of its time). I recall with relish one scene in which an oldtime actress, wise in the ways of white theatre, wearily gave a valuable piece of advice to an inexperienced mummer waiting in a producer's outer office. Her advice was, in paraphrase: "Just tell them you were in *The Green Pastures*, honey; they won't know the difference."

A very special event in American culture occurred in March, 1959: the first play by Lorraine Hansberry, a twenty-eight-year-old black author. *Raisin in the Sun* was a landmark, for it was the first major play by a black about black life to be produced on Broadway. Here were no Porgys and Besses rolling their eyes in green pastures, but honestly etched black people in a variety of guises, from the old-fashioned, conservative Mama (out of Gorky or O'Casey) to the rebellious, college-bred daughter excited by revolt in Africa. Miss Hansberry's characters were involved in their own personal clashes (the clash of generations, the educated versus the unschooled, Americans versus Nigerians, etc.) as well as a collision with White America; they were full-bodied and real, and the author employed laughter and irony as well as tearful affection to give them all individuality and dimension. Sidney Poitier, Ruby Dee, Diana Sands, Claudia McNeill, Ivan Dixon, and Louis Gossett glistened with beauty in the full knowledge of the drama's pioneering destiny. The players were directed with loving attention to nuance by a new black director, Lloyd Richards. The drama's detractors (and there were many) loftily dismissed it as soap opera—and thereby missed the point.

The unifying issue in this domestic drama was open housing. The Younger family had bought a house in a middle-class white neighborhood in Chicago, and they were determined to hold on to it. The title of the script was taken from a poem by the late Langston Hughes: "What happens to a dream deferred?/Does it dry up/Like a raisin in the sun?/Or fester like a sore—/And then run?/Does it stink like rotten meat?/Or crust and sugar over—/Like a syrupy sweet?/Maybe it just sags/Like a heavy load/Or does it explode?" The play was prophetic, for in the sixties the black urban ghettos did explode in race riots and open housing was one of the decade's most burning issues. But was the play about injustice in housing? Yes—and more. It was about human beings fighting for dignity. Coming at the end of the fifties, Miss Hansberry's pivotal drama coincided with the burgeoning black militancy, and in a sense she heralded a new era in theatre and in life. She was a harbinger. Never again would black people allow chocolate dandies or Carmen Joneses to represent them. Such cultural uncletom-foolery would be gasoline-bombed by the young militants.

The playwright offered the fitting and final epitaph for all theatre stereotypes in a 1960 article in *Theatre Arts*, during one of the various unsuccessful attempts to revive that sterling magazine: "Finally, I think that American writers have already begun to believe what I suspect has always been one of the secrets of fine art: that there are no simple men. Chinese peasants and Congolese soldiers make drastic revolutions in the world while the obtuse and myth-accepting go on reflecting on the 'inscrutability and eternal placidity' of those people. I believe that when the blinders are dropped, it will be discovered that while an excessively poignant Porgy was being instilled in generations of Americans, his truer-life counterpart was being ravaged by longings that were, and are, in no way alien to those of the rest of mankind, and that bear within them the stuff of truly great art. He is waiting yet for those of us who will but look more carefully into his eyes, and listen more intently to his soliloquies. We must not be intimidated by the residue of the past; the world is paying too large a price for the deception of those centuries; each hour that flies teaches that Porgy is as much inclined to hymns of sedition as to lullabies and love songs; he is profoundly complicated and interesting; everywhere he is making his own sounds in the night."

Miss Hansberry herself did not fit the stereotype manufactured by disordered whites. She was a cultured, worldly rebel, and her deep commitment to civil rights was a part of a larger social commitment. Miss Hansberry spoke for all of us. Her words remain a challenge to all artists, black and white.

Indicating her astonishingly catholic range of vision, Miss Hansberry's second play was *The Sign in Sidney Brustein's Window*, which was not about blacks and not about prejudice. This study of a Jewish intellectual, an editor of a small but potent liberal weekly newspaper in Greenwich Village, and his involvement in local reform politics, was about caring, about commitment. With a stageful of unstereotyped characters (a conservative suburban matron, for example, who turns out to be more liberal than a liberal), she surveyed the situation of the Western intellectual in a time of chaos, apathy, and disenchantment and reaffirmed that one can indeed change the world. It was a *tour de force* in both its subtle, complex writing and its philosophical premises. The script, however, seemed unfinished, wandering alarmingly and in need of cutting and tightening. Moreover, the Broadway production was fumbling and its demise came shortly after cancer destroyed Miss Hansberry in the first month of 1965.

Following Lorraine Hansberry's lead, other black playwrights have emerged in recent years. James Baldwin was previously best known as a novelist obsessed with sex and color and as a proselytizing essayist obsessed with racial injustice. *The Amen Corner* was written in 1954, but it did not get to Broadway until 1965. There are awkward passages that display Baldwin's immaturity as a dramatist, but *The Amen Corner* also displays a rugged honesty, a fierce poetry, and an elemental emotional power that puts it above ordinary Broadway fare. Here is a storefront preacher in Harlem, a woman preacher who has been frozen into a false and cold piety through the death of her baby, the waywardness of her husband, and brutal poverty. She finally breaks out of her rigid patterns of fake sainthood into a deeper, more understanding love of mankind. The play is about our illusions, our lies to ourselves, and, on occasion, our liberation. It is undoubtedly autobiographical in part. Baldwin's father was a minister, and he himself was a boy preacher in a storefront church. Another Baldwin play, *Blues for Mister Charlie*, was presented on Broadway in 1964, under the sponsorship of Actors Studio and the direction of Burgess Meredith. It was melodramatic and creaky and uncontrolled. Yet there was beauty. Some of Baldwin's deep anger came out in incredibly poetic and moving arias, most particularly a searing monologue for Diana Sands. Baldwin, it now appears, is better as a prophetic essayist, warning of the coming race war, than he is as either novelist or dramatist. But he may yet produce a great stage testament.

Adrienne Kennedy, too, may surprise the theatre world. Her *Funnyhouse of a Negro*, presented in 1964 at the Cherry Lane in Greenwich Village, was a scorching report on the agony of being black in a hostile world. Within a macabre shadow world of fantasy and nightmare, Miss Kennedy evoked a surrealist vision of an "invisible" person, a woman without a country.

Ed Bullins, a disciple and sometimes associate of LeRoi Jones, showed more than mere promise in 1968. Three of his short plays, *A Son Come Home*, *The Electronic Nigger*, and *Clara's Ole Man*, were presented off-Broadway first at the American Place and then the Martinique. Bullins is an acute observer of character, and his dialogue is fresh and true. He does not prettify life but shows slum and ghetto degradation in all its horror. There is no fake preaching or sentimentalizing. This is the way it is. Below the surface of his work is a fine humanist sensibility that somehow reminds one of Sean O'Casey. Best of all, the young playwright returns lusty laughter to the stage.

There were also simple but powerful hallelujah spectacles by the late Langston Hughes, half-drama, half-exultation. In a sense, they restored drama to its earlier function of myth and ritual. *Jerico Jim Crow* was Hughes's best, and in 1965 it shook the sanctuary of a Greenwich Village Presbyterian church with it foot-stomping joyousness. When young bass-baritone Gilbert Price sang a slave block song, "Mother, Will They Sell Me Today," he conjured up the rich voice and personality of Paul Robeson. Poet Hughes, in these evenings of song and chronicle, offered a rare spiritual sermon, far more profound than institutionalized pieties.

Ossie Davis used the weapon of laughter. Actor-playwright Davis starred in his own *Purlie Victorious* on Broadway in 1961. This was an oddity—a comedy about segregation and integration. It poked fun at all stereotypes, black and white, and it caught the wild, bittersweet humor inherent in the subject. Prejudice is ugly, but it is also so ridiculous as to be funny. Professional liberals didn't quite know how to react to *Purlie Victorious*. In this warm, very broad comedy, combining Molière farce and O'Casey fantasy, Ruby Dee limned a delicious caricature of an ignorant backwoods girl and Godfrey Cambridge fashioned a perfect Rastus cartoon.

There were several staged readings in the sixties. *In White America* was compiled with admirable finesse by a white professor, Martin Duberman, but it was, in large part, a collection of original material (letters, speeches, songs, etc.) by blacks. Duberman shared the authorship with authentic black voices, and, to anyone who would listen, it was an illuminating recital of three centuries of virulent racism. It introduced Gloria Foster, an electric actress who later appeared in a number of Broadway and off-Broadway productions. In an off-Broadway staging in 1965 of the Euripides-Robinson Jeffers *Medea*, Miss Foster proved to be a more haunting and subtle Medea than the role's long-time custodian, Judith Anderson.

A Hand Is on the Gate, a luminous and affecting evening of poems and songs of the Negro people from the days of slavery to the present time of revolt, opened the 1966–67 Broadway season. In evening dress and sitting on chairs of varying heights, an elegant octet of our finest black players (Roscoe Lee Browne, Leon Bibb, Josephine Premice, Gloria Foster, Ellen Holly, Moses

Gunn, Cicely Tyson and James Earl Jones) faced the audience as though preparing for a minstrel show. It was, however, a long way from minstrelsy. Roscoe Lee Browne served as the urbane, witty, and sometimes mocking master of ceremonies. The poems covered a wide range, from Countee Cullen to LeRoi Jones. Here were James Weldon Johnson's "My City," surely one of the finest sonnets ever written to Manhattan; here too was the sardonic "We Wear the Mask," in which Paul Laurence Dunbar succinctly and heartbreakingly describes the masks that black Americans have been forced to wear in front of white Americans. To the uninitiated, it was a revelation of the riches and variety found in our black poets. But it folded quickly.

A new theatre opened in Harlem in late 1967, the first professional playhouse there in twenty years. The New Lafayette was inaugurated with Ronald Milner's *Who's Got His Own*, which had first been produced at the American Place. A bitter picture of the psychological high-pressure chamber in which black Americans live out their lives, the drama ends on a forlorn note: "Nothing has changed . . . not a God-damned thing." The sum of $50,000, mostly from foundations, was raised to insure a first season and to present works primarily by black playwrights about black people. One wished these brave ghetto impresarios well. Those with long memories recalled the noble failures of Harlem's proud past: the Lafayette Players, the Negro Playwrights Company, the Rose McClendon Players, and the American Negro Theatre. From these and similar groups have come many of the nation's most talented actors, including Rose McClendon, Charles Gilpin, Inez Clough, Robert Earl Jones, and Ossie Davis.

One actor became a playwright of distinction in 1965. A newcomer from Louisiana, Douglas Turner Ward, had earlier appeared on Broadway in *Raisin in the Sun*, where he impersonated a moving man and had no lines at all. However, he made up for the silence when his two short plays, *Happy Ending* and *Day of Absence*, opened in an off-Broadway showcase. His comedies sparkled with an uncommon wit. Young playwright Ward has the precious gift of irony, of double vision. Whites are often startled and, in their smug self-righteousness, more than a little disconcerted to learn that blacks have been laughing at them and their primitive color prejudices for generations. To many black people, whites are rather ludicrous. It is with this special insight that Ward created these masterly comedies. He is hilarious—with point. In *Happy Ending,* one sits in a kitchen of a Harlem tenement and gets the lowdown on the downtown whites for whom the domestics work. It offers a good healthy belly-laugh at the whites, with (and this is because Ward is an artist with more than one tune in his repertory) a few pointed barbs at the blacks as well. In *Day of Absence* Ward offers an even more revealing look at "Charlie," "Whitey," "The Man." *Day of Absence* is a minstrel show in reverse, the funniest minstrel show I ever saw. The entire black cast plays in whiteface. In an unnamed Southern town, the blacks—hotheads and Uncle Toms alike—have disappeared overnight. It is a calamity. In countless homes, whites wake up without seeing the cheerful, familiar grin of mammy. Who's to do the dirty work? Who's to nurse the children? In a quick succession of cartoons, the black actors impersonate the Southern whites to a fare-thee-well.

A handsome, unusually talented young actor starred in Ward's evening of black-white humor. He was Robert Hooks, who had earlier impressed the critics in LeRoi Jones's *Dutchman.* In 1964, Hooks started a theatre workshop by literally taking to the streets. He discovered that youngsters in his impoverished neighborhood hungered for theatre but found the usual settlement-house psychology barren and unpleasant. The impromptu classes held in his apartment grew, and by early 1965 his Group Theatre Workshop unveiled several productions in an off-Broadway playhouse. Though he soon became financially secure and highly successful on Broadway, in the films, and on television, he consistently returned to his dedicated dream of a theatre of, by, and for Afro-Americans.

In Douglas Turner Ward, Hooks found a man who was thinking along the same lines, and they teamed up to form the Negro Ensemble Company in New York. Ward is the artistic director, Hooks the executive director. In mid-1967 they were given a $434,000 Ford Foundation grant. Housed in an off-Broadway theatre, the company opened in early 1968 with nothing less than the American premiere of Peter Weiss's *The Song of the Lusitanian Bogey*, ostensibly a mirror of the brutal Portuguese colonialization of Angola but by extension, a harrowing and compelling picture of the modern world. The actors, employing both song and dance, were supple in mind, speech, and movement. The premiere indicated that this young company may well change the face of New York theatre.

The Negro Ensemble Company has a nucleus of fifteen permanent actors on annual salary, special workshop groups for playwrights and directors, and a large cadre of apprentice performers. The theatre is not in the Negro ghetto, but the company hopes their subscription lists will include a vast number of Harlem residents. The major emphasis is on Negro culture and on an unapologetic Negro viewpoint, a correction of three hundred and fifty years of stereotypes. The company plans to revive some of the neglected plays by Negro authors as well as present new scripts. Though it will primarily offer themes of black life, it hopes to be resilient enough to incorporate the best of world drama—whatever its source—into the repertory. Whites will not be altogether excluded from company membership. This is a theatre with a black identity, rather than a segregated, separatist theatre. Ward is neither a rabid white-hater nor an Uncle Tom. "I'm an integrationist only because—not that I exactly want to be one—because the realities of life make it seem the only feasible way for Negro and white to make it in this society. I don't think the U.S. is going to give us Utah. I don't think white people love us or we them. It's just that, after a couple of hundred years, there's no place to hide. If we think this is doomsday, that's one thing. If not, whether we like it or not, whether it's hard or not, we have to sit down together, after the shouting's over, and work on policy."

But the man who has cut deepest in baring the living hell of race prejudice is LeRoi Jones, playwright, poet, critic, teacher, and magazine editor. In a number of plays both produced and unproduced, he has fashioned a frenzied, soul-splitting cry of hate and despair aimed at the zombies and sleepwalkers of both races. His best drama to date—and a beautifully constructed work of art it is—is *Dutchman*, which appeared in an off-Broadway showcase in

1964. The scene: a subway car; the time, now. A white girl, both predator and provocateur, picks up a black youth. To her, he is a fleeting plaything. He is at first annoyed and then intrigued by her boldness. But she goads him into a hysterical harangue of hate. Revenge, he declares, is in every Negro's heart. The girl then proceeds to stab and kill him. She is, of course, a symbol of America—hip, forever babbling, spouting liberal clichés, empty, insensitive, and a killer. *Dutchman* is surely one of the finest pieces of writing of the 1960's—perfectly cut, gem-hard, and dazzling. Some are shocked by Jones's constant use of obscenities. He answers, "The lies of today begin with the lies of language," and he refuses to tone down his dialogue. He is absolutely right. When a sanitized version of *Dutchman* was presented at Howard University, Jones's alma mater, he jumped onto the stage and declaimed all the deleted words.

Though Jones's *The Toilet* and *The Slave* were presented in an off-Broadway theatre the year following *Dutchman*, they were actually earlier plays. They are not so polished as *Dutchman*, but the authentic fires of revolt rage within them. *The Toilet* takes place in the boys' rest room of a New York high school. The scene is ugly, the vocabulary consistently four-letter. Two boys, one white and one black, are secretly in love with one another, but, conforming to reality, they nearly beat each other to death. *The Slave* is the story of a black poet turned revolutionary assassin, who during a war between the races returns to take his revenge on his white wife and his idolized white professor who has won her love. Many have been shocked by its central premise: the play assumes the inevitability of war between the races. Jones has written other unproduced plays. One five-hour drama reportedly promises to stir up controversy. Requiring a large cast and many changes of scenery, the play concerns a black soldier stationed in Puerto Rico. There is a scene in a whorehouse with intercourse taking place on a sofa and a sequence on the masturbatory fantasies of soldiers. In one scene, a black girl kills a white man with a bottle in bed; in another, Negro drag queens sit in a row on johns. Jones follows Terence's motto with unusual devotion: I am a man, and nothing in life is alien.

Who is this angry American? Little is known about LeRoi Jones and that is by his own choice: he is withdrawn and not given to talkative sessions with interviewers. Thus speculation about him grows. He has been professor at both Columbia University and the New School for Social Research. His poetry is read and quoted by thousands of young militant Negroes. He is a jazz pundit, devoted to the styles of John Coltrane, Ornette Coleman, and Cecil Taylor. His acknowledged literary debts are to William Carlos Williams, who "taught me to use everyday language," and to Nathanael West for his blending of horror with sardonic humor. One tale is persistent: something crucial happened to Jones in the summer of 1960 after he was invited with a group of Negroes to tour Cuba. The uncommitted poet became the engaged man. The happy, unsegregated crowds he saw deeply impressed him, and from that beginning, he became involved not only with the new Cuba but with the other new nations of Asia and Africa. Today, he bitterly attacks the black middle class of America for trying to become white and cover up their African roots. In 1966, Jones founded the Black Arts Repertory Company in Harlem, and the new theatre project was awarded a $40,000 federal grant. But both the government and his cultural-moderate enemies were enraged by his extreme anti-white attitudes, and his repertory idea eventually failed. LeRoi Jones remains a profound influence on the thinking of young blacks, and he may yet produce other plays with the bitter power of *Dutchman*.

There are those who do not see the need for a special discussion of blacks in any account of the theatre. To some, LeRoi Jones is merely paranoid and obscene. A few even argue that the blacks are now free. This is simply not so—and it is these blind who are the sick Americans. Those who use their eyes and ears in the urban jungles as well as on the redneck plantations measure our culture against the brutal, ugly realities of the theatre of life. They understand the key role to be played by the Negro, if a flowering of culture is ever to come to our nation. We are a long way from a society in which men are no longer divided into "we" and "they." Dozens of black playwrights are now standing in the wings. If they are allowed to tell their story in all its savagery and all its beauty, in all its horror and hope, they will create one of the richest and most dramatic epics in American history. They might help heal a sick and divided nation, and they might give vital restorative powers to a moribund theatre, bringing sanity to a neon madhouse of trivia. The time is very late, perhaps too late. The communion of black and white is still possible, if improbable. It remains a hope.

CHAPTER 11

THE CASE OF BROADWAY'S MISSING PLAYWRIGHT

WHERE ARE THE American playwrights? Can't anyone write worthy scripts anymore? What's the matter with our dramatists? These are the questions still most frequently asked about the Broadway theatre. It is tacitly assumed, with little thought about the matter, that the problem of Broadway is the problem of finding "good" plays. The producer, when criticized too sharply about the trashiness of his offerings, will almost invariably offer the customary glib and insincere answer: Find me a good script. It is at once a retort, a challenge, and a convenient excuse.

This popular answer is based on a Big Lie, a clever Broadway legend which has prevented too many sleuths from examining the facts about the sorry state of the drama. What most producers really mean by their "find-me-a-playwright" answer is that there are not enough plays that suit their tastes and that will guarantee them a fast buck. In the dismal sixties, one must ask more abrasive questions and demand more candid answers. If a challenging and significant script came along, would it get produced—and in a manner true to its concept? Does Broadway give a damn about art? Are the producers, surrounded by a wall of rising costs and stern-visaged theatre-party ladies, actually afraid of anything that seems truly fresh and provocative? If a distinguished drama with outrageously sharp social comment and a delightfully original style, were somehow produced, would Broadway audiences go to see it? The answers to all these questions are unhappy ones. The best material has small chance for attention, production, or survival on Broadway. To put it even more bluntly, inferior products sell better. The audiences have been brainwashed to prefer the second-rate. Canny producers, with dollar signs for eyes, are not looking for the best; they are looking for that Big Hit. And so the case of the missing playwright takes on quite a different dimension when one brushes aside the misleading premises usually assigned to the issue. It is sadly true that American playwrights of quality—probing, imaginative, exciting, inventive, subversive, committed, entertaining —are missing from Broadway. However, they do exist. The problem is that they are not really welcome on Broadway.

Thus it is quite clear that one cannot discuss Broadway playwrights in a social vacuum; one must also point to producers and audiences. These groups form a commercial tandem, and an obvious and inseparable chain links them together. Don't mistake me—the matter is not simple. The producer, for example, comes in two distinctly different versions. One is the producer whose real interest is in making a killing. He will often coyly hint that he himself desires great art but that the public is stupid and couldn't care less. He is seldom honest enough to appear in public in his pirate's costume and raise the flag of the dollar rather than the banner of art. The second type of producer is, of course, interested in making a living, but more importantly he is wholeheartedly involved with the theatre as an art form. There are only a handful of these leaders in a generation. Arthur Hopkins was such a man, and he astutely and successfully combined commerce and art. Winthrop Ames and John D. Williams also belonged in this precious category. The producing team of Eugene O'Neill, Kenneth Macgowan, and Robert Edmond Jones was of this persuasion, but they were, after all, rather special—a playwright, a critic, and a set designer. The early Theatre Guild, the Group Theatre, Eva Le Gallienne's Civic Repertory, the Playwrights' Theatre, and various other special troupes have marched under the banner of Producer-Artist. These voices from the not-so-distant past were deeply convinced that the public would enjoy and eventually demand quality—if given a proper chance to view it. The two kinds of producers represent two differing ways of looking at the theatre public, one with cynicism and the other with respect. Actually they represent two radically opposed views of America. In the Broadway theatre today, the second kind is as scarce as God's grace. And yet this creative producer is desperately needed if we are ever again to have a genuine playwrights' theatre on Broadway.

Audiences can create playwrights, too. True, they cannot create geniuses, who come along in the theatre every century or so—during depression and boom, fair weather or foul, seemingly unexplainable other than as accidents of history. But the overall texture—the average—of a nation's theatre is determined in large part by the kind of consumers it has and the quality of their demands. It has long been the practice to flatter American theatre audiences with smug sermons telling them they deserve better than they get. But don't Broadway audiences deserve precisely the dormitives sold them? Can a commercial theatre ever be much better than its audiences? If they prefer moldering products, can they be forced to accept true entertainment of the mind and senses? Perhaps; perhaps not. These are questions never seriously debated.

Thus viewed, Broadway is a vast middlebrow (or low-middlebrow) shopping center, offering gaudy gimcracks to gullible consumers and advertising them with all the hucksterism of the circus barker. There is barely a hint of lively dissent on Broadway stages. After all, the real issues in American politics are muddied by both political parties and their millions of followers who endlessly expound on the same stale pieties with only superficial variation. All that really takes place is a jockeying for position. This void is perpetually reproduced on the Broadway stages and in the audiences. When August Heckscher resigned as President John F. Kennedy's special consultant on the arts, he made a trenchant and haunting statement: "The majority in political life still tend to talk of culture as if they were telling an off-color story."

The most chilling group portrait of Broadway audiences came from playwright Lillian Hellman, in a *New York Times* interview in February, 1966: "I feel like a stranger in the theatre now. Whenever I go to see other people's plays and have a look at the audience, I ask myself 'What am I doing here?' I don't understand the people sitting next to me. Everyone seems to me old and square and rich. If the play is serious, they are so glum they look almost crazy, and if the play is a comedy, they laugh at nothing, as if they were in another ward of the hospital." Years earlier, Bernard Shaw had summarily dismissed the matter of audiences with his usual acerb wit. Asked whether one of his plays would prove a success on Broadway, he retorted, "Undoubtedly, but the question is whether the audience will be."

Once upon a time, in the twenties, thirties, and well into the forties, the intellectuals, the cultivated professional people, and the disdainful, dissentient young attended the Broadway theatre with some regularity. More and more, they have found their entertainment and intellectual stimulation elsewhere. Their defection has been a rebellion based on artistic principles and economics. They constitute a small portion of a lost audience which, because of the prohibitive costs of theatre tickets and the lures of films, radio, and television, has deserted Broadway en masse. The annual audience has dwindled from roughly thirteen million in the twenties to seven million today. So who is left in those theatre seats? An audience affluent and complacent. A ticket-buyer never pays less than $3 for the poorest seat (and poor most of them are) and never less than $7 for the best. Orchestra tickets to some musicals have soared to $15. In large part, today's audiences are cold and tired and spiritually torpid, and they do not care to be emotionally or intellectually stimulated. They have lost perspective; they view the theatre as another brand of tranquilizer or as a means of conspicuous consumption. Often they go to solidify a business deal. In this coldly commercial context, the inviolate canon of Broadway is widely accepted: a good play is one that makes money; a bad play is one that does not.

To an astonishingly high degree, I have enjoyed the box-office flops on Broadway more than the hits, and I have often felt somewhat like a Quaker at an American Legion convention. Three of the most fascinating, provocative, and original scripts of the sixties were resounding failures at the box office, each lasting only a few nights. They were Jack Richardson's *Xmas in Las Vegas*, Lillian Hellman's *My Mother, My Father, and Me*, and Jules Feiffer's *Little Murders*.

New playwright Jack Richardson created a splendid *The Prodigal* in the fifties, a fresh, sparkling, witty re-examination of the Orestes legend, and it was given a solid off-Broadway production. The author was justifiably encouraged by the Other Theatre audiences. In 1963, he invaded Broadway with *Lorenzo*, an intelligent if verbose and rambling look at those who romanticize, who live in the world of illusion. This not unworthy parable for today was revealed through the eyes of traveling players accidentally involved in a small Renaissance war. It was a flawed but promising play. However, *Xmas in Las Vegas* (1965) proved Richardson to be Broadway's most exciting—and unwelcome—newcomer. Nobody has attacked our cherished and false values with such gleeful gallows humor and corrosive wit. Richardson is a keen observer of our national neuroses. In a black comedy mood, he presents Las Vegas as the town that best exemplifies the hopes and dreams of the U.S.A. The crap table, the blackjack board, and the slot machines become symbolic terrain in the battle for Success, the Big Money, and the American Dream. Each year at Christmas time, the American Everyman (beautifully impersonated on Broadway by Tom Ewell) brings his family to Las Vegas to hit the jackpot. *Xmas in Las Vegas* is more American than apple pie. But director Fred Coe, used to television realism, simply did not know how to handle this excursion into expressionism. He did direct one scene brilliantly, a telling sequence in which he staged a tense gaming-table session like a larger-than-life championship prize fight. Throughout the play, however, Richardson's inventive mind darted about nervously in mercurial fashion, leaping from realism to fantasy, and he needed a director to match his changing moods. Furthermore, most critics as well as audiences did not appreciate the play behind the direction. Jack Richardson was last observed pursuing the dubious pleasures of theatre criticism for *Commentary*. Yet I expect to see *Xmas in Las Vegas* again—on the off- or the off-off-Broadway stages or in the new resident theatres or perhaps in London or Berlin.

Lillian Hellman's *My Mother, My Father, and Me* (1963) was a hilarious satire of uncommon merit. The critics, in the main, panned it, and the audiences were equally negative. The play failed simply because it was too good for Broadway. It was glowingly praised by our most discerning and erudite literary critic, Edmund

Wilson, who correctly pointed out that it was a "novel kind of entertainment." "It is harsh, ironic, and shocking, but also extremely funny, a satirical commentary on the kind of lives we are living in the United States," he added. "No one except Miss Hellman could have written it." The nation's unofficial poet laureate Robert Lowell was equally enthusiastic: "One of Miss Hellman's most fascinating and surprising plays ... I was delighted by its weird invention, its wit, and the gay variety of its anguish." But did their literary opinions really count on Broadway?

Based on *How Much?*, a Burt Blechman novel, *My Mother, My Father, and Me* is a bitter study of the middle class, a slashing, merciless look at a very American papa, mama, son, and grandmother in a cheerless New York household. Mama is a brainless lady with a compulsion to buy everything. The "hidden persuaders" have done a thorough job of brainwashing. She must shop every day, even though she buys spurious goods she doesn't need, has no room to store, and cannot pay for. The apartment is crammed with stuff from mama's shopping sprees. This mama has nothing in common with the cloyingly sentimental, loving, impossibly wise woman of our folklore. The father is a sniveling, harried bore, too busy cheating the government and borrowing to pay his bills to notice his family. The son is a walking wreck, trying to find himself in folk music, beatnik literature, and other frenzied pursuits. His liberalism is as phony as a three-dollar bill. Grandmother is quite unwanted, and finally the hypocrites place her in a home for the aged. The son finally loses his identity among the American Indians, though—along with other noble savages—he must don war-paint and sell cheap trinkets to the tourists.

My Mother, My Father, and Me is a high point of theatre in the 1960's. Sardonic, Voltairean, Lillian Hellman recognizes the rot in the social fabric, and she is magnificently angry. Here are the puny descendants of Miss Hellman's little foxes. But this scathing satire was disastrously mauled on Broadway. Gower Champion, former dancer and now a deft director of musicals, was the wrong man to stage a bitter portrait of the middle class. Everything needed to be done in an exaggerated, stylized fashion, in the Molière manner of the Comédie Française. The settings could have been suggested rather than detailed. The play probably should have been done in the off-off-Broadway theatre, where it would have been understood and admired. Talented playwrights rightly question whether Broadway is the proper place for dramas of serious intent.

One of the funniest and wittiest Broadway comedies of the decade closed in an outrageous hurry. Jules Feiffer's *Little Murders* (1967) needed a younger and more aware audience—in brief, an off-Broadway audience. The cartoonist-turned-playwright has written a thinking man's comedy of remarkable resonance. Liberating and bracing, Feiffer has presented a reality seldom encountered in our dulled and escapist Broadway theatre. His irreverent, off-beat cartoons had already shown him to be a first-rate social critic, our contemporary Daumier. In his cartoon-drama, he pondered the joys of living in the urban jungle. In a series of grotesqueries by turns bittersweet, mordant, ironic, despairing, and hilarious, he limned a New York replete with noise, dirt, muggings, lewd telephone calls, air pollution, hypocritical homosexuality, government snooping and witch-hunts, and murder, murder, murder. Cultural life is exemplified by a photographer who makes a brilliant career out of camera close-ups of excrement. The theme of *Little Murders* is basically the growing violence in our cities: sub-themes are concerned with the less obvious psychological murders happening within the Great American Family. The women are busily castrating the men; the men vainly follow a ridiculous concept of manhood. Frustrated wives turn to their sons for love; equally frustrated husbands turn to their daughters. It is a major American comedy, a fiercely alive, rollicking, uncannily accurate cartoon.

It was small comfort to know that one could see *Little Murders* in London in the same year as its Broadway failure. The comedy was produced by the Royal Shakespeare Company in its London home, the Aldwych. Here the audiences were more accustomed to strong and original fare, and the Feiffer farce was welcomed. Perhaps this marks a new direction for unwanted American playwrights. As was the case with American opera and concert singers until recently, our playwrights might better display their talents in

Europe, where they may or may not be "discovered" by America but where they will find interested audiences.

A growing number of playwrights have found radical answers to the questions implicit in the Broadway experiences of Richardson, Hellman, and Feiffer. They increasingly echo the Provincetown Players' demand fifty years ago for nothing less than revolution. These iconoclasts simply do not bother to submit scripts to Broadway producers; they do not care to write for the present Broadway audience. They know from painful experience that they will fare much better in the livelier and more flexible off-Broadway theatre. A pleasant run in a small, somewhat plain showcase is far more desirable than an overnight flop in a large, luxurious one. Even if by some miracle the superior scripts of these new playwrights reached the Broadway stages, they probably would be horribly emasculated in production. This attitude among playwrights marks, of course, an extraordinary change. Only yesterday Broadway was a goal and a zenith for the aspiring author. A few years ago Arthur Miller penned a loving essay extolling the glories of Broadway, even suggesting that glamour and wonder were part of its mystique. Today the very idea of glamour associated with Broadway provokes wry laughter among the young. Oddly and surprisingly enough in our commerce-oriented culture, many of our young playwrights value art and independence above the Big Money. Thus they may be creating a new theatre culture. "You could cover the whole world with asphalt," the late Ilya Ehrenburg once remarked, "but sooner or later green grass would break through."

Two separate clusters of dramatists and two distinctly different audiences have now formed in New York theatre, and they represent two increasingly antagonistic, seemingly irreconcilable cultures. The off- and the off-off-Broadway dramatists regard uptown writers as Organization Playwrights manufacturing products to the specifications of the Commodity Theatre. Will the two cultures remain forever separate and unequal—Broadway with the money, the mindless crowds, and the indifferent products; the Other Theatre off Broadway with little cash, a small but dedicated following, and exciting, relevant, experimental scripts? The case is no longer one of the missing playwright; it is really the case of the clashing cultures.

The playwrights in the two cultures even talk a different language. On Broadway an entire cast of characters is missing, and whole areas of modern life are omitted or falsely presented. The major social issues of our times are still awaiting treatment on the Broadway stages. To most playwrights the phenomenon of McCarthyism (still with us in varying degrees and several disguises) has not been proper subject matter for the theatre, even though this raging plague is one of the most dramatic events of the last few decades. America's role of Policeman to the World has been similarly ignored. The Vietnam war, which has dominated the sixties and has rent our own nation as well as Vietnam itself, is a theatre unmentionable. Of the missing cast of characters, the nation's industrial worker has been the stage's forgotten man ever since the thirties. When a socialist, an atheist, a black or white civil rights worker, an antiwar protester, or a draft dodger is depicted on the stage (and a rare occasion that is), the portrait is invariably stereotyped and basely inaccurate. Man as sex partner is seldom presented in his rich and infinite variety. The Broadway stage still views him as a sexual primitive or, with a leer and a snicker, as an adolescent acting out a dirty joke. Any casually observant New Yorker can point out the ludicrousness of this willfully obtuse view of sexuality. And, of course, the nation's poor and dispossessed are not considered at all: they simply do not exist.

The young of today—both the New Leftists and the Hippies—are blandly ignored or crudely caricatured. When they do get into such Broadway comedies as William Goodhue's *Generation* or William Inge's *Where's Daddy?*, they are not painted with any special insight. After all, an honest and searching look at the young would lead the dramatist into dangerous areas of American life, and this would not please the complacent Broadway audiences. They come to the theatre to be flattered, not provoked. Instead the young are gaily presented as amusing kooks, problem children all parents must somehow endure. Isn't it awful what parents have to put up with these days? Thus the entire moral struggle of today's youth is conveniently ignored. The popular generation-gap comedy is merely a gimmick to soothe the egos of the elderly.

On the other hand, the unsmiling aspects of American life are being examined by the Other Theatre's playwrights with great subtlety. The cheap, uneasy, and violent quality of American life is at the core of such plays as Jean-Claude van Itallie's *America Hurrah*, Leonard Melfi's *Niagara Falls*, and Frank Gagliano's *Night of the Dunce*. The Other Theatre's *MacBird*, for example, breathes more of the vivid reality of American political life than a season of obsolete Establishment dramas. *MacBird* is concerned with morality in an angry way Broadway has long forgotten. In the showcases of off-Broadway, America is presented as it is; in the gilded cages of Broadway, the U.S.A. is a peculiarly lifeless, antiseptic terrain which has never existed.

A few men who genuinely cherish the American theatre and who value Broadway's past and its still dazzling potentialities are desperately trying to halt this artistic *apartheid* and bridge the ever-widening chasm between the two cultures. The most hopeful believe that the off-Broadway movement can somehow spill some of its gaiety and vigor and irreverence onto the Establishment stages. Edward Albee, the one playwright who has successfully leaped from the Other Theatre's small change to Broadway's Big Money, is acutely aware of the revolution. He once stated that the audience is so dead he has had to shake life into it. I'm afraid he has not done this with his own plays. However, he has encouraged young dramatists through his Playwrights' Unit and by offering promising writers professional off-Broadway productions, with paying audiences and reviews by the city's leading critics.

In the fall of 1968, Albee announced a startling attempt to heal the cultural rift. Fanatical rebels who see the present clash between Broadway and the Other Theatre as final and irreconcilable will undoubtedly dub Albee the Kerensky of the revolution. For this somber, tight-lipped playwright introduced off-Broadway to Broadway. With his producing partner Richard Barr, he transformed the Billy Rose Theatre into a non-profit performing arts center, presenting Beckett's *Krapp's Last Tape* and *Happy Days*, as well as several of his own more experimental works. None of these dramas had previously been displayed on Broadway. Later in the season, he sponsored a festival of Modern Dance and brought Merce Cunningham, José Limon, Alvin Ailey, and Meredith Monk to Broadway. One might seriously question whether Broadway will welcome this conciliatory maneuver for very long, but one cannot quarrel with Albee's concerned effort to unite the opposing armies—if that means a peaceful victory for the experimentalists.

A stop-gap (and, to many outraged conservatives, profoundly un-American) plan to save Broadway's battered playwrights was evolved in 1968. The Theatre Development Fund, with grants totaling $400,000, including both foundation and federal money, purchased tickets to adventurous Broadway shows it considers meritorious and in dire need of precious time to find its audience. This is the first subsidy plan actualized for America's commercial theatre. Who chooses which play and why will be questions guaranteed to provoke bitter controversy during the early years of the rescue mission—*if* it continues.

Belatedly, haphazardly, dimly, and reluctantly, individual philanthropists, the foundations, and the city, state, and federal governments are beginning to perceive that the basic solutions lie with the rebels. Perhaps the real saviors of the American theatre will be the off-Broadway visionary playwright-as-artist. Certainly the millionaires who built the spectacular New Theatre in 1909 were on the wrong track. The New Theatre failed because it was based only on money, vanity, and a foolhardy desire to produce instant culture. Monetary first aid must always start at bedrock—with the nurturing of young playwrights and young theatre groups in revolt against today's dry rot on Broadway. This is only half-understood, and the money afforded them is usually an absurd trickle. It is, however, a welcome first step.

A number of foundations, most notably the Ford and Rockefeller Foundations, have awarded grants to young playwrights. They have also helped broaden the professional opportunities for young playwrights by contributing moderate sums of money to a number of off-off-Broadway theatre groups, including the Chelsea Theatre Center and the New Lafayette Theatre in Harlem. In 1967, the American government finally recognized the existence of the Other Theatres in New York. Through the National Endowment for the Arts created by Congress, a cautious, tentative experiment was inaugurated, and grants were made to the Chelsea Theatre Center ($15,000), the Albee workshop ($10,000), the Judson Poets' Theatre ($2,500), the New Theatre Workshop ($2,150), and the American Place ($25,000). The last-named group knew precisely where one of theatre's major problem lay, so it planned to use the money "for audience development and subsidized theatre tickets."

Two off-off-Broadway groups that have played key roles in the nurturing of new and expressive playwrights, Ellen Stewart's La Mama and Joseph Chaikin's Open Theatre, received a paltry $5,000 apiece. Ironically, it has been these two groups that have best bolstered America's faltering cultural prestige abroad. Among Europe's dissident young, these wandering minstrels come as prophets of the New Theatre. La Mama has been the hit of European festivals for several seasons, and it is respected for its originality and its contemporaneity in theatre journals from Stockholm to Prague. One critic on the London *Observer*, after viewing the defiantly joyous La Mama troupe in Rochelle Owens' *Futz* and Leonard Melfi's *Times Square* at the Edinburgh Festival, exulted: "The most exciting American theatre we've seen since the advent of Miller, Williams, and Albee." Chaikin of the Open Theatre has achieved an international reputation for his bold experimentation, including his midwifery of *America Hurrah;* he even journeyed overseas to assist Peter Brook with his Royal Shakespeare production of *U.S.*, a controversial happening markedly critical of the American stand in Vietnam. In 1968, the Open Theatre toured a grateful Europe for four months, offering works by American newcomers as well as by Brecht and Ionesco.

These theatres have fostered dozens of young playwrights, many of them sharply anti-government in their writings. It is encouraging that Washington, however cagily, supports them even in their dissent. Perhaps the government might someday even come to see the error of closing the Becks' Living Theatre. When will Washington welcome them with Federal funds?

The care and feeding of playwrights—at least for three weeks during the summer—has been taken quite literally by the Eugene

O'Neill Memorial Theatre Foundation at Waterford, Connecticut. Since the summer of 1966, the Foundation has housed and fed gratis some twenty playwrights. The young authors are also given a small cash subsidy. Too, the Foundation invites professional critics, directors, set designers, and actors to work with the play-wrights. In a barn on the ninety-five-acre estate, professional per-formances of each writer's work-in-progress are offered to the public. Plays by Frank Gagliano, John Guare, Sam Shepard, Lan-ford Wilson, and Leonard Melfi have been tried out here. Israel Horovitz, who earlier had been playwright-in-residence with Eng-land's Royal Shakespeare Company, presented his *It's Called a Sugar Plum*. It was later produced in an off-Broadway theatre as a companion piece for his brilliant study of fear and violence in the urban jungle, *The Indian Wants the Bronx*. Ron Cowen's *Summertree*, later an off-Broadway hit, was first exhibited in Waterford. Created by a 22-year-old newcomer, this memory play about a young man who had been killed in Vietnam was flawed and derivative, but it displayed a remarkable reverence for life.

Not only the foundations and the government are expressing sudden interest in the new playwrights whom Broadway chooses to ignore. Even the publishing houses are beginning to print the phenomenally prolific outpourings of these young dramatists. In 1967 alone, there appeared entire volumes devoted respectively to the plays of Rosalyn Drexler, Leonard Melfi, Lanford Wilson, Megan Terry, and Sam Shepard. A flurry of anthologies saluted the playwrights of off-off-Broadway, including not only such cur-rent experimentalists as Tom Eyen and Carolee Schneemann but also such Other Theatre veterans as the late Gertrude Stein and e. e. cummings.

But a disquieting and nagging question persists to becloud this flattering attention to the rebellious American playwright. Are we creating dramatists with no place to go? Already the American theatre has more trained actors, directors, and set designers than can ever find work in any given year. Now the nation possesses playwrights in ever increasing number, and it is not at all clear that it wants them. In the sixties, the off-off-Broadway theatre in New York has produced scripts by more than five hundred new playwrights. But these artists cannot live on bread and water. Plays in the experimental theatre net next to nothing. There are only a handful of seats, and the nominal admission fees do not always cover the rent. Take the example of Playwright X. He is a busy member of the Playwrights' Unit, the Actors Studio, and the New Dramatists Committee; he has enjoyed free staged readings of his works at the Eugene O'Neill Memorial Theatre Foundation; he has been awarded both a Guggenheim Fellowship and a Ford Foundation grant; he has been produced at La Mama, the Judson Poets' Theatre, and Theatre Genesis. From all this activity he has made little money, and more often then not he is heavily in debt to his friends and well-wishers. As he gets older and takes on family responsibilities, he despairs of ever making a living. Must he spend a lifetime living a marginal existence, a pauper in his own land? Is the adulation of a minority culture sufficient to keep one at the arduous task of playwriting? All too often the would-be dramatist decides to forgo the theatre and try something else.

He is clearly unwanted on Broadway, where the money is, unless he turns out safe commodities. Lanford Wilson's *The Rimers of Eldritch* and Tom Eyen's *Tom Paine* have not been done on Broadway, even though they are clearly superior to most anything on the Establishment stages. From Sam Shepard to Rochelle Owens, the new playwrights go unproduced in the nation's major showcases. Robert Lowell, the nation's greatest living poet, has written several distinguished dramas. None has come to Broadway. His creative version of Racine's *Phèdre* is the most masterly literary adaptation of the century. Lowell captures the fires raging within the classic boundaries of the poetic drama in a dazzling, diamond-hard style. Veteran experimentalists are equally ignored. *Many Loves*, a witty and audacious play by another great American poet, William Carlos Williams, is not considered Broadway material. The long list of plays you are not allowed to see on Broadway—important works by authors as different as Alice Childress and Paul Goodman—grows lengthier each season.

One must sadly conclude that the Other Theatre is strictly for the very young, for those who can afford to work under near-starvation conditions. In their mammoth compilation of statistics,

Performing Arts: The Economic Dilemma, William J. Baumol and William G. Bowen clearly indicate the plight of the American playwright. In the years 1953–57, the annual median income for the American playwright (and this includes Broadway) was $684. This figure is for theatre writing alone—not for income from other sources, including help from working spouses. And for today's playwright in the Other Theatre, this figure is fantastically high.

When one is aware of these dismal facts, the interest of the foundations, the universities, and the government in the Other Theatre takes on another aspect. Are these well-meaning forces falsely encouraging an unwanted man—the playwright? Isn't something radically wrong in a culture which has fine new plays and playwrights but a limited audience? Should a playwright work forever in the Other Theatre, with its miserable economic returns, uncomfortable auditoriums, rickety stages, and poor technical equipment? It is a happening compounded of irony and despair. Must our best playwrights forever remain part of a minority and underground culture? It is no use pretending this culture represents America. The Other Theatre is a minuscule segment of the nation, of a country forever boasting that it is the world's richest. Hopefully change will come from the young, those mad pioneers who live on a few dollars a week. Many of them see morality in new public terms, not as a matter of who should be allowed to sleep with whom, and they may create a new kind of sophistication and a new kind of moral beauty. Perhaps in time they will reverse the theatre decline. Or perhaps (and this is more likely) theatre culture will die out— except on little slum stages.

Whatever happens, let us know the truth. It is not at all a case of the missing playwright. It is, more accurately, a case of missing audiences. Perhaps in a larger sense, it is an even sadder case—a nation that does not care about the dramatic arts, a nation without a soul.

CHAPTER 12

TAP
DANCING
AND
TOTAL
THEATRE

BROADWAY IS NOW chiefly given over to the musical. Drama as a serious art form seems to be slowly and inexorably disappearing. A pretty girl, a song and dance, and a joke or two—this is largely the Broadway stage. European visitors invariably exclaim, with elaborate condescension, that Americans are absolutely marvelous at putting on musicals. Implied in this left-handed compliment are two unflattering provisos: musicals are all that Americans can do well, and musicals, though sometimes diverting, are really a rather unimportant genre.

Intellectuals, both foreign and domestic, are quite right to deride the current musical. The song-and-dance show has become big business, and the form has settled into a familiar pattern, unimaginative, trivial, and distinctly second-rate. On any given night at least two-thirds of all Broadway theatregoers are applauding musicals. The long-running hits net millions of dollars, and indeed the advance sales alone often total more than a million. With the Hollywood producing companies and the television giants underwriting musicals, the profit potential is compounded. The film corporations occasionally make second fortunes on the film versions; the television companies can net new millions on original-cast albums through their subsidiary record companies. The contemporary musical is a mass commodity manufactured to please everybody. Thus it is carefully designed *not* to be too good.

The libretto of most musicals is alarmingly high in sugar content. For example, the numerous collaborations of composer Richard Rodgers and librettist-lyricist Oscar Hammerstein II have been graced by glorious Rodgers scores, but the banal books have all too frequently resembled road-show Shubert operettas. Hopefully, there will come a time when *Oklahoma!*, *South Pacific*, *Carousel*, *Flower Drum Song*, *The Sound of Music*, etc., will be laughed off our stages. Our "beloved" American musicals are, in fact, ephemeral and they rarely hold up in the decades after their overpraised premieres. Though critics and journalists notoriously lavish superlatives on them, most are rubbish when judged as art. I am condemning not only the obviously squalid ones, such inartistic stews as *Buttrio Square*, *Portofino*, *Whoop-Up*, *Pousse Café*, *Anya*, and *Kelly*, but the entire musty musical-comedy catalogue. No wonder that one of America's most reflective critics, the late Stark Young, seldom attended a musical.

And yet—is this the whole of the matter? Can the musical be dismissed so airily? In my own years of aisle-sitting, I have discovered (somewhat to my chagrin) that I often enjoy Broadway musicals much more than Broadway dramas. Perhaps it is an exercise in relativity. Our serious dramas are pretentious, puffed up with stale ideas passed off as profundity. The dramatist ambitiously poses as an artist and thus falls with a more reverberating thud. The insult is the fiercer when one pays for art and receives instead a simulacrum. On the other hand, one expects very little of a musical and thus the knowing, value-conscious consumer is never cheated by misrepresentation. In fact, one is sometimes unexpectedly delighted at a song-and-dance show. The parts are always greater than the whole. One can usually find a bright moment— an inspired bit of clowning, a sweepingly expressive dance, an astonishing bit of scenic invention, a song of compelling beauty. These magical moments often happen in the flimsiest of shows. *Funny Girl*, for example, was quite routine, with an asinine book purportedly based on the life of Fannie Brice. But an artist, Barbra Streisand, made it glow with her presence. With a Nefertiti exoticism, a nose-thumbing arrogance, and a sweetly awkward grace, Miss Streisand is an authentic harlequin, a special blend of the funny and the sad, the ludicrous and the stirring, and she sings with an unfailing sense of drama and a rare attention to mood. How she made "Sadie" sound like a vintage phonograph record, the kind that was once pressed onto a cylinder! In many another yawn of a musical, great clowns have fashioned unforgettable turns. With the remembered ache of laughter I conjure up Nancy Walker hopelessly misdirecting Holland Tunnel traffic in *Copper and Brass* and Beatrice Lillie nonchalantly toying with an Ouija board in *High Spirits*. David Wayne, Gwen Verdon, Zero Mostel, Alfred Drake, Charlotte Rae, Barbara Harris, Jack Cassidy, Richard Kiley, Lotte Lenya, Jack Gilford, and the late Bert Lahr are among the merlins who have vastly improved musicals in which they have appeared.

Often intellectuals snobbishly neglect to see the art in the popular song. Not all songsmiths are Tin Pan Alley hacks. The popular composer, at his best, is an artist we can be proud of, and he is often at his best in the theatre. Jerome Kern's "All the Things You Are," Cole Porter's "Were Thine That Special Face," or Harold Arlen's "Ill Wind" are not songs of the moment. These works are *lieder*, or art songs, as much as any heard at Philharmonic Hall. Frank Loesser's "Fugue for Tinhorns" from *Guys and Dolls* is an eminent ode to gamblers, laced with contrapuntal graces and a delicious musical wit. His score for *Most Happy Fella* is studded with operatic arias, duets, quartets, and recitatives of distinction. Leonard Bernstein, at home in classical composition and a charismatic symphony conductor, has created several superior scores for Broadway, including *On the Town, Wonderful Town, Candide,* and *West Side Story*. George Gershwin, Burton Lane, Arthur Schwartz, and Jule Styne have now and then presented us with music of quality.

Lyricists of merit have been scarcer, but they have on occasion graced the Broadway songbook. Lorenz Hart wrote notably adult, biting, urban-tough verses with more than fleeting relevance. His *Pal Joey* poems remain a model for lyricists today and tomorrow, perfectly blending words with the scene's action and feeling. A modern madrigal one part wit and one part venom, "To Keep My Love Alive," adorned the updated version of *A Connecticut Yankee* in 1943. One of the last songs Hart wrote before he died, it presented him at his most typical—unhackneyed and unsentimental. Howard Dietz, Ira Gershwin, John LaTouche, Sheldon Harnick, and Stephen Sondheim have been among the Broadway bards not content to rhyme moon and June. E. Y. Harburg, with his wry understanding of the way social systems work, is the wittiest of all the versifiers. In the rakishly audacious *Finian's Rainbow*, Harburg happily intermingled the dream world of leprechauns with the real world of greed and bigotry. His "God's Country" from the 1938 *Hooray for What!* is still a freshly puckish paean to Popeye and Gypsy Rose Lee and a thumbs-down judgment on such celebrities of that moment as Benito Mussolini and Oswald Mosley. The late Cole Porter, though his ideas tended to be cold, brittle, and glossy (and just a mite collegiate), penned intricate rhymes and ingenious inner rhythms; he employed an erudite vocabulary rarely encountered in the Broadway lexicon. In a few instances, a lyricist, composer, and librettist have come together to form a splendid trinity. Alan Jay Lerner, Frederick Loewe, and George Bernard Shaw (though Lerner was erroneously given the major credit for the book) turned *My Fair Lady* into one of the century's best musicals, and "The Rain in Spain" and "I've Grown Accustomed to Her Face" constituted an almost-perfect blend of lyrics and music, character and plot. Only the misplaced "On the Street Where You Live" spoiled the remarkable unity of style.

Dance has bestowed prestige and quality on many a musical. An inspired soft-shoe or tap by Jack Whiting, Ray Bolger, or Paul Draper has hushed many an audience into devotion. These are dancers of blessed grace. Broadway now and then produces ballets of surpassing originality, ballets that should be preserved in the permanent repertory of a dance company. A most ordinary musical, *Skyscraper*, contained a Michael Kidd ballet that was extraordinary. In a joyous contemporary salute to the welder and the riveter, a group of men danced as they proceeded to construct onstage several floors of an office building. Ever since 1936 and *On Your Toes*, with its pioneering "Slaughter on Tenth Avenue" sequence by George Balanchine, Broadway has increasingly, if somewhat patronizingly, turned to talented choreographers to impart a Tiffany air to the musical comedy. Agnes de Mille, Herbert Ross, Jerome Robbins, Helen Tamiris, and Hanya Holm have made vital contributions to Broadway as well as to the world of "serious" dance. Perhaps De Mille will be remembered almost as much for her haunting Civil War ballet in *Bloomer Girl* as her "Rodeo" for the Ballet Russe de Monte Carlo. The late Helen Tamiris will be canonized for sparkling dances in *Annie Get Your Gun* as well as "Adelante," her warm embrace of the Spanish Loyalists in the Civil War.

The musical theatre is first and last the theatre of the craftsman, and the skill in production invariably exceeds that in the drama proper. Nowhere is this more strikingly evident than in the wonders of elaborate costuming, scenery, turntables, lighting boards, etc. The American stagehands and lighting technicians effect changes of tempo and mood with incredible deftness and speed. American musicals offer the spectator an old-fashioned cornucopia of color and splendor and pageantry; they offer something too often absent from the stage—a gratification of our visual appetites. I have often left a musical humming, in effect, not the tunes but the lavish *look* of the show. Only in the more recondite worlds of opera and ballet does one find the spectacle equaled or bettered.

However, I do not wish to mislead. Not for a moment has our Broadway musical theatre arrived at any summit of overall excellence. The past and present are merely overture. A look backward indicates how little, really, we have accomplished. In the nineteenth century, such spectacles as *The Black Crook* were untidy pastiches rather than marriages of style, and this has remained true in the 1960's. Commerce almost always triumphs over art. In point of fact, the pioneering mixture of drama with song and dance in *The Black Crook* was an accident rather than a conscious artistic union. A ludicrously vulgar melodrama loosely based on the Faust legend was scheduled to open at New York's Niblo's Gardens in 1866. In that same year, a French ballet company had been signed to appear at the Academy of Music but was left without a stage when that theatre burned down. An enterprising impresario hired the hundred-member ballet company, with its pretty girls in daringly brief costumes and its elaborate scenery, as an extra lure to ticket-holders for *The Black Crook*, and thus drama and ballet were quickly and crudely grafted into a new kind of American theatre. Another long-running spectacle was an unlikely "girlie" extravaganza of 1875, *Evangeline*. Ostensibly a burlesque of Long-fellow's poem, it was one of the first musicals with an American theme. After *The Black Crook* and *Evangeline* came the operettas, most often based on European models—a flurry of pretty and insipid formula divertisements by Victor Herbert, Rudolph Friml, Sigmund Romberg, and their imitators. (In the 1960's, the mind-less operetta plots were to receive an affectionate parody by Rick Besoyan with *Little Mary Sunshine*, one of the longest-run musi-cals in off-Broadway history.) A Yankee-doodle dandy, George M. Cohan injected a special American bounce and cheekiness into his book shows, but unfortunately he settled happily and noisily for innocuous platitudes and the third-rate. Complete integration of music, dance, and drama was neither pursued nor understood.

In 1927 one musical did slightly jar this never-never land. Based on Edna Ferber's novel, *Show Boat* was a most unusual creation by two gentlemen of the old-style candy-box theatre, Oscar Ham-merstein II (book and lyrics) and Jerome Kern (music). Produced by—of all unlikely pioneers—Florenz Ziegfeld, the musical is, in part, a pretty evocation of the nineteenth-century showboats along the Mississippi, but it is much more than that. The curtain rises on a startling scene of black dock workers hauling bales of cotton and openly discontent with their fate. (The Negro Joe has a most pointed and poignant line in "Ol' Man River"—"De lan' ain't free.") The plot involves two unhappy marriages and miscegenation (with an implied criticism of our laws against it), certainly a radical change from Victor Herbert's chocolate creams. The integration of drama and music, with identifiable characters and situations, marked a notable if not major breakthrough. Would that Ham-merstein and Kern had continued to grow, rather than to become congealed into subsequent show-business formulas.

However, ever since that historic night of December 27, 1927, the reign of the mechanical musical has been threatened. It still reigns but more uncertainly, with a timid step forward and another backward, forever advancing and retreating. An impressive roster of talents joined hands for another significant musical, *Four Saints in Three Acts*, first produced in 1934 and later revived in 1952 at the Phoenix. The wittily jumbled words were by Gertrude

Stein, and they were not meant to be taken literally but rather as an artfully strung necklace of phrases designed to evoke a feeling and mood. For Virgil Thomson, a leading American composer and music critic, the words recalled church music and a kind of sophisticated naiveté about the saints. Thomson himself had once been a church organist. Added to this felicitous pair was painter Florine Stettheimer, who created imaginative, childlike settings and costumes. The all-black cast was uncannily right in interpreting the stylish Stein-ish nonsense, at once solemn and gay, into song and dance. Dancer-choreographer Frederick Ashton, in later years himself a saint of Britain's Royal Ballet, was imported to supply the overall dance patterns for the work. Here was an unusual and unified theatre piece that began properly with the choreographer, who in turn gave the production its formal unity and beauty. It was an important lesson for the future—but few were listening at the time.

The late Marc Blitzstein was another harbinger, offering social protest in a fresh, sparkling package. His *The Cradle Will Rock* (1937) is a work of special merit. An off-Broadway revival in 1964 showed conclusively that the score of *The Cradle Will Rock* was as delightful as ever and that its saucy Brechtian style (also related to the American minstrel and vaudeville forms) was still exhilaratingly effective. Its theme of inhumanity is, of course, no more dated than today's little gifts of jellied gasoline.

Certainly *Pal Joey* (1940) is a landmark in the uneven history of the American musical. With an ironic musical commentary by Richard Rodgers and Lorenz Hart and a tough-minded book by novelist John O'Hara, here at last was neither syrupy romance nor phony piety but a candid portrait of an anti-hero. Joey was a third-rate nightclub hoofer who prodded money from a rich and aging society dame; she in her turn used the heel to procure some momentary amorous delights for herself. Joey and Mrs. Simpson were authentic, native monsters, recognizable inhabitants of our urban jungle. Vera Simpson's aria, "Bewitched, Bothered, and Bewildered," was honestly self-critical and sharp in a new city-cynical way. The musical's audiences were confused by its vitriol, and its run was brief. *Pal Joey* was so misunderstood in 1940 that critic

Brooks Atkinson was vexed enough to ask, "Can you draw sweet water from a foul well?" The difference between *Pal Joey* in 1940 and *Oklahoma!* just two years later, both of which were graced with scores by chameleon Richard Rodgers, was the difference between the mordant observation of Lorenz Hart and John O'Hara and the fake folksiness of Oscar Hammerstein II. The first was an important step forward in Broadway music history; the latter, despite its celebrated dream ballet by Agnes de Mille, a step backward toward treacly operetta.

Plausible cases might be constructed for many another production which has slightly extended the artistic boundaries, in form and/or content, of the musical. The excessively praised *Porgy and Bess* (1935) was a laudable attempt at folk opera, but it marked no notable advance in American operatic composition. Worse, it encouraged racism. *Johnny Johnson* (1936), which contained Kurt Weill's first score for Broadway, was a bitter yet funny antiwar play. Paul Green was the dramatist, and the cast included Lee J. Cobb, John Garfield, Robert Lewis, Elia Kazan, Luther Adler, and Morris Carnovsky. It was not a commercial success, but it was a fascinating fusion of music and words, fantasy and satire. *The Golden Apple* (1954) by composer Jerome Moross and lyricist-librettist John LaTouche spawned a cult of fervid admirers. The ambitious endeavor was no less than a breezy and very American adaptation of both the *Iliad* and the *Odyssey*, and it was ingenious, gay but, sadly, too cute. Yet at least it did not altogether insult the intelligence.

Three musicals, *West Side Story*, *Gypsy*, and *Fiddler on the Roof*, were choreographed and directed by Jerome Robbins, a former dancer and choreographer for Ballet Theatre. Each production resoundingly proved the wisdom of having one man (and especially a dance-trained one) impose a unity and style on all the elements of a musical work. *West Side Story* (1957), splendid in its silken-smooth integration of production elements, was a somewhat self-conscious effort to translate the Capulets and Montagues of Verona into the Sharks and the Jets, Manhattan street gangs. Though *Gypsy* (1959) fudged and gave way to obvious tricks and commercial considerations, it was a truer-than-usual picture of show-business life. If the emphasis had been focused more sharply and courageously on Rose, the anti-heroine, *Gypsy* could have become a sort of Mother Courage of backstage life. *Fiddler on the Roof* (1964) was a sentimentalized, impure evocation of the richer, far more flavorsome Yiddish bittersweet of Sholom Aleichem. Jerome Robbins could not, of course, single-handedly throw off all the mildewed Broadway baggage weighing down these musicals. He did succeed, however, in offering astonished audiences a tantalizing glimpse of how dance and drama, properly wedded, could create magic.

A number of musicals have pretended to criticize our social structure but, in actual practice, have blunted their blows. An overpraised political spoof of the 1930's, *Of Thee I Sing,* poked tiresomely broad and irritatingly feeble fun at congressmen and presidential campaigns. Broadway has continued to emasculate provocative themes. *How to Succeed in Business Without Really Trying* (1961) and *How Now, Dow Jones* (1967) were really quite conventional musicals for the tired businessman, though they posed as satires on business. In the forties, *Finian's Rainbow* had boldly attacked racial prejudice with delightful wit and sting, but in the sixties, neither *No Strings* nor *Hallelujah, Baby* really examined the harrowing subject. In fact, these musicals were scandalously blithe about it, as though race hatred were merely a minor irritation that would soon disappear. Often great literary legends have been diluted. *Man of La Mancha* (1965) did attempt to portray some of the ironic nobility inherent in the saga of Don Quixote, but the production was painfully Broadwayed. Cervantes and his Don were sadly compromised, though critics and audiences pretended not to notice. The classic tale (a satire once considered subversive by the religious-military Establishment of Spain) was cheapened into a sentimental study of an oddball old man pursuing a whore with a heart of gold. A routine, unimaginative gang-rape dance was added as obligatory Broadway spice.

A relatively recent musical pointed in the right direction was *Cabaret,* which made me a bit more hopeful about the future of the American musical. Its ambitions were enormous and laudable— to recreate the tacky, degenerate, divided world of Berlin just before Hitler. Miraculously, *Cabaret* embodied the brilliantly bilious, vomit-smeared George Grosz drawings of the period. Though it had little to do with the Christopher Isherwood novel nor the play taken from that novel, the musical fiercely traced, in its own original way, the downward journey from pre-fascist depravity to the stygian jaws of the Nazis. *Cabaret* scalded one with sadism, profligacy, prostitution, alienation, abortion, and—most unsettling —social commentary with prophetic overtones. One of the musical's stars, Joel Grey, later recalled how producer-director Harold Prince tacked up on the cast bulletin board a photograph of a rioting Chicago mob throwing rocks at black demonstrators. "We all kept that image and remembered it," Grey said. "Berlin, 1929, is no more decadent than America, 1967."

Cabaret was a lusty reversal of all the basic ingredients of the "hit formula" show. How did it ever make it to Broadway? This was a musical about commitment; it was about the "it-can't-happen-here" people, the "what-has-this-got-to-do-with-me" people. *Cabaret* was a most useful guide on how to achieve stylistic unity in a musical, but even in this superior sample the collaborators vacillated between uncompromising artistry and Broadway mass-commodity values.

The promise of *Cabaret* partly explains my own stubborn affection for the musical genre. I have enjoyed a song, a dance, and a joke in countless overpraised hits, but the Broadway musical excites far less by what it delivers than by the potentialities inherent in the form. From this tilted angle, the continuing dominance of Broadway by the musical may someday be seen not as a bane but a boon. Out of the current musical could come a revolutionary new form. The basic ingredients are there, waiting to be transformed into art.

By its nature (a union of song, dance, drama, and decor), a musical is unrealistic, fantastic, expressionist. If an actor suddenly breaks into song in the middle of a love scene or dances his amorous intentions, he and the production have departed from naturalism. By artifice, one can paradoxically come closer to the real. The miracle of life is too sprawling, too contradictory, and too explosive to be contained within the old-fashioned thesis play. Life is infinitely more complex than most cardboard, one-dimensional problem plays suggest. Indeed, American theatre, from Belasco to Chayefsky, has long been cramped by a dull literalism. O'Neill tried valiantly to open new doors of expression, but few followed his lead. Theatre should not try to offer a photographic reproduction of life. For films and television, the camera can roam freely over on-location settings and in closeup it can capture the detailed manifestations of emotion. The musical stage, however, can express deeper truths about reality, nuances about the hidden drama of life that are impossible to convey through documentary, tape-recorder methods. In brief, the musical theatre can be poetry of the highest order.

The possibility of poetics is not understood on Broadway, but elsewhere it is boldly inscribed on the banners of the experimentalists. In the off- and off-off-Broadway theatres, the young Balboas are impatiently searching for ways to better express the complexities of our time and our moment. They are creating "total theatre" in which all the elements are mixed more freely and imaginatively. These pioneers are certain that the present pigeonholing of theatre forms into separate categories is a false and restrictive fragmentation of the consciousness. They are intent on breaking down all artificial barriers and transforming theatregoing into a poetic incantation, an unfettered, sensuous experience. The musical, the drama, modern dance, ballet, the "happening," "environmental" art shows, and even perhaps religious ritual should all be merged into one. Will the despised Broadway musical and its tired hacks ever catch up with the fresh visions of the young, the dreams of total theatre?

I am not suggesting that the total-theatre concept is new. Myth and ritual, dance and poetry, constitute the earliest impulses of theatre. The classic Chinese theatre, the ancient Greek drama with masks and choruses, the medieval morality plays, *commedia dell'arte*, and especially Shakespeare—all are rooted in the union of music and movement and language. In this century, Sean O'Casey has penned several powerful expressionist dramas, still misunderstood, which masterfully combine the spoken word with music and dance.

The father of total theatre in its contemporary form is unquestionably Bertolt Brecht, and it is no accident that he is one of the great poets as well as playwrights of this century. Brecht's Epic Theatre is his personal version of the new grammar. In his instance, he did not wish to heighten emotion with a song but rather, as he stated again and again, to dispel cheap realism, simpering sentimentality, and easy tears by using music and song as alienating devices. He wanted literally to stop the show with songs, to provoke furious thought and not surface emotion. Greatly admiring Oriental theatre for its elaborate disdain of naturalism, he sought to destroy the illusionist theatre by openly employing artifice. Of all the seminal works influencing America's young total-theatre promulgators, Brecht's slashing, grating, acrimonious *The Threepenny Opera*, first produced in Berlin in 1928, has had the most profound effect. Though it was loosely based on John Gay's *Beggar's Opera*, with the scene changed from Hogarthian to hypocritical Victorian London, the musical's unmistakable mood was that of pre-Hitler Germany. Here, too, was a remarkably supple score of Kurt Weill—sweetly syncopated, ironic, bitter, and devastingly clear-eyed about the rotten nature of the modern Establishment. When *The Threepenny Opera* appeared on Broadway in the 1930's, its heady flavor and style were lost on the unprepared audiences. It closed after twelve performances. When it was produced off-Broadway in 1954, however, it proved to be a musical to which young America could relate. The production was a shade too genial, and the cast, excepting Lotte Lenya, was not a great one. But the youthful dissenters enthusiastically applauded the mocking manner of *The Threepenny Opera*, and it ran for five years. The only other work that has produced as many echoes among American experimentalists is the more recent import, Peter Weiss's *Marat/Sade*, with its slashing, explosive use of total-theatre techiques.

Today, Brecht's admirers are everywhere, and they are evolving ever-freer, more swinging theatre forms. Director-explorer Tom O'Horgan's actors at La Mama leap like acrobats, make music on medieval oboes and flutes, dance like Merce Cunningham troupers, and chant with the zeal of recently cloistered monks. O'Horgan subtly transformed Paul Foster's *Tom Paine* and Rochelle Owens' *Futz*, first off-off-Broadway explorations and later off-Broadway hits, into musicals. He also worked a miracle on Broadway in the spring of 1968. He restaged the off-Broadway musical *Hair*, dispensing with its confused plot and transforming it into a hallelujah happening, catching both the sweet vulnerability and the new mood of joyful defiance among the young. Broadway audiences were alternately startled, angered, delighted, and confused by this rollicking, mind-blowing musical with its nudity and its four-letter word impudence. The Galt McDermot score offered musical sounds new to Broadway, a mélange of New Orleans, Nashville, rock, spiritual, folksong, madrigal, and raga. It was an infectious score, and it brought a whiff of what's happening to tired Broadway. It will probably remain an exception to the Broadway rule.

The iconoclasts—Judith Malina and Julian Beck of the Living Theatre, Joseph Papp at the Public Theatre, Joseph Chaikin and Jacques Levy at the Open Theatre, and many an unsung pioneer in the drama workshops that dot Manhattan Island—are all combining sound (rock, raga, and what-comes-next), movement, films and photographs, improvisation, psychedelic lighting, ritual, even children's games in sensuous, visual, poetic new ways. *The Coach with Six Insides*, the James Joyce fantasia under the direction of modern dancer Jean Erdman; Gertrude Steins's *In Circles*, with gleeful music by the Judson Memorial Church's dogma-free minister, Al Carmines; the "Motel" sequence from *America Hurrah*—they are a part of the theatre revolution, with varying degrees of commitment to the total-theatre cause.

One of the most satisfying achievements of total theatre is *Dynamite Tonite*, performed all too briefly in 1967 at the Martinique, an off-Broadway showcase in a hotel. This antiwar play, employing both music and dance, is an admirable attempt at the Americanization of Brecht. Arnold Weinstein sets his expressionist work in a bunker during an imaginary war, and by mixing Karl Marx with the Marx Brothers, he fashions a novel and haunting addition to the growing antiwar literature. The script is laced with a childlike naiveté that makes the killing all the more absurd and the dying all the sadder. William Bolcom's dissonant, jagged score, reminiscent of Kurt Weill's threepenny bittersweet, includes a tango, a waltz, and even a little soft-shoe music. Who can forget the poignant "Enemy Children" or the ironic "After the War I

Change"? Despite the lame reception of *Dynamite Tonite*, Weinstein and Bolcom must continue their collaboration. Audiences are often wrong-headed. Certainly this musical/opera/vaudeville/drama—the label is unimportant—is imperfect, but it possesses a depth of feeling and a flowing beauty seldom encountered on our stages. Perhaps these gifted Americans might yet produce a masterpiece out of native materials.

Mind-expanding ideas for the total-theatre buffs are often derived from quite unexpected sources. Interestingly, several of the best models for today's firebrands have come from what historians unimaginatively call the Middle Ages. Two of the hottest tickets in New York during the 1960's have been for twelfth-century musicals, *The Play of Daniel* and *The Play of Herod*. These medieval morality plays, produced with a rare perfection by the New York Pro Musica, have been presented in local Episcopal churches and at the Metropolitan Museum of Art's Cloisters. The devoted artists boldly use aisles, choir lofts, and all available space in and around the audience with a theatrical flair that makes Broadway seem plodding and hopelessly square. The actors not only sing *a cappella* chants and motets; they sometimes use medieval musical instruments as part of the stage action. Another sumptuous example of medieval total theatre has been *Noye's Fludde*, a pageant-like enactment of the Old Testament legend of Noah and his Ark, with a strikingly original and deceptively simple score by England's Benjamin Britten. Using the entire church space, singer-actress Marie Powers, a cast of amateurs, and one hundred children performed the work in naive style. Unencumbered by the baggage of naturalism, they employed neo-primitive make-up, costumes, and settings as fresh and color-splashed as Matisse in his late period. The musical instrumentation included Chinese blocks, recorders, bugles, and a gong. Hopefully, these medieval musicals in churches will in time profoundly affect our commercial theatre.

Sooner or later the total-theatre adventurers of the future must pay homage to the considerable accomplishments in the more daring worlds of ballet, modern dance, and jazz. The Joffrey Ballet, the New York City Ballet, and Ballet Theatre, which have long surpassed Broadway in their artistic explorations, have all created marvelous models for the young experimentalists. Eliot Feld's evocative ballet "At Midnight," based on a Gustav Mahler song-cycle, with the singer in the orchestra pit, is fortified by a stunning collaborator, modern American painter Leonard Baskin. Robert Joffrey's very contemporary theatre-piece, "Astarte," demonstrates the visual splendor of two superb dancers supported by psychedelic lighting effects and a pulsating rock ensemble. Playwright-chore-ographer George Balanchine and his actor-dancers of the New York City Ballet capture, through movement and music, a con-temporary relevance and a dramatic variety missing from most musical stages both on and off Broadway.

If a European, for example, were to ask one who are the greatest theatre artists in America, one would have to answer George Balanchine and Martha Graham. Attend a Graham evening and you will begin to understand how drama can be heightened by the dazzling union of music and dance, costume and sculpture (often a stark Isamu Noguchi construction). This modern dance sorceress, now in her seventies, is a master of total theatre. Frequently she has introduced spoken texts into her special theatre world (for example, the impassioned Emily Dickinson poems in "Letter to the World"). With her magnificent company ("acrobats of God," she had felicitously called them), Martha Graham has created some of the most profound dramas in today's theatre. She is a dramatist in the deepest Greek sense, for she has explored the geography of the human heart, where gods and demons war. She has pursued drama through its most fundamental element—movement—and she creates no less than the dance of life. The Broadway musical has yet to mirror the nuances of the universal drama with such urgent artistry. Ironically, in the world's richest nation, we are deprived each season of seeing this incandescent artist because she cannot afford regular seasons of repertory on Broadway. We are similarly deprived of viewing repertory seasons of another towering artist of the modern dance, José Limon. In his "The Moor's Pavane," he has told the story of Othello with an economy, beauty, and power that is truly astonishing, and in "La Malinche," he has recreated a complex and gripping Mexican legend with unfor-gettable fervor. Both Limon and Graham have been shamefully neglected. All their works should have been filmed and notated for future generations—but that would involve money. The late Doris Humphrey, perhaps the greatest architect of stage space this nation has produced, was never given the national honors and plaudits due her. We waste our artistic treasures on a colossal scale of indifference. I dream of a unified theatre, where a Graham, Limon, Paul Taylor, Merce Cunningham, Robert Joffrey, Gerald Arpino, or Alwin Nikolais might stage an entire evening of musical theatre. Can one imagine the artistic triumphs for America if these inspired choreographer-dancers, completely in charge of every detail of production, could present full-length musicals on our Broadway stages?

The music of youth, the rock beat of today, is largely ignored on Broadway, for the smug, square audiences do not understand the new sounds, nor the reasons for them, and do not find them to their tired tastes. Just as the rock variations have been neglected, so all jazz has been despised from its beginnings. Broadway has always been shockingly satisfied with a watered-down, saccharine version. Jazz and modern dance are America's priceless, indigenous contributions to world culture, but Broadway couldn't care less. Nor has our folk music elicited any real response from old Broadway hands. As far as Broadway is concerned, such magnificent artists as Bessie Smith, Jelly Roll Morton, Billie Holiday, Leadbelly, Charlie Parker, Woody Guthrie, Dizzy Gillespie, and Miles Davis have not existed at all. However, they all have had invaluable lessons to teach about the authentic rhythms of American Life. Imagine a Broadway musical with decor by, say, Robert Rauschenberg, with direction by Eliot Feld (whose galvanic "Harbinger" for Ballet Theatre caught precisely the half-joyous, half-anxious hippie quality of today), with Nina Simone and Joan Baez in leading roles, and with a score by either Thelonious Monk or the Mothers of Invention. It is, of course, quite unthinkable, for Broadway antiquarians stubbornly refuse to use today's talent to produce art.

The musical theatre must become a place for passionate propaganda, incantation, communion, ritual, or that most difficult of achievements, pure joy. We must break down the barriers, rid ourselves of formulas, storm the Broadway prosceniums. In the next few decades the new musical could well become the most significant form in the American theatre. A fresh musical form at this moment in history might contain within it the seeds of progressive content, if it came out of the young and their instinctive dissent. When the young themselves learn how to combine blazing form with blazing protest—what an exciting conflagration that will be. Then the rest of the world could truthfully say that Americans do musicals better than anybody else, and they would mean it not ironically and condescendingly but *con amore*.

CHAPTER 13

THE COLLABORATORS

TOO MANY SELF-STYLED aficionados of the stage fail to understand a simple truth: theatre is, first and last, a collaborative art. Certainly a partisan of the drama should properly extol the playwright and place fervent emphasis on content and form; certainly he should care about the drama as literature. But if he ignores the actual staging of a play and the various elements that go into the magical transformation of a literary work from the printed page to three-dimensional reality, he is not truly a theatre man.

A play may be for all time, but it is also very much of the moment. It urgently demands a viewing here and now. The playwright needs actors, a director, a set designer, a costumer, a lighting expert, carpenters, stagehands, and a long list of fellow-artists before his script is ready for the final collaborator—an audience. The writer is only one of the many collaborators necessary to provide the exciting group experience we call theatre. Truman Capote, a sometime playwright, defined the special communal world of the stage. The novelist-journalist-social butterfly candidly declared that he could not work in the theatre. He liked to work alone, and he found the theatre to be the product of too many people's labors. It remains an apt observation about the collective nature of the dramatic arts.

There will always be those who argue endlessly about the relative importance of each member of the theatre collective. It is a silly game, a waste of time. From the prop man to the director, they are all precious, and together they create the dramatic event. Stanislavsky once stated that there are no bit parts—all roles are important. This axiom applies equally to everyone connected with any theatre venture.

But there's the rub. Though theatre is by its nature a group effort, true collaboration between the various artists is an impossible dream on Broadway in the 1960's. As theatre does not exist apart from the rest of society, it is ridiculous to discuss the drama without reference to America's politics, economy, and cultural values. Vietnam and theatre subsidies, urban blight and the lack of repertory—they are all interrelated. Price-fixing in business, thievery in Congress, our imperial arrogance abroad are reflected in the dramatic arts in labyrinthine ways. The men and women of the theatre have become contaminated with the same hit-and-run, each-man-for-himself virus that infects the rest of us. One cannot expect these artists to be immune from the worship of the Holy Buck. Directors, for example, are all too often far more interested in making a meretricious success for themselves than in faithfully evoking the author's intentions; stars and would-be stars are less concerned with the overall artistic effect than in cheaply attracting the attention of the critics and Hollywood agents; set designers are so enamored of their eye-popping scenic effects that they sometimes forget there is a specific drama at hand on which their talents should be centered. The aggressive thrust of contemporary American society is in direct conflict with the essentially cooperative nature of the theatre arts, and the artistic quality of our stages will change only with a qualitative change in the state of the union. So long as the theatre is regarded by Americans as merely another division of private enterprise, a business and not an art, the collaboration of its artists can never be total.

How show business has effectively squashed art is most strikingly evidenced in its crippling effects on American actors, the most conspicuous of the collaborators. The art of acting is seldom practiced on Broadway. Ensemble acting is unknown. An actor learns all too quickly that thorough training is unessential in our mechanical theatre; he soon discovers that he—not the play—is the thing. To succeed, he must stand out from the rest of the company in whatever clever way he can devise; he must ceaselessly employ tricks to exploit his personality; he must nurture his mannerisms.

He becomes uninterested in character acting, which is the essence of all good performing. He does not want to play all kinds of persons in many periods of history and many styles, for he knows that he must forever play one man—himself—if he is to make it in the Broadway theatre. Thus we have plenty of stars but few actors.

Most members of Actors' Equity are trained for only one kind of acting—the hysterical, showy naturalism now in vogue. Our actors are best at frustration and violence. (Perhaps in this way, too, our stages reflect American life and the prevailing national hysteria.) Even our finest artists—Kim Stanley, Geraldine Page, and Maureen Stapleton, for example—have been given little room to stretch; they must be content, in the main, with flashy, neurotic parts. Mistaking a coarsened and hopped-up intensity for true feeling, most of our actors rant and rave with melodramatic monotony. Many have forgotten—if indeed they ever knew—certain basic tenets about the acting art. First and foremost, acting is far more than a selfish and excessive wallowing in one's own role. Performers must practice the most exquisite refinement of their art: they must listen and react to one another on the stage. They must act as a group. Too, an actor must understand his character's time and place, how he dresses, how he makes a living, even how he makes love. He must also seek out the play's style. He must discover the emotional orchestration of the drama, and then integrate his own role into the total design. Many actors today do not select the telling moments for their emotional peaks; they are so busy being neurasthenic the play loses its rhythms. Acting demands sharp intelligence, sustained discipline, enormous sensitivity, and hard work. One can't really expect a rootless exhibitionist with one eye cocked on Hollywood and cheap fan-magazine success to take these requirements seriously.

The fact is that with few exceptions the American actor is not trained for world dramatic literature—for the Greek classics, Shakespeare, Molière, and Racine, for the long reach beyond naturalism. Indeed, all too often the American actor knows neither how to speak nor to walk. Perhaps he is not altogether to blame: he has had little opportunity to explore his possibilities or to widen his range. With no permanent troupes and no sense of tradition, he is isolated. Were it not for the occasional visits of foreign actors, Americans would scarcely know what a glorious art acting can be. I recall with relish the performers of the Moscow Art Theatre, the Vienna *Burgtheater*, the Piccolo Teatro di Milano, the Comédie Française, Japan's Grand Kabuki, and the Hamburg Opera. What an ambience of mellow chamber music emerged from the English players in Anouilh's *The Rehearsal* and Sheridan's *The School for Scandal*. The group mummery in Wesker's *Chips with Everything*, a Royal Court production, was a revelation to Broadway audiences.

Acting is appreciated as an art in many countries, if not in America. In England, an actor might become a Sir or a Dame in recognition of his or her contributions to the nation's culture. The virtuosity of the English actor is the result of repertory training. John Gielgud, Laurence Olivier, Edith Evans, Michael Redgrave, Dorothy Tutin, Ralph Richardson, Joan Plowright, Alec Guinness, Paul Scofield, Maggie Smith, and Peggy Ashcroft could never have become the transcendent artists they are if they had not spent years working in subsidized and quasi-subsidized repertory theatres. Attuned to the word magic of native-son Shakespeare, the English actor is verbally splendid, with an easy appreciation of fanciful language and of the voice as a delightful instrument to be played in many keys and modulations. Too, he is vitally interested in playing a variety of roles, not himself, and he displays a wondrously trained eye for the idiosyncrasies of character. At the moment, such an approach to acting is largely ignored in our theatre. It is no accident that two of the most supple and subtle actors who sometimes appear on Broadway, Rosemary Harris and Christopher Plummer, are not native Americans at all. Miss Harris was born in England, and she has graced many an English repertory production, including those of the Old Vics in both Bristol and London. Toronto-born Plummer, equally at home in a sweatshirt or tights, has appeared at both the English and Canadian Stratfords.

Yet I do not count myself as a narrow Anglophile. Given the same cultural ambience, Americans might possibly act as well as or better than the English. Uta Hagen, Zero Mostel, Barbara Harris, Seth Allen, Kevin O'Connor, Alan Arkin, Dustin Hoffman, George Grizzard, Sorrell Booke, Frances Sternhagen, Martin Balsam, Stacy

Keach, Robert Symonds, Fritz Weaver, Nancy Wickwire—they are artists all. Every nation possesses the raw talent which could produce great actors. The vital factor is always the manner in which the talent is nurtured—or neglected. It is the waste in our blighted commercial theatre that appalls me.

The average American sees the theatre as a business, and the average actor naturally goes where the Money is—Hollywood. Even in the twenties, the thirties, and the early forties, when Broadway had a certain éclat and some artistic pretensions, regiments of actors joyfully trekked westward to sell their souls. Broadway once boasted of its Royal Family, but Lionel Barrymore fled the stage in 1925 and John weaved uncertainly through third-rate films. Only Ethel remained faithful. The saddest contemporary symbol of the sellout is Marlon Brando. Once a potentially great theatre artist, he fled to Hollywood for keeps, becoming not so much an actor as a very busy businessman. At present, no one bothers to count the theatre's losses to Hollywood, for the exodus has become epic in its proportions. Many actors also turn to television. The performers in soap operas and situation comedies eat well—and dream of their return to the stage. Some augment their income by doing television commercials. Two magnificent comics, Jack Gilford and Charlotte Rae, immediately come to mind. Television dramas are, for the most part, banal and insipid, but working in these inferior efforts at least flexes a few acting muscles and pays the landlord.

The situation today is ironic. Broadway producers frequently import television and Hollywood names, often money-makers with little or no acting experience or ability, to make their box-office profits soar. The reasoning is that, with today's spiraling costs of production, one needs big names to insure hits. Often these names are synthetic personalities created by expensive publicity, glossy make-up, protective camera angling, soft lighting, and the unsung artists of the cutting room. The irony is compounded in that a dedicated Broadway actor may have served the stage with distinction for many years, but one appearance in a film or on national television may bring him more money, fame, fan mail, and man-in-the-street recognition than he has ever known.

A few performers, miraculously, remain loyal to the stage, still responsive to the special joys of the discredited art of acting and still eager for live audiences; they have discovered that there is something, albeit elusive and momentary and probably subversive, that is more satisfying than pots of money. Julie Harris, Anne Jackson, Robert Preston, Eli Wallach, Jason Robards, Anne Bancroft, and Geraldine Page are examples of actors who have picked up the lush Hollywood paychecks while still enriching our stages by frequent appearances. George C. Scott once put it succinctly: "I make movies for financial reasons, and this allows me the luxury of acting on Broadway. . . . We might as well exploit Hollywood as much as it exploits us." One of the stage's staunchest defenders is magnificent Colleen Dewhurst, who has worked in both films and television. Miss Dewhurst acted for a few dollars a week in two of the most exciting off-Broadway groups of the fifties, Joseph Papp's Shakespeare Festival and José Quintero's Circle-in-the-Square. Today a Broadway star, she is still defiantly proud that she is not a supermarket star (i.e., she is not recognized in the supermarkets by the housewives). She speaks for all true theatre artists in these ringing words: "I have no regrets. Money isn't important. I'll do a television show for thousands just so I can afford to work for Joe Papp in Central Park or do something off-Broadway for fifty dollars a week." The truly committed actor goes wherever theatre is, on or off Broadway. Mildred Dunnock and Ruth White, two of Broadway's most versatile actresses, do not hesitate to appear in small, shabby, out-of-the-way theatres for small change when this gives them a chance to do plays of quality.

Is the actor who dedicates himself wholeheartedly to theatre a saint or a lunatic? Certainly the serious actor today feels an enormous sense of bewilderment and impotence. The number of theatres, productions, and acting jobs dwindle alarmingly each season on Broadway. There are nine thousand members of Actors' Equity in the metropolitan New York area; the number of Broadway roles each season covers no more than a minuscule fraction of the union membership. Fast figuring indicates that it would take more than fifteen years to insure each Equity member one role in a Broadway drama or musical. And so actors turn to whatever they can get—

waiting on tables, pounding an office typewriter, driving a taxi. Behind the publicized success stories are often bitter years of struggle. Jason Robards, for example, has found fame in all media since he impersonated Hickey in the 1956 off-Broadway revival of O'Neill's *The Iceman Cometh*, but he was desperately knocking about the theatre for a decade before that. Indeed, at the time of the O'Neill drama, he was considering a permanent job as a small-time radio announcer. In an unusually good year, Robards earned $4,000. One year, the sum was a little over $1,000. To imagine yet the insecurity of the off-off-Broadway actor, one must view Robards' $1,000 as an enormous figure. Actors at Ellen Stewart's La Mama feel lucky if they are fed, clothed, and housed. And they accomplish this in the only way possible—by living together in spartan communal style.

If any of these off-off-Broadway actors did achieve a modicum of economic security on Broadway, they might sometimes wonder if the ends justified their sacrificial efforts. For Broadway offers few artistic satisfactions, and many a serious acting career is wasted on commercial trivia. The American actor is without honor in his own country, a rootless waif without permanent, subsidized theatres and without repertory. This is the opposite of the state honors heaped on actors in England, France, Germany, and most of the socialist countries. Only yesterday in America the acting profession was equated with sin, and actors were considered whores and adventurers. This attitude has not entirely vanished, and actors are material more for vulgar newspaper columnists' gossip than for respect and love as treasured national artists. The serious actor, with or without money, deeply desires artistic dignity and a sense of continuity in his work.

Perhaps this is why one single organization, the Actors Studio, dominates the American theatrical landscape with such fanatic adherents. If American actors cannot have honor in their own land, they can at least have a home, a private cult all their own. Lee Strasberg, with charisma and the Word, has given actors a sense of belonging. He has become father, analyst, and god to actor-orphans in an indifferent culture. Perhaps this compulsive loyalty also explains why so many Studio actors are impatient with and rude to non-Studio mummers and why they show rank favoritism to each other. After all, they have been tapped by Strasberg.

All discussions of acting inevitably lead to debates about the Studio. No topic elicits such extravagant praise and such fierce denunciation. Now the reigning Establishment academy of acting in America, the Studio is a shrine located in a chaste Greek Revival building in New York's Hell's Kitchen. Appropriately, it was once a church. Headed by guru Lee Strasberg, the Studio promulgates his Method, an American variation of Constantin Stanislavsky's System. Started in 1947, the Studio became in the fifties and sixties a vast talent factory for the stage, films, and television. From its sessions have come, enchanted or disenchanted, many of the fan-magazine names, including Marlon Brando, Shelley Winters, Anne Bancroft, Montgomery Clift, Ben Gazzara, James Dean, Jane Fonda, Paul Newman, and Marilyn Monroe. Many other stars, including Joan Crawford, Eva Gabor, and Rock Hudson, have dropped by for a peek, grateful to be admitted to the temple.

Has the Studio been a vitalizing force in the American theatre? Is Lee Strasberg hero or villain? Has the Studio encouraged actors' neuroses and discouraged ensemble acting? It may be decades before a balanced view of the Studio is forthcoming, with a careful catalogue of what it has accomplished and where it failed.

Strasberg, it appears to me, is not a villain of our theatre. He is, in a way, as much a victim of our stunted theatre culture as any-body else. His Studio has been isolated, without a permanent com-pany of actors and an opportunity to essay the collaborative art of repertory. Unlike the great Stanislavsky, who was a teacher-theorist-actor-director-producer with his own theatre, Strasberg has been unable to practice what he preaches with any significant continuity.

At its best, the Studio has been a place where professionals in a society inimical to the theatre arts could stay in touch with their craft, and where they might try parts they otherwise would prob-ably never get the opportunity to play. Patricia Neal once did Juliet beautifully, Eli Wallach and Anne Jackson tried Noel Cow-ard, and Anne Bancroft and Kevin McCarthy acted and sang songs from *My Fair Lady*. The Studio has at least kept alive the idea of acting as an art. Perhaps Strasberg's Method has simply filled an urgent need demanded by our commercial and naturalistic theatre, a special kind of excessively hysterical actor. A wag once told me the Studio was "all about crying." It is an oversimplification, but there is truth in it. The Studio has not produced many versatile theatre artists, but it has produced many striking personalities. It has been particularly effective in the films and on television, where the close-up is vital, and it has improved the performances of several screen and video actors. The mumbling, scratching, and anguished mannerisms associated with the Studio are ideally suited to the screen.

At its worst, the Studio has fostered a kind of arrogant, self-centered actor who is the exact opposite of the Stanislavsky ideal. Everyone has seen at least one fanatical Methodist ruin a play by egomaniacal concentration on his own role to the detriment of ensemble playing and the values of the drama itself. The actor, with a half-digested knowledge of Stanislavsky's celebrated "emotional memory" (the performer recalls an episode from his own life which in turn sheds light on his present condition, and he then uses this to better achieve an emotion in a particular scene), often promotes the "cult of the personality." A scene can become too interior. Often the art of acting becomes psychoanalysis and therapy. Every little acting school in New York and around the nation (not just the Studio) is now teaching a variation of Stanislavsky's System in who knows how many misinterpreted and mutilated versions. Stanislavsky's "true feeling" has been coarsened and distorted. Self-appointed gurus with a thirst for power have become dangerous amateur psychoanalysts.

There have been a number of warnings that we were making a fetish of Stanislavsky. Even during the heyday of the Group Theatre in the thirties, certain bold members of the Group were wary. The Group was rocked by intramural struggles, and many were troubled by Strasberg's dogmatism and fanaticism. Stella Adler went to Paris and studied daily for five weeks with the great Stanislavsky himself. Upon her return Miss Adler confronted the Group with her uneasiness about "emotional memory," which she felt could be used in ways inimical to art. She had found Stanislavsky undogmatic and in agreement. He himself was beginning to understand that his theories could be grossly misused by power-hungry and uncreative followers.

Today, many theatre people are taking a second hard look not only at the Studio but at Stanislavsky himself. Michel Saint-Denis and many other theorists who knew the great man feel he would be the first to modify his own System. During his lifetime, Stanislavsky was constantly testing and revising his ideas within the context of a working repertory company as well as a school. From the founding of the Moscow Art Theatre in 1898 to his death at seventy-five in 1938, he was an invaluable reformer, in open revolt against the false posturings and the empty rhetoric of nineteenth-century theatre. He cleared the way for a new and deeper awareness of character acting, and he can be read today with enormous profit. Essentially a poet, he was not a systematic thinker. But he did plan, fight and win the battle for a repertory network throughout Russia. It was a spectacular victory. Stanislavsky was a fervent naturalist, and he worked best in the illusionist or realist theatre. But he wanted his ideas to be applicable to the classics and to highly artificial works as well as to realism. It was a problem that bothered him all his life. In fact, in his later years, he developed a method of physical actions as a key to approaching a role and dispensed more and more with "emotional memory." He began to stress theatricality in the theatre, the style of a production, and the intent of the author more than the psychology of the actor. That, however, has been largely ignored by his "disciples."

In Russia, as in America, his theories have become congealed. He has suffered the same fate as Marx—dogmatization. The pernicious stricture labeled Socialist Realism included an entombed and deified Stanislavsky. The rebel became academic, comfortable, safe, and even bourgeois. From its beginnings in freshness and daring, the System soon degenerated into sterility. Today, a startling new development is taking place among young Russian actors and directors. Many privately admit the Moscow Art is old-fashioned, and they speak scathingly of the past as an era of "gray realism." They feel Stanislavsky concentrated on a reform most necessary in his time, but that the pendulum swung too far in the direction of inner feelings. They now seek a balance between theatricality and naturalism to fit a new age. Art is forever revolutionary.

Just as in Russia, the young in America are becoming increasingly restive with the fetish-worship of Stanislavsky and the Studio. They see Stanislavsky's ideas not as an infallible grammar of acting but as an insightful, creative guide. They now recognize the imperative need for more stylization, for more rigorous training in body movement and voice. In the off-off-Broadway workshops of the Other Theatre, rebel mummers may be initiating a more sophisticated phase of playacting. Indebted in various ways to Brecht, the young keenly understand that naturalism is simply not adequate to convey the horrors and intensities of today. Theatre is not life, theatre is theatre—a heightened revelation of our lives by means of style. In the Brechtian anti-illusionist theatre, the actor is, in a sense, an extrovert. He makes a study of human relations and conduct rather than human nature. There is a subtle shade of difference. A whiff of fresh air is coming into the cult of introspection. The new-style actor must learn to sing, dance, play musical instruments, perform acrobatic feats, and possibly discuss war and peace with the audience. Some workshops are even experimenting with children's games to teach actors the true sense of "play," the art of talking to each other. There is today among actors a slight swing from "me" to "us," and an unmistakable, though slow and torturous, return to politics. Perhaps the newcomers will discover the special joys of commitment.

Out of the workshops and schools will come, hopefully, a renewed respect for the acting art. It has certainly occurred abroad. Many of the great repertory companies have developed directly from schools and workshops. I am pinning my special hopes on the new School of Dramatic Arts at Lincoln Center's Juilliard School of Music. The first freshman class began in the fall of 1968, and it will take at least a decade to test the school's vitality and significance. The co-directors are John Houseman and Michel Saint-Denis, two theatre men of distinction. Houseman was, of course, associated with Orson Welles in the Federal Theatre and the Mercury Theatre projects. Saint-Denis, a Gallic gift to New York, acted in and staged plays first at the Vieux Colombier under Copeau and later with his own Compagnie des Quinze. A man of culture with an elegant and precise sense of language, he established and directed the celebrated London Theatre Studio from 1935 to 1939 and later was a leading force in the Old Vic schools. His 1936 staging of Chekhov's *The Three Sisters*, with John Gielgud, is still considered in London the definitive production of that work. He also directed Laurence Olivier in the Old Vic *Oedipus Rex*, in which Olivier later electrified New York audiences at the end of World War II. A considerable part of the credit of the National Theatre in London must hark back to Saint-Denis and his lectures and pioneering workshops. At Juilliard, Saint-Denis will stress rigorous training in movement, dance, acrobatics, wrestling, speech, singing, and work with masks, all areas scandalously neglected in American theatre training. This French *maître* is not a man satisfied with mere naturalism. In fact, he once stated his position with elegant precision: "Style is liberation from the muck of naturalism." Hopefully, out of the Juilliard experiment might come a production group significant for the future of the American theatre arts.

Many of the problems which bedevil the serious actor apply equally to all the other artists working in the American theatre. Our highly advertised way of life stifles artistic collaboration right down the line. Not only is the art of ensemble acting impossible, but the director, the set designer, the costumer, the lighting man, and the others are equally stymied. The director, for example, is not given the opportunity on Broadway to present a truly creative, collaborative work. He is subject to chilling economic and artistic pressures; he is at the mercy of the producers, the angels, and the hit-or-flop philosophy of Broadway. His actors have seldom worked together before and may never again. They are chosen for box-office, not artistic reasons. There is no group feeling. The director himself must think first of his own economic security; he must produce a smash hit—or suddenly find Broadway doors closed to him. He could courageously stage a drama with integrity and artistry, carefully evoking the mood and the style found in the play. Perhaps the play might be ruminative and gentle, perhaps Chekhovian. Even an innocent knows, however, that if a new American play with a flavor and a pace not unlike that of Chekhov's

The Three Sisters were presented on Broadway today, it would surely close Saturday night. So the director had better jazz it up, add a touch of sex (remember those recurrent musclemen in Joshua Logan's successful efforts?), and pace the play at breakneck speed. "Entertain" the fools: give them cheap and vulgar success, not art. The director must make a choice between quality and the box office—or, even worse, a debilitating compromise. Only in a permanent company, probably a repertory troupe semi- or fully-subsidized, could a director make artistic choices without thought of the ruinous hit-or-flop economy of today's Broadway. It is an ugly story.

The contemporary director is largely a creature of the twentieth century. Since the arrival of such striking and forceful theorists as Craig, Appia, and Stanislavsky (and later Piscator, Reinhardt, and Brecht), there has been increasing talk of the importance of the director and his individual interpretation. In the American theatre the director was seldom mentioned in the playbill before World War I. A new respect for the director was created by the insistent demands for artistry by the Little Theatre partisans in the 1910's and 1920's and through the development of such off-Broadway companies as the Provincetown and Washington Square Players. However, it was only after World War II that the director began to assume commanding stature on Broadway. Elia Kazan, in the forties, achieved marquee prominence following his intense direction of plays by Tennessee Williams and Arthur Miller. The debate still rages in a compartmentalized theatre—how much of the playwrights' work was theirs and how much the contribution of the director? In general, our Broadway directors seem best suited to a sensationalized naturalism. Remember the artistic debacle which nearly destroyed the new Lincoln Center company when Kazan was entrusted with the staging of the dark, sardonic seventeenth-century tragedy *The Changeling?*

The director, when he is not hamstrung by paramount economic pressures, can be gloriously creative. It is no accident that the most exciting directorial ventures in the past two decades have been in the off- and the off-off-Broadway playhouses, which are less dependent on large bankrolls and affluent audiences. The work of

directors José Quintero, William Ball, and Gene Frankel immediately come to mind, for they gave us memorably original productions of quality in the fifties. José Quintero was at his best
when he was making $50 a week and when he headed the ambi-
tious young group called Circle-in-the-Square, with its wonderful
and mad dreams of art. Since his rapid leap to fame on Broadway
and in Hollywood, where the economic life is less free, his talent
has been somewhat restrained. At the moment, the truly creative
directors are not the big Broadway names at all. They are instead
the cultural descendants of the Little Theatre movement—Tom
O'Horgan at La Mama, Joseph Chaikin and Jacques Levy at the
Open Theatre, Julian Beck and Judith Malina at The Living
Theatre, Joseph Papp and Gerald Freedman at the now-year-round
Shakespeare Festival, and a small band of rebel directors far from
Broadway. They are artists intensely interested in breakthroughs
and new directions in communication; they have little money and
yet they somehow attract semi-permanent companies of actors.
Most are aiming for permanent group theatres. Importantly, a number of these directors are also becoming more and more involved
with political and social issues; they are beginning to mirror the
connections between the stage and the world drama outside.

The new breed of directors accepts Stanislavsky as another help-
ful contributor to the theatre arts, but Brecht is the true god. They
have devotedly studied, too, McLuhan and Artaud, and they are
not unfamiliar with the radical yet undogmatic American philosophers Herbert Marcuse, Norman O. Brown, Staughton Lynd,
and Paul Goodman. Finding that naturalistic styles are best suited
to films and television, they seek instead a wild, visual, irreverent,
expressionist theatre. These new directors delight in the use of
masks, puppets both small and life size, swirling lights, rock scores,
and other boldly theatrical devices, and they demand actors skilled
in song, dance, acrobatics, and improvisation. They constitute, in
a sense, a network of laboratories in which they search for the
limits of contemporary theatre experience.

Two productions at Joseph Papp's Public Theatre, a handsome
indoor playhouse in an unfashionable part of the city, illustrate
current trends. In late 1967, Papp directed a courageous, outra-

geous production of *Hamlet*. Taking a cue from Polish poet-critic Jan Kott and his revolutionary study, *Shakespeare Our Contemporary*, Papp valiantly tried to rescue the Bard from the frozen posturings of the nineteenth century. Shakespeare, Kott avers, was a fierce, bawdy, and intensely alive existentialist. Kott's thesis is that Shakespeare was murdered by the prudent, prudish Victorians and that we must return him to lusty life. With his recent *Hamlet*, Papp attempted an actual phantasmagoria of the modern consciousness. In an evocation of the brutal quality of the American military presence around the world, Claudius was a bluff military officer, and the palace guards were beer-swilling G.I.s. Gertrude was an insipid floozie in a negligee, Polonius a top-hatted platitudinous politician, and Ophelia a mini-skirted frugger. High on methedrine, Hamlet first appeared in a cradle (which contained a transistor radio) near his mama's bed. Later he did vaudeville turns, and sold peanuts and ballons to the audience. Horatio photographed the play within-a-play with an 8-mm camera. The duel scene was transformed into a deadly game of Russian roulette. With it all, the "feel" of the production was perhaps closer to Shakespeare, but the language was lost in the frenzy. Our actors desperately need more training in voice and the rhythms of speech. However, Papp's provocative and ambitious staging of *Hamlet* was a hundred times more interesting than practically anything else in town.

A 1968 production at the Public Theatre of *Ergo* introduced Austrian playwright Jakov Lind to New York. It was directed by Papp's compeer, Gerald Freedman. Gross gargoyles of middle-class respectability and phony piety copulated onstage while they heiled *der Führer*. A band played Viennese waltzes gone sour, punctuated by sounds of rifle shots and bombs. Here was a Siqueiros shriek, a Grosz grimace, a Bosch belch. The nightmare appropriately ended with a man digging his own grave. Freedman evoked a world gone mad, using sounds, lights, and even life-sized puppets to capture a poet's vision. The director presented hell in a disjointed rush of surrealist imagery. Forget logic, he seemed to suggest, and let the play overwhelm one in its Artaudian totality. In Freedman's creative hands, this bitter, ribald import was more exhilarating and original than anything bloated Broadway, with pocketsful of money, could offer. It was *Cabaret*—with far more anger and guts.

Another startling attempt at Total Theatre was offered at an off-Broadway bandbox, the De Lys, when a brutal, vulgar, and erotic *A Midsummer Night's Dream* was staged by John Hancock. The director cut through the nineteenth-century sentimentalities which have covered this play with a virgin-white scrim, and restored it to its original randiness. Conservative critics howled, complaining that it was obscene, bad taste, and all that. Of course, it was obscene. Bawdy William Shakespeare is a very obscene writer, if one listens carefully. Hancock, who had earlier directed a sharp-eyed, tough version of *A Man's a Man*, now gave us a very contemporary and arresting bit of erotica, much closer to the play's spirit than the familiar cosmeticized fairies Disneyed beyond endurance. For Shakespeare wrote bluntly about the sex urge in all its incredible varieties and vagaries, about man's inner life of wild fantasy. On the left of the stage was a huge, gaudy jukebox, and it "played" snatches of Mendelssohn, Mahler, and Richard Strauss. A Brechtian circling ramp dominated the simple set. In an enchanted-forest scene, luminous butterflies, moths, fireflies, and snakes were held on poles by actors in black, à la the Apparition Theatre of Prague and classic Japanese convention. A tall young man in a blonde wig played Helena. Demetrius' fitful passions were registered by a codpiece which lighted up from time to time. It was the most delightful of the Dreams and an important exploration into interpreting the play.

Irony pervades Broadway. Some of the most successful and best-paid Broadway directors, sensing the artistic decline (indeed the impossibility of operating as an artist at all) in the uptown theatre, now and then sneak away to work in the small out-of-the-way houses. One of the most sensitive of Broadway men, Alan Schneider, does not hesitate to go way off Broadway to pursue Beckett. The true artist is learning a sad lesson—the excitement is far from the big, fancy, and spiritually empty theatres we boast of under that tarnished catch-all, "Broadway." Give my regards to Broadway, but take me, please, to Sheridan Square or Bleecker Street for real enjoyment of the theatre arts.

Almost everything I have said about actors and directors applies equally to the set designer. Appia and Craig liberated the stage from literalism, but you'd never know it on Broadway. Today's settings are not too far removed from that exact copy of Child's Restaurant which Belasco so proudly displayed in *The Governor's Lady*. Broadway designers are often simply interior decorators, and their efforts resemble department-store displays. The setting seldom comments on the play or evokes any particular mood or style.

There have been exceptions. Robert Edmond Jones, who died in 1954, was a genuine artist among set designers. He was forever preaching that the theatre must create a sense of wonder, that it must be an extension of life, not a duplication. He once put the battle against naturalism this way: "A setting should say nothing but give everything. Scenery as rule seems to me too definite. It should possess powerful atmosphere but little detail." No Broadway careerist today would publicly accept that noble statement about collaboration in the theatre. There are those who cherish his settings for *The Jest*, John Barrymore's *Hamlet*, *Anna Christie*, *Desire Under the Elms*, *The Green Pastures*, *The Green Bay Tree*, and *Lute Song*. Jones, appropriately enough, started his rich career designing for both the Provincetown Players and the Washington Square Players. Another fine scenic artist, the late Lee Simonson, first designed settings for the Washington Square Players and later became a founding director of the Theatre Guild. Other notable designers have included Norman Bel Geddes, who once turned the Century Theatre into a Gothic cathedral for a Max Reinhardt production of *The Miracle*, and Howard Bay, a graduate of the Federal Theatre who, in the sixties, gave *Man of La Mancha* an extra dimension with his awesome drawbridge-ramp. Playwright Thornton Wilder, borrowing from the Orient, gave all set designers an important lesson in stagecraft with his bold ideas for the 1931 *Our Town*. He magically created a New England town with a bare stage, a minimum of props, and a few lights.

The leading set designer on Broadway today is unquestionably Boris Aronson. He is, however, not at all taken in by Broadway fame, and he states the problem grimly: "Productions in our theatre are organized calamities." Aronson came to America from his native Russia in 1922. He designed first for Eva Le Gallienne's Civic Repertory Theatre. In 1940 he did settings for the Ballet Theatre's "The Great American Goof," and it marked one of the first times film projection served as scenery on our stages. His magnificently brooding settings for a Phoenix Theatre production of Ibsen's *The Master Builder* remains a contemporary model for stage designers. In more recent years, his celebrated mirror for *Cabaret* was especially striking. At the rear of the stage, Aronson tilted a huge mirror towards the audience, suggesting both the distortion and the voyeurism of pre-Hitler Berlin and, more subtly, showing American audiences their own images in a parable for now. But the basic lessons taught by a few gifted men from Jones to Aronson have gone unheeded. Broadway is far behind Europe East and West in stage design.

Nowadays, it is only in the off- and off-off-Broadway theatres, where art is the goal and collaboration is an admired way of life, that scenic work of originality and lasting interest is being created. Here scenic designers do not hesitate to become free and fanciful, and they work wonders with little. Remy Charlip, one of the founders of the Paper Bag Players, the best children's theatre in America, has also done remarkable work for the Judson Poets' Theatre. His settings for Paul Goodman's 1966 *Jonah*, presented at the American Place, were extraordinarily creative. In primitive-painting style, he deftly suggested a ship tossed at sea, and he used puppets with verve and childlike joy. Ming Cho Lee has been the principal designer for the New York Shakespeare Festival since 1962; his work for *The Comedy of Errors* and *Ergo* are high points of design in this decade. He has also designed for the Martha Graham Company, the City Center Joffrey Ballet, and the New York City Opera. He is a poet and never a naturalist, and he works in complete collaboration with all the artists involved in a new work. His settings can never be separated from the total production: they are organic to it. But such men are in the minority, and they are rarely found on Broadway. They are unwanted men in our commercial theatre, for they are collaborators.

The same misunderstanding of the cooperative nature of the theatre arts prevails in the field of lighting. Someday, all lighting and sets will be done or supervised by one person. It should always be so, for the two are complementary elements in the total design. Appia was right, although few have paid attention. Light is sculpture, emotion, tempo. Appia often spoke of the musicality of lighting. Today, most of the best lighting artists prefer to work with modern dance and ballet. Jean Rosenthal, long the lighting artist for Martha Graham, is unsurpassed in America. Fortunately for all of us, she lights a Broadway show now and then. Jennifer Tipton, who does the lighting for the Paul Taylor dancers, is a gifted magician with lights. Thomas Skelton has done exceptionally skillful lighting for the Joffrey Ballet. Recently, more and more off-Broadway companies have experimented with psychedelic lighting (Appia would have approved). But lighting artists cannot work alone. Only by consistent work with a company for a long time can a lighting artist become truly part of the ensemble, making lighting, in a sense, another member of the troupe.

Costumers, too, fare best when they can collaborate in a group theatre. Costumes must be carefully designed with the role and the individual actor in mind. The most intelligent actors in a first discussion of a new work often ask what they are going to wear. It is not as superficial a question as it might first appear, for how an actor is to look is a valuable clue for him about how he is going to play his part. The ideal costume should be a physical extension of the actor's role and performance. But more often than not, Broadway's top designers are far more anxious over whether the audience raves about their clothes than whether they are right for the particular play and the particular actor.

Nancy Potts, a busy costumer for the APA, first served a period in dress design for a Seventh Avenue fashion house. Now she is one of the few genuine artists in the neglected world of stage costuming. (Only Theoni V. Aldredge, costumer for the New York Shakespeare Festival since 1960, rivals her in dedication and virtuosity.) She has designed, and splendidly, the clothes for productions as diverse as Sheridan's *The School for Scandal*, Chekhov's *The Cherry Orchard*, and Kaufman's *You Can't Take It With You*. With enormous insight, she stated the need for profound collaboration among theatre artists: "If the object of the designs for a number of shows is primarily to show off the designer, for his own personal aggrandizement, he will not last long in a repertory setup. The play, the collective concept, is of primary importance, and it is toward this that all of us work. My costumes, therefore, should always be meaningful to the play and to the concept of the play. For me to superimpose a style which may be diametrically opposed to it would be defeating the very idea of a repertory theatre."

By extension, Miss Potts is talking about the collaboration of all theatre artists. She is indeed fortunate to be a part of a struggling repertory company. But in general, theatre collaboration cannot blossom in current America. By some miracle of the human spirit and against all odds, it sometimes does happen, but it cannot yet happen on any significant scale. During my lifetime I will see very few examples of total collaboration of the actor, director, designer, costumer, and the other individual artists in our theatre. Such joys will be denied us until we have a true flowering of our culture, and a profound understanding of the collective nature of the theatre arts. The expectations are dim.

CHAPTER 14
FATHEADS AND CRETINS

WHAT IS A critic? Actress Kim Stanley, with flamboyant brevity, has pronounced the aisle-sitters "fatheads." Playwright Elmer Rice observed that the Broadway arbiters of taste "are, for the most part, men without intellect, perception, sensitivity, or background." Maxwell Anderson dubbed them "the Jukes family of journalism." Edward Albee surpassed his fellows in condemning the judges. In a 1968 speech at the University of Florida, the ill-tempered creator of *Who's Afraid of Virginia Woolf?* informed the startled students that if the critics could be bought off, we would have decent theatre in this country in five years. E. B. White, the resident philosopher of *The New Yorker*, looked more wisely and less cholericly at the critics in this quatrain: "The critic leaves at curtain fall/To find, in starting to review it/He scarcely saw the play at all/For watching his reaction to it."

Critics themselves have often attempted to describe their grim profession. George Jean Nathan, that sad-faced, pint-sized gadfly of another generation, pontificated on the theme: "Criticism is the art of appraising others at one's own value... No chronically happy man is a trustworthy critic... Impersonal criticism is like an impersonal fist fight or an impersonal marriage, and as successful. Show me a critic without prejudices, and I'll show you an arrested cretin." Clive Barnes, current critic for *The New York Times*, has underlined Nathan's asperity:"No man has a right to be a critic unless he can slit his grandmother's throat." Perhaps iconoclast John Simon, who writes in acid for a number of publications, has supplied one of the most thoughtful and, surprisingly, tender definitions of a worthy critic: "With cogency, suasion, passion, and charm, he induces us to think, to widen our horizons, to open yet another book, to reconsider a snap judgment, to see something from a loftier vantage point, in historic perspective, and using more and truer touchstones . . . Good criticism of any kind—of movies, ballet, architecture, or whatever—makes us think, feel, respond; if we then agree or disagree is less important than the fact that our faculties have been engaged and stretched."

But, of course, there can be no final definition of a critic. At its best, criticism is an art, not a trade. There can be no instruction sheet or ten easy lessons. It is a humanistic concern, quite different from repairing a television set or constructing a high-fidelity unit. Reviews can be no better or worse than the critic's mind and taste and politics. Expatriate T. S. Eliot once tersely summed up the critic's way of work: "The only method is to be very intelligent." Instead of forever imprisoning the critic into a useless formula, I prefer to probe the actual everyday practice of Broadway reviewing. In truth, most dramatic criticism on Broadway is trivial and for a very good reason. One must look at the larger stages of life itself to place the American critic in proper focus. Selling shopworn goods which its brainwashed and culturally disadvantaged audiences do not seriously question, Broadway all too accurately reflects the sick society outside its doors. It is a truism that America and Broadway deserve each other. Broadway also gets, more often than not, the kind of critics it deserves. These gentlemen, in the main, mirror the prejudices, desires, and goals of the public. Judging the feckless fare of Broadway is hardly a satisfactory occupation for a man of sense and sensibility, unless he has fallen into masochistic habits. Few men of stature express interest in the practice of drama criticism. More and more, it has become a job a man has every right to be ashamed of.

Yet the Broadway Establishment blithely pretends not to notice this ugly fact. Instead the producers and their publicity machines have transformed the critics into seers. Critics' adjectives culled from Roget are puffed up as oracular messages from Delphi. I find these maneuvers deeply offensive, and it tells much about the low estate of the theatre. The critics are, after all, average citizens whose special claim to fame is that they have endured a lot of plays for a number of years; they are, by and large, honorable men simply doing their job the best they can. Some are quite good, some are deplorable. Most of them are grossly underpaid for their grisly assignments. To elevate them to some exalted Parnassus is nonsense. Americans do nothing by halves. Actually, upon close scrutiny of the reviews, most critics are not very critical. They are a kindly crew, much too tolerant of Broadway's débris, and they seldom desire the destructive power thrust upon them. It is distressing, but a vulgar few actually identify with the producers, becoming shills for show business, failing to understand that the profits and losses of the backers have nothing to do with the art of criticism. The Broadway producers hypocritically rail at the poor critics when they dismiss an obviously dismal creation even a mother couldn't love, and yet it has been the producers who have fostered the myth of the all-powerful critics. It has been all but forgotten that the critics never close a show: that fateful decision rests with the producers.

Ironies tumble over ironies. Through their hired drum-beaters, the producers consistently misquote the critics in their advertising. The most common distortions are changing lower-case adjectives to capitalized words or adding exclamation points that never appeared in the reviews. The critic might have stated in his notice that the setting was "great," but that the play was "impossible." His quote for the play might then appear in advertisements as "GREAT!" Nobody seems to care in the Barnum and Bailey world of Broadway. The producer demands something known on Broadway as a "money review," and he dislikes critics who pepper their notices with ifs, ands, and buts. Indeed, the Broadway Establishment has employed all sorts of subtle and not so subtle ruses against publications which audaciously hire honest critics rather than disguised advertising copywriters quick with such adjectives as "superb," "brilliant," "magnificent," "hilarious," and "incomparable." Critics have sometimes been barred from opening nights by both theatre-owners and producers. One husband-and-wife team was barred because they had the temerity to dislike a vapid Rodgers and Hammerstein hit musical, which was tantamount to revolution

in America. In another instance, a producer forced a major newspaper, through veiled advertising threats, to edit a critic's review
in a later edition.

The Broadway world of instant success or instant defeat sooner
or later infects everybody and besmirches art. Acutely aware that
$500,000 for a musical or $300,000 for a drama are often at stake
on opening night, the critic himself, consciously or unconsciously,
can be influenced in his deliberations. He can lose his nerve. Shall
he tell the world that this lavish and inordinately expensive venture
is junk—or shall he compromise? A classic example of how the
Establishment misunderstands the mission of the critic was long
provided by the show-business bible, *Variety*. For many years
this newspaper conducted a kind of racing sheet of the critics, a
dopester's past performance sheet at the track. At the end of each
season, the weekly published a solemn charting of each critic's
acumen. A critic was judged great if he praised the shows that
became hits and vetoed the shows that turned into flops. He had
called the shots right. This is, of course, completely absurd. Box-
office gold does not necessarily spell artistic success, and inversely,
box-office defeat does not mean lack of quality. All too often the
flops are far better, artistically, than the hits. *Variety* has discon-
tinued this stupid practice, but the degrading attitude the poll
symbolized continues to dominate our theatre.

Now there is a brand-new breed of critic for whom one can
feel sorry—for a new reason. As the newspapers disappear one by
one (New York will probably fall into the dismal situation of other
cities), the importance of television critics increases. During the
newspaper strikes of the sixties, television newscasters began moon-
lighting as drama critics. There are now half a dozen celebrated
television critics in New York, all of whom proclaim their views
within an hour or two after the opening night curtain goes down.
They are allotted sixty seconds for their mighty critiques. It is
salutary to break the domination of the newspaper critics, but not
in this dangerous and insulting way. How can a responsible critic
review a production in one minute? Edwin Newman, the best of
television's instant critics, has calculated that a one-minute review
contains roughly one hundred and eighty to two hundred words;

as Arthur Miller summarized the absurd situation, "If you belch, you lose one act." Yet the television critics are being courted with sickening sycophancy, for they speak to the largest potential theatre audience in the land. But that audience is cheated with mini-reviews. It is not, however, the poor critic's fault. It is definitely the shirking of responsibility by the station and its advertisers. Surely before the century's end these electronic reviews will be at least five minutes long. Or will they be cut down to a grunt of disapproval or a burst of applause?

Unromantically observed from this inside perch, perhaps critics should be applauded for courage and endurance in performing a forlorn and unpleasant task. The heavy toll on the critic's mind and nervous system is frightening. The best suffer periods of depression and explosive anger. The more sensitive critics suddenly and dramatically express their deepseated dissatisfaction with Broadway in anguished and devastating terms when they depart from reviewing for more rewarding jobs, or upon their retirement. When Louis Kronenberger quit theatre reviewing for *Time* after twenty-three years at hard labor, he agonized in print: "How could one not feel relieved when so much of one's job was not merely dull but degrading; not just clumsy but cheap?" Howard Taubman, former critic of *The New York Times*, pronounced on his departure from that exalted post: "Vastly dispiriting to sit through a seemingly endless succession of clumsy, abortive, shockingly expensive efforts. The disappointments, alas, have outnumbered the satisfactions by a landslide margin." When Richard Gilman resigned in 1967 as the drama critic for *Newsweek* to accept a teaching position at the Yale Drama School, he, too, had no illusions about what he was leaving behind: "Much of what is staged on Broadway is mediocre and boring. The occasional good drama has become accidental."

Thus it has become painfully clear that all of us—the critic, the producer, the actor, the public—are trapped together in an airtight balloon, suffocating from want of air. The good theatre critic today must prick the balloon. He must be a rebel. Perhaps at no other time in American history has the critic become so crucial. He has a leading part to play, if he would but try. He must perform a larger social task as well as the customary, purely esthetic functions: he must be a dedicated revolutionist. He must blast away at the very foundations of our dangerously corrupt society as well as our rotting theatre. Of course, he will be vilified by people in and out of the theatre who misunderstand his historic role.

The situation is fraught with irony. The Broadway Establishment sometimes complains that critics are destroying the theatre. The well-liked are usually those who flatter the most and disturb the least. In fact, the critics are killing the theatre with kindness. To love the theatre today is to attack frontally the Broadway Way of Life. Honest passion does not waste its time on false and mealy-mouthed flattery.

Perhaps the American critic who has best perceived and performed this heroic task in the nineteen-sixties has been Robert Brustein, a radical theatre dissenter for *The New Republic* from 1959 to 1965. A first-rate mind, he clearly understood that the theatre needed shock treatment. His testy reviews have since been collected in book form under the apt title, *Seasons of Discontent*. In the preface to that disturbing and invigorating volume, he looked backward at his confreres with obvious distaste: "I was astonished that the standards of our theatre were being arbitrated (often in less than two hours of hurried scribbling) by newspaper reporters, many of whom had prepared for dramatic criticism through stints in such departments as music, foreign affairs, dining and dancing, and sports." He recalled: "I was soon convinced that the commercial system would never encourage real dramatic adventure, indeed was preventing such adventure from taking place. And so I joined the ranks of those who had warred upon Broadway as a cultural institution, underlining its inadequacies, exposing its values, atomizing its fakeries, and attacking its heroes and saints . . . Now this art was in the hands of the spoilers and profiteers: one style dominated our stage, and one system of acting; plays had lost their relevance to the deeper realities of contemporary life; and the only debate the theatre was stimulating (this issue rages week after week in the Sunday *Times*) concerned the rude treatment of theatre-lovers at the hands of the box office." Brustein was a constructive destructive critic. He expressed a rare quality among critics, a moral concern for the quality of American life. It is the theatre's great loss that he has fled the critic's seat. Perhaps he will make equally significant contributions, in another way, as the Yale Drama School's dean and the impresario of the Yale Repertory Theatre.

I do not wish to imply that Brustein has been alone. *The New Republic* and *The Nation* have served as America's most remarkable outposts for quality criticism. Brustein was preceded on *The New Republic* by, among others, Stark Young and Eric Bentley. The late Stark Young, a discerning appreciator of acting and a first-rate translator of Chekhov, was a keen critic, but he lacked broad social vision and a wide knowledge of international politics. His love for stage stars was genuine, but it often contained a kind of magnolia-scented, almost feminine gushiness associated with the Old South. Brustein's immediate predecessor on *The New Republic* was English-born Eric Bentley, a professor of dramatic literature at Columbia University. His pungent books, documenting his long and personal search for quality theatre both here and abroad, and his prolific outpouring of anthologies of lesser-known plays have incalculably enriched American theatre life. He has brought a quirky, fiercely independent quality to local criticism, and like two other uncommon English critics, George Bernard Shaw and Kenneth Tynan, he has made no bones about his commitment to socialism. It has been mainly through Bentley's dogged persistence that Bertolt Brecht is now getting rapt attention from the young. Harold Clurman has contributed, via both *The New Republic* and *The Nation,* urbane, perceptive, and concerned criticism. He sees a play whole, its immediate impact, its point of view, and its probable place in dramatic literature. Too, Clurman views Broadway from a truly international perspective, remarkable in a critic in any country. Moreover, he brings a vast backstage knowledge to his critical comments, having been an actor, playreader for the Theatre Guild, and a founder of the Group Theatre. He has directed more than fifty Broadway plays, his hallmark being a special civilized sensitivity to the play's style and intent.

Criticism has been best on the weeklies, monthlies, and scholarly quarterlies. Elizabeth Hardwick, in the searching *New York Review of Books,* has scattered provocative insights, but she has sometimes seemed too literary at the expense of a play's production values. Certainly *The Drama Review* (now published under that name at New York University and previously the *Tulane Drama Review*) has contributed to the growing sophistication of the young theatre partisans. Though *TDR*'s editors and writers have often been sophomoric, they have always been angry and irreverent and urgent; they have demanded change and have plotted ingenious ways either to destroy or to take over Broadway, the seat of power. They have performed a scholarly task, too. In the quarterly's several special issues (Brecht, Stanislavsky, Eastern European Theatre, Black Theatre in America), they have presented firsthand information available nowhere else.

There have been other American critics and publications deserving praise and attention, but they have been the exception and not the rule. Luckily for us, foreign aid has sometimes rescued our faltering critical contingent in several surprising ways. The most welcome aid came in the misleadingly Mayfair personage of Kenneth Tynan. In 1958, he joined *The New Yorker* as drama critic, and he stayed in America for two seasons. He had been the theatre pundit for *The Observer,* and he was perhaps the most quoted critic in the English-speaking world. Though sometimes too free with bad puns and sometimes too much of a compulsive entertainer, Tynan was a graceful and witty stylist. He wore his immense erudition lightly, and he obviously relished shocking and outraging a complacent populace. He himself had gone through a typically English esthetic period, with drama elegantly separated from life. Proudly calling himself Brecht's only convert, he came to politics through art and "became aware that art, ethics, politics, and economics were inseparable." His two years of weekly criticism in this country constituted important lessons for Americans, and hopefully a number of younger critics have absorbed much from him.

Tynan's reviews for *The New Yorker* were models of the critical exercise. His longish review (December 20, 1958) of Archibald MacLeish's *J. B.,* a modern version of the Book of Job, was one of the best ever to appear in any American publication. One section illustrated how beautifully drama criticism can blend into a broader social view: "The truth is, of course, that he [MacLeish] has stated the right problem in the wrong way. We are all vitally concerned with any search for the causes of human pain, but when needless agony is inflicted (as it is on J. B.) by bombs, bullets, drunken drivers, and psychotic adolescents, our first impulse, if we are rational beings, is surely to see an explanation in human terms—to ask how the war could have been avoided, why the man drank, what pressures sent the boy mad. Not many of us, I think, immediately ascribe our sufferings to the judicial acumen of the Old Testament God, who could never be ranked among the more sympathetic characters of world literature, and who appears in the Book of Job at his worst—arrogant, bombastic, and casually cruel. Yet Mr. MacLeish's hero thinks of nobody else. The emphasis on guilt is obsessive . . . Long before the final curtain, I was bored to exasperation by the lack of any recognizable human response to calamity." Tynan noted elsewhere that he appreciated the flawless acting, setting, and direction, but "the same, unfortunately, cannot be said of the thing presented."

His American sojourn was not without its drama outside of the Broadway theatres. Though he was welcomed by the critical fraternity, he was *persona non grata* in certain official quarters. In May, 1960, he was subpoenaed by the Senate Internal Security subcommittee and questioned about his views on Cuba and other matters. The secret interrogation lasted an hour and a half, an echo of the earlier experience of his hero, Bertolt Brecht. Tynan later recalled that Senator Thomas J. Dodd from Connecticut was clearly convinced he was a Communist. Perhaps Kenneth Tynan returned to the relative sanity of England because of our restrictive politics. Or perhaps it was because of our ailing theatre. The visiting critic did state that he quit local reviewing because Broadway was a contracting horizon: "Having looked into the economics of it, I thought it was written by, and addressed to, the middle classes. It will be increasingly dominated by light comedies and heavy musicals." Presently he is the literary manager of England's showplace, the subsidized National Theatre—the longtime dream, now realized, of every stage buff from the days of David Garrick onwards. Sir Laurence Olivier is the theatre's director, and Tynan is, in his own words, "playing Boswell to Larry's Johnson."

Two European theatre men, although not professional critics, lent welcome aid to two unusual American plays during the 1960's. Sweden's German-born Peter Weiss, here to attend the Broadway premiere of his *Marat/Sade*, visited a small walkup theatre on Second Avenue to view Douglas Turner Ward's explosive, hilarious double bill about Negro life in America, *Happy Ending* and *Days of Absence*. He pronounced this "the most wonderful night I've spent in a New York theatre." Many native critics had either ignored these plays or reviewed them with far milder plaudits, and so Weiss' rave was promptly used to excellent advantage in the theatre's advertising. He was of inestimable help. England's incorrigibly bad boy of the Royal Shakespeare Company and the National Theatre, Peter Brook, took time out during a New York holiday to attend Barbara Garson's controversial *MacBird* in Greenwich Village. He was entranced—unlike most uptown reviewers. In a glowing article in *The New York Times*, he stated that his evening with *MacBird* was the closest he had ever come to the Elizabethan theatre. The audiences were on easy intimate terms with the actors, and common references were exchanged through a nod or a hint. He concluded it was "the most powerful piece of *pro-American* theatre in a long time" (italics added). He was, of course, quite right, the play's publicity men eagerly seized on such Brook bravos as "exuberant," "biting," and "explodes with theatricality."

In Europe critics are likely to become involved in colorful quarrels about plays and players. Often critics write with passion from an openly acknowledged stance, and the reader is given, for example, a Catholic, a Communist, and a Fascist view of a particular drama. This is unfamiliar practice in America. Our critics are neither passionate nor nettlesome, and they usually write from some rather tenuous vantage point called "objectivity," whatever that is. But most American plays are lightweight and unconcerned with the drama of life and with global politics, our critics have nothing to argue about, really, so our reviews are too bland to invite controversy. Even the highly publicized battles of producer

David Merrick with the critics are all sham and not really interesting; they are merely publicity gimmicks. However, Peter Brook again came to the rescue in the sixties and provided us with our only critical fireworks. Walter Kerr, who was then critic for the now-defunct New York *Herald Tribune*, called *Marat/Sade* "an entertainment devised by director Peter Brook for the infinite pleasure of Peter Brook." Brook answered the critic on a coast-to-coast television show a few days after the opening of the Weiss drama: "Well, I think I wouldn't normally, in any circumstances, hold against a man his choice of words, but I think that in the case of the Kerrs [he included Kerr's playwright wife Jean] this is a family, and there is a strange coincidence that Walter Kerr's attitude in every review I've ever read, toward any form of avant-garde or experimental theatre, should reflect so typically the middle-of-the-road bourgeoisie that is so affirmed in a charming and light way in his wife's plays. There is a connection. It is a family; it is a package. And these are the very people who, in our play, are the middle-of-the-road French who come to look at the play and get up and say: 'I think that plays were meant to be entertaining, and the play, Mr. de Sade, that you presented is even pessimistic.' Worst middle-class crime of all." Brook on another occasion remarked on Kerr's Catholic ideology, though religion is a forbidden topic never discussed in polite American critical circles. The feud, along with the play, enlivened another dull season, but generally theatre controversy is as rare as justice in a Mississippi courtroom.

I have danced around the subject of the critic, and I have suggested that he must have something of a rebel in him. He should be, at the very least, a little bit subversive. Indeed, I have gone further to point out that Broadway desperately needs revolutionists today—if Broadway is to have any relevance at all. However, I do not for a moment imply that rebellion alone is enough. There is infinitely more to the good critic than the commendable wish to change the world. It is how the world is changed that is crucial. The admirable critic will be concerned with the script as message, but he must be equally intense about every aspect of the play's production. One must care fervently about the quality of the happening. Ideally, the critic should be alert and ardent in discussing the nuances of an actor's individual performance and his artistic growth as he goes from one role to another—or, in other words, the continuity of his career. The aisle-sitter must make fine distinctions. For example, an actor may have given a dazzling performance when it is analyzed separately from the play, and yet the turn may have been atrociously inartistic in that it destroyed the delicate balance of the script. Sometimes a quiet turn is better than a showy one. One should properly discuss the director in the same careful manner. Rarely do critics conjure up the mood or the texture of a particular production, and then proceed to analyze the elements which jar within the attempted unity of style. In addition, too little attention is generally paid the designer, costumer, and the lighting expert, yet they are crucial elements of a production's success in evoking the author's particular view or specifics of time and place. In brief, the art of criticism is rarely practiced.

Our critics (and the public at large) have spectacular difficulty with a notoriously overused and misunderstood adjective, "entertaining." It has been a cover for all sorts of tasteless junk. What is entertaining and for whom? *Oedipus Rex* may spell sheer joy for one man, splendid entertainment of the mind and senses; another man may avoid it with fanatical distaste. One must define one's terms and carefully describe each play for which "entertaining" is used, else the adjective tells us nothing. *Barefoot in the Park* is forgettable cotton candy—and entertaining; Wedekind's *The Awakening of Spring* is memorable, rich food—and entertaining.

Similarly, a critic must do more than state that a play is "good" or "bad." This is not very enlightening to his readers, and it is certainly not drama criticism. It is fitter material for newspaper gossip columns. The critic must explain why he admires or detests a production. He must present a reasoned brief, or his opinions are of no particular value. (Incidentally, the poor critic is often hamstrung by the tyranny of space on those journals where editorial space is determined solely by advertising lineage. It is most difficult to explain anything in twenty lines.)

The good critic should describe for readers what kind of play he is discussing and—out with it—he should educate. The educational role of the critic is one that is bitterly attacked these days from both the right and left, from the Broadway do-nothings to the Sontagian free-formers. There is danger, of course, in interpretation, for the educator is likely to be a pedantic, pompous, and presumptuous man eager to force his sermon on others. And yet all critics are pushers of one opinion or another; they propagandize in spite of themselves. The Sontagians are, in effect, educators who pretend not to be educators, sensitive minds who have understandably been turned off by the contemporary dogmatisms and brainwashing techniques of both Russia and the United States. For after all, a critic without opinions would be a vacuum. Instead he is a living person with a past, a present, and a future, and he responds to the issues of change and status quo, of peace and war. His birthplace, parentage, formal and informal education, religion, and politics have all created a complex man, not a typewriter. However, the large-circulation newspapers and magazines severely discourage any signs of *aliveness* in their critics. They do not want individuality. After all, these pap-pocked journals are carefully planned to please everybody. They demand blandness from their staffs, and they seek safely conventional, unoriginal men who will not shock or outrage or display strong emotions of any kind. This is bad for art, and it makes dead souls of critics. It is one of the many reasons for Broadway's descent into nothingness.

The sheeplike readers of the critics are also deserving of contempt. Too many have voluntarily surrendered their minds. In some truly free utopia, readers would of course decide for themselves what to see and not see. In the meantime, readers might profit by a few guidelines. The intelligent approach is to read as many critics as possible. If there is not time, the reader should find, by trial and error, a man he likes best, a critic who shares with him a common view of art and reality. Even then, a reader must be careful; he must learn the idiosyncrasies of his chosen critic. Being human, all critics have peculiarities. One may be tone-deaf and hence utterly untrustworthy at musicals; another may have no feeling for body movement, for dance; a third may be a bit of a prude, appalled by good old Anglo-Saxon four-letter words or playful lasciviousness. A critic might be such a religious fanatic that he cannot tolerate blasphemy on the stage. The reader must also discover for himself if his critic knows anything at all about painting or music or dance. Few theatre critics attend the ballet, opera, concerts, or the art galleries. Personally, I cannot fathom how a man can be a good critic without some knowledge of these related fields. After a month or two, the faithful reader will also find out whether the critic displays any sophistication in matters of global politics and commitment. It's all a matter of getting to know him, and the reader who follows a critic's recommendations without checking his credentials is quite foolish and often misled.

At bottom, the fault with native drama criticism is with a society in which originality and audacity are discouraged. Critics will truly change when the general tone of American life changes, when the nation changes. Of that you can be certain. Perhaps in the 1970's, hopefully, with younger, brighter, and more irreverent judges, criticism will improve. In the meantime, many aisle-sitters will be content to reflect the tastes of the audiences. They are not leaders in the Shavian sense, and they are absurdly well-mannered. If ever a country needed a few ungentlemanly men, guerrilla fighters outraged by the ghastly blight on Broadway, that time is now.

CHAPTER 15
OUT
THERE

BEYOND NEW YORK CITY's borders is, from a theatre perspective, a vast land thought of as "Out There." At the moment, theatre theorists are excitedly talking and writing about Out There as our artistic salvation. Expensive cultural centers and university stages, many of them with professional acting companies, are mushrooming in practically every state in the union. Through the din and the smog, one hears brave and sometimes nonsensical chatter that the banalities of Broadway are now being successfully challenged, that year-round repertory troupes will soon grace all the nation's leading cities, and that campuses will be afire with theatre magic. Perhaps culturally deprived, suddenly provincial New Yorkers will then journey around the nation to visit these great centers of the theatre arts. At last, theatre will spell more than just a few tawdry and joyless blocks of real estate called Broadway.

To anyone familiar with the history of the American drama, all this is somewhat *déjà vu*. The Little Theatre frenzy in the years just before and after World War I, most especially, in the tempestuous twenties, was quite similar to today's brouhaha in its goals and its evangelicism. In Boston, Chicago, and even as far south as Chapel Hill, North Carolina, there were heated manifestoes about saving the nation from Broadway through the passionate nurturing of regional drama and the Little Theatre Movement. Before one could say Herbert Clark Hoover, the dream had vanished.

Here again, in the 1960's, is that same siren incantation, the recurrent dream, the undaunted desire to festoon our withering cities with theatre of quality. The actuality, however, is as uncertain and elusive as ever. In fact, the present pioneers of Out There are bitterly fighting for their artistic lives and for economic survival. The stage one praises today may not be there tomorrow. The Pasadena Playhouse folded after heroic labors; Margo Jones's theatre in Dallas vanished after her death. Within various organizations there are frequent and disheartening clashes between trustees, still consumed by babbittry, and adventurous artistic directors. In the second half of the sixties, John Hancock and André Gregory, both directors of uncommon skill and originality, were forced out of, respectively, the Pittsburgh Playhouse and Philadelphia's Theatre of the Living Arts: they had committed the crime of trying to create *living* theatres and not safe museums. Many of today's art centers are mere façades of culture: the politicians and social butterflies who run them desire showplaces for status and prestige. Too often they know little about theatre and care even less. The spectacular new buildings are all that money can buy, but the actors and other artists inside are grossly underpaid as well as unappreciated. Sooner or later many directors throw in their backstage towels and present safe, routine hits "direct from Broadway." Many of the centers become no more than what were once called stock companies. To hail then the present commotion as a renaissance would be outrageous Fourth-of-July rhetoric. The long-heralded Golden Age has not arrived. Am I being too astringent and cynical about what may prove to be a vital direction in American culture? I cannot be a fuzzy sentimentalist in a theatre which merits only the bleakest pessimism.

However, one continues to dream. There are several good omens. The current resurgence just might, after all, amount to something; never rule out the improbable. A surprising number of regional dreams have stubbornly become reality during the sixties. The most ambitious of these provincial ventures is the Minnesota Theatre Company in Minneapolis. The man responsible for this bonanza is not a Minnesotan but a canny Scot, outsized in body and mind—Sir Tyrone Guthrie. He had been managing director of the Old Vic and Sadler's Wells in England; he was a highly successful director both in London's West End and on Broadway. In 1952, he organized what is now the most celebrated theatre in the Western Hemisphere, the Shakespeare Festival in Canada's Stratford. (This is not to be confused with the dismal Shakespeare Festival in Stratford, Connecticut.) Seeking a new frontier, he recognized the desperate need for quality regional theatre in the United States. With two other experienced theatre men, producer Oliver Rea and stage manager Peter Zeisler, both of whom were fed up with the New York stage, Guthrie went city-shopping. After an exhausting and exhaustive cross-country junket (a haze of Chamber of Commerce conviviality, creamed chicken, and cocktails) in search of a site, they finally chose Minneapolis. The Minnesota Theatre Company, a resident professional troupe, opened at the new $2,500,000 Tyrone Guthrie Theatre in May of 1963. It was—and remains—a miracle in Minnesota.

The Guthrie is the largest of the new non-profit, tax-exempt civic theatres of the 1960's, and its 1,437 seats equal the capacity of the big houses on Broadway. The building's exterior is an imaginative blend of steel, wood, and glass in a timeless but contemporary style; inside the audiences surround the polished-oak thrust stage on three sides. Technically as well as esthetically, the Guthrie is superior to most of the antiquated Broadway houses. Too, Minneapolis was fortunate in securing the services of Tanya Moiseiwitsch, the remarkable artist who designed with Guthrie the extraordinary stage at Canada's Stratford. She was the design consultant for the Minneapolis stage, and she has been the principal designer for the company's productions.

Since the opening, the Minnesotans have offered highly skilled and sometimes brilliant productions of plays by, among others, Shaw, Williams, Shakespeare, Chekhov, Congreve, Miller, and O'Neill. They presented the first professional production in America of both parts of Strindberg's *The Dance of Death*, with compelling expressionist designs based on Edvard Munch's paintings. In the first years, the directors decided on a classical program (on the theory that local audiences needed a grounding in drama), with every fourth play an American work of potential classic status. They are now evolving an admirable plan to produce new American plays not yet seen on Broadway. In 1967 the troupe produced Barrie Stavis' drama about John Brown, *Harpers Ferry*.

Stavis is the author of two other plays about great men in history, *Lamp at Midnight* (Galileo) and *The Man Who Never Died* (Joe Hill). The company is still without a strong unifying style, but it has already attracted many distinguished actors from the Broadway stage. Hume Cronyn, George Grizzard, Jessica Tandy, Zoe Caldwell, and Nancy Wickwire have all appeared here in a number of roles. In 1968 the troupe branched out, offering an auxiliary season at a newly acquired second theatre in the twin city of St. Paul. The supplemental house was opened with both a safe choice, Goldsmith's *She Stoops to Conquer*, and a more daring one, Slawomir Mrozek's *Tango*, a Polish black comedy on the decline of the Western World. (*Tango* was later staged by London's Royal Shakespeare Company, but Broadway has yet to see it.) In December of 1968, the Minnesota Theatre Company made drama history by making a visit to New York. Perhaps someday many regional troupes will make national tours and include disadvantaged Broadway on their schedules.

At the moment, one must applaud the Guthrie as the best civic theatre in the nation. Because of its existence, many persons have seen good theatre for the first time in their lives, and thousands of high school students have attended its special, reduced-price performances. There have been grave problems, however, and nobody can safely predict the company's survival. Financing has been precarious. Without grants from the foundations, government aid (via the National Endowment for the Arts), and local fund-raising drives by private citizens, the theatre would not have survived. The citizens of Minneapolis are learning that the maintenance of a good repertory company is very expensive. There have been other difficulties. Sir Tyrone has left to conquer new worlds, and his galvanic presence is sorely missed. Another Scot, actor-director Douglas Campbell, succeeded Guthrie as artistic director in 1966, but the future pattern for the company was unclear. Rea was not wildly optimistic about regional theatre after his Minneapolis experience, and he has since put this most bluntly: "I don't think much art is flourishing: many of the theatre institutions are turning into poorly operated museums, catering to a static, middle-class, chauvinistic audience." At an ANTA luncheon in New York in the fall of 1967, he told the assembled resident theatre representatives that the major problem was American acting: "[In the early days at Minneapolis] we all wondered whether or not American actors would leave New York to venture out to the Midwest. They came and they were found wanting. They were untrained for a serious repertory of world plays, whether comedy or tragedy. After thirty years of misuse of Stanislavsky . . . , voice and body-movement teachers were engaged in an attempt, mostly futile, to teach old dogs new tricks." It was apparent that sooner or later, the Minnesota Theatre Company would need vast sums of money for a full-time acting school or workshop. The informal alliance with the University of Minnesota, in which a certain number of graduate students were given a season with the theatre in an apprentice capacity, was clearly not the answer.

Incidentally, Minneapolis is also the home of perhaps the only authentic avant-garde theatre between New York and the West Coast—the Firehouse. The artistic director of this Midwestern outpost of off-off-Broadway is Sydney Schubert Walter, a graduate of the Open Theatre. Most of the playwrights promoted here are from New York's Other Theatre, including Sam Shepard, Jack Gelber, and Jean-Claude van Itallie. With less than two hundred seats, sporadic attendance, and a shoestring budget, the Firehouse Theatre has made a courageous stand for innovation and the New Morality. One of its artistic successes has been Megan Terry's *The People vs. Ranchman,* and the company triumphantly visited New York's La Mama with it. Ranchman, a "polymorphous perverse" character reminiscent of Caryl Chessman, is tried, convicted, and executed for sex crimes. Yet he emerges as the play's hero, with the villain an uptight American society. As the play concludes, Ranchman makes a triumphant plea to his destroyers and to the audience: "Someone sits next to you; enjoy him while you can."

William Ball's American Conservatory Theatre, now happily ensconced in San Francisco, is another experiment of the 1960's that deserves top billing and bravos. Starting with his staging of Chekhov's *Ivanov* in a small off-Broadway house in Greenwich Village back in 1958, it has been increasingly evident that gentle,

scholarly, and deceptively quiet William Ball is a director of
enormous sensitivity and unlimited invention. In the spring of 1965,
he was given the rare opportunity of forming his own repertory
company, the ACT, with the financial support of the Rockefeller
and Mellon Foundations and under the sponsorship of the Carnegie
Institute of Technology and the Pittsburgh Playhouse. The Playhouse, after years of being a second-rate theatre with a local, semi-
amateur company, suddenly wanted to upgrade its efforts. However, Pittsburgh proved to be an unenlightened city and Ball and
his newly formed ACT were out in the cold the next year after
bitter artistic and financial disputes. Then followed a period of
gypsy life, with the company appearing on the Ann Arbor campus
of the University of Michigan, the Playhouse in Westport, Connecticut, the Ravinia Festival near Chicago, and a drama festival at
Stanford University in Palo Alto, California.

In an amazingly short time, Ball has again put San Francisco on
the theatre map. (The city was once the home of the now-defunct
Actor's Workshop, which was born in 1952 and died in 1966.)
Fortified by more than $1,000,000 in aid from the Ford Founda-
tion, the national government, and other sources, Ball dazzled San
Franciscans with a rotating schedule of productions in two local
showcases. He has averaged 65 per cent of capacity in the 1,448-
seat Geary and 90 per cent in the 640-seat Marine Memorial
Theatre. In a matter of a season or two, he has more than doubled
the subscription list of the Actor's Workshop at its peak. His reper-
toire has included unassailable plays, such as *Under Milkwood, Six
Characters in Search of an Author, Tartuffe, Uncle Vanya,* and
Death of a Salesman. But he has made up in sheer theatricality for
the safeness of his choices. Ball is definitely not a social polemicist
but he is a man with a cause—the cause of attention to detail and
quality in each production. His staging of Miller's *The Crucible*
makes that seemingly dull and platitudinous tract leap to fiery stage
life. Ball's startlingly lavender version of Albee's *Tiny Alice* is
much more openly and melodramatically homosexual than the cautious Broadway edition.

That word conservatory in the title of Ball's company is not just
a fancy verbalism. He considers the American Conservatory Thea-

tre to be both a school and a company, and he constantly trains his actors as well as directs them in actual production. Ball feels strongly that many Method actors have all too often employed a convenient crutch: "I don't feel it." These Methodists have been encouraged in this stress on feeling, to the virtual exclusion of technique, by teachers whose artistic roots go back to the Group Theatre. "Let's say these people didn't have an affinity for comedy; they are all geared to a certain kind of theatre." Ball has observed, "I'd like to add a few things to the curriculum." The ACT's training program is based not on the Studio's hallowed emotional memory but on behavorial movement, a Ballian version of Rudolf von Laban's complex teachings. There is also intensive speech training, since Ball finds American actors sadly lacking in musicality of speech.

Ball enthusiastically endorses the Alexander technique for his actors. Developed in London sixty years ago by an Australian actor to release the inner tensions that constrict an actor's voice and movement, this system has been generally applied to all kinds of muscular tensions. Ball's actors, trained in the approved Alexander manner, have improved in several ways. They are now shedding their cramped, pinched style of walking and are beginning to move like dancers; they are looser, not frozen with fear. Another of Ball's theories fits nicely with his present San Francisco residence. He strongly feels that actors work better away from New York. "They become freer, more natural," he has declared. "Actors need to be close to nature for some period of the day. Broadway is inhuman. The theatre is a hit-or-miss arrangement, filled with opportunism and quick judgment...A creative person becomes a Ping-Pong ball."

William Ball's heroic labors may or may not succeed in San Francisco, but at the moment the love affair between his company and the city is rapturous. However, the director should ponder Herbert Blau's bitter remark that San Francisco is built on the hard rock of provincialism and not on cosmopolitanism. Blau and Jules Irving, professors at San Francisco State College, had begun their pioneering Actor's Workshop in the early fifties, and in time they won international fame with a European tour under State Department auspices, notably for their production of *Waiting for Godot*. Irving and Blau produced *The Birthday Party* long before it came to Broadway; they presented the first professional production in America of *Mother Courage*, as well as the American premiere of Arden's *Serjeant Musgrave's Dance*. San Franciscans were also fortunate to play host to Dürrenmatt's *The Marriage of Mr. Mississippi*, a play yet to be produced in New York. Blau and Irving regularly invited leading local painters and sculptors to do sets and costumes for them, a wise custom still unpracticed on Broadway. Despite all this and nationwide attention, San Francisco was indifferent to the Actor's Workshop, failing to come to the rescue when money was crucial. Naturally, Blau and Irving responded with pleasure when they were invited to take over New York's Lincoln Center Repertory Company just eighteen months before the Actor's Workshop expired. Hopefully, San Franciscans will behave themselves this time, and salute the American Conservatory Theatre with affection, pride, and lots of money.

The Minnesota Theatre Company and the American Conservatory Theatre are the most impressive of the resident professional troupes, but evaluations must be tentative. At the moment, there are about fifty such theatres around the nation, most of which exist in a perpetual state of crisis. Three comparatively stable ones have their roots in the 1950's—the Arena Stage in Washington, D.C.; the Alley Theatre in Houston, and the Milwaukee Repertory.

The nation's capital is a city notoriously indifferent to culture, but somehow the Arena Stage has thrived. The director is Zelda Fichandler, and she is now the national heroine of the regional movement. In recent years, Mrs. Fichandler has received several large foundation grants and smaller donations from the national government. The Arena Stage began in 1950 in a converted movie house, fled later to an abandoned brewery, and in 1961 moved into its present custom-made, 773-seat home. The award-winning, million-dollar building, a tasteful combination of brick, glass, and concrete in a park-like setting, is the first theatre to be built in Washington in sixty years. A genuine theatre-in-the-round, the Arena has rows steeply banked, with excellent sightlines. A million-dollar satellite, which will concentrate on new American plays, will be completed in late 1969. The Arena Stage has never been content to revive stale works already pawed over by Broadway, and it has been the scene of several world and many American premieres. In December of 1967, Mrs. Fichandler presented the world premiere of Howard Sackler's first full-length play, *The Great White Hope*. This sprawling, lusty chronicle play is based on the life of Jack Johnson, who in 1908 became the first black man to win the world's heavyweight crown, and it contains some striking insights into racism by a white playwright. The ironic title indicates the racist search for a challenger who could capture the coveted belt for the Caucasian race. One vividly sees how the sporting world and the civil authorities force the champion into exile and destroy his mind and body. Johnson's love for a white girl is explored in moving, flaming scenes. During this powerful wallop of a play, one is sometimes reminded of a more contemporary situation, the raw public attitudes toward Muhammed Ali (Cassius Clay). One of the most significant dramas of the sixties, *The Great White Hope* came to Broadway in the fall of 1968, with James Earl Jones repeating his searing, soaring impersonation of the black champion.

Houston's Alley Theatre was started in the fifties by tough-minded, theatre-mad Nina Vance, one-time assistant to the late Margo Jones. She used her last few dollars to pay the postage for the initial subscription mailing. Some two hundred plays, both old and new, were performed in the cramped old Alley, but by late 1968 Miss Vance was settled in the splendid New Alley, part of an enormous multi-million-dollar civic center. What might happen in this impressive cultural complex is as unpredictable as Texas itself. Except for the Alley, the Milwaukee Repertory has a history longer than that of any resident professional company between Cleveland and the Pacific. The theatre in a converted movie house was founded in 1954 by a group of concerned local citizens, and it has offered everything from *Waiting for Godot* to last season's Broadway hits. In late 1969 it will open in the inevitable new center for the performing arts, an eleven-million-dollar building of travertine marble, situated in a park setting along the banks of the Milwaukee River. Along with such amenities as restaurants, cocktail lounges, heated sidewalks, a fountain, and sculpture along a promenade, there will be a large hall for symphonies and operas as well as the 527-seat, thrust stage theatre for the Repertory Company.

Unlikely soil for quality theatre is the myopic Deep South. Yet by the 1970's, Atlanta might possibly emerge as an important drama capital. The Georgia city boasts not one but two major theatre projects. Although Theatre Atlanta has produced many plays of the *Boy Meets Girl* variety, it has not been afraid to offer such biting, compelling works as *MacBird* and *The Investigation*. At the opening of the 1966–67 season, the group moved into a sparkling million-dollar theatre, a 765-seater with a thrust stage. During the production in the new house of Shaw's *Caesar and Cleopatra*, Broadway's Diana Sands substituted for injured Kathryn Loder. It marked the first time in Atlanta that a black performer played a major role not written specifically for a black. A rival resident company, the Municipal Theatre, was installed in late 1968 in another new complex, the multi-million-dollar Atlanta Memorial Arts Center, which includes auditoriums for the city's ballet, symphony, and opera groups as well as an 890-seat repertory theatre. Metropolitan Atlanta has a population of one-and-a-half million people, 40 per cent of whom are black. It will be most interesting to see if these rival theatres pursue a potentially valuable new customer, the Southern black.

There are professional theatres in several other Southern cities, including New Orleans, Dallas, Louisville, and Baltimore. Stuart Vaughan, who once performed directorial wonders for New York's Phoenix and Joseph Papp's Shakespeare-in-the-Park, launched the New Orleans Repertory during the fall of 1966, primarily with money from the Federal government. Begun in 1960, the Dallas Theatre Center is housed in an elegant building designed by Frank Lloyd Wright and ideally situated in a grove of trees. The 444-seat playhouse has been the scene of several premieres of American plays, including Robert Anderson's *The Days Between* and Paddy Chayefsky's *The Latent Heterosexual*. The latter trifle starred Zero Mostel and was directed by Burgess Meredith. The Actors Theatre of Louisville, Kentucky's only resident professional stage, has shown signs of awakening in recent seasons after a long spell of torpor. Baltimore's Center Stage, founded in 1963, has produced a rich variety of dramas including Lowell's *Benito Cerino*, John Whiting's antiwar *A Penny for a Song*, and Genet's *The Balcony*, the last starring Julie Bovasso, a virtuoso actress-playwright-director who introduced New Yorkers to Genet and Ionesco in her own avant-garde theatre back in the 1950's. The Center Stage's subsidiary workshop also discovered a playwright in Baltimore-born C. Lester Franklin. His *A Scaffold for Marionettes* was based on an incident in 1963 when a wealthy white man caned a black waitress to death at a society ball. (Bob Dylan later wrote a song about it called "The Lonesome Death of Hattie Carroll.")

Boston's resident professional theatre, the Charles Playhouse, has offered the obligatory Beckett and Lorca, but they have also been more adventurous in presenting such off-off-Broadway classics as LeRoi Jones's *Dutchman* and Lanford Wilson's *The Madness of Lady Bright*. New Haven's the Long Wharf has combined safe Broadway hits with such experimental plays of the Other Theatre as Sam Shepard's *Icarus's Mother*. The Long Wharf, incidentally, has also found time for a children's theatre and for tours of the Connecticut public schools. In March of 1968, Buffalo's Studio Arena Theatre was suddenly the center of national attention when the company offered the world premiere of Edward Albee's *Box-Mao-Box*. This unusual fugue pits the empty, futile lives of several Americans against the droning voice of Chairman Mao Tse-tung mechanically reading his own *Quotations*. Its theme of the total corruption of our times is presented with rich irony and a haunting melancholy. The Repertory Company at the Trinity Square Playhouse in Providence, Rhode Island, presented Robert Lowell's masterly adaption of Racine's *Phèdre* in 1968. These Rhode Islanders concentrate on quality. In 1968 they dismantled the 1,145-seat ANTA-Washington Square Theatre, a temporary home of the Lincoln Center Repertory in New York, and had it shipped to Providence. It was New York's loss. In blighted Los Angeles, there was no real relief in sight, but perhaps the Ahmanson Theatre and the Mark Taper Forum in the plush new arts center might someday bring drama distinction to Southern California.

The ferment in a number of civic theatres in the 1960's is being augmented by an exhilarating vitalization of the university stages.

What was once pedantically called the educational theatre is finally joining the universal revolt of the young against both hypocrisy and pomposity. In fact, the universities may well lead the way to the stages of tomorrow. The spiritual leader of this welcome rebellion is Robert Brustein, the dean of the Yale Drama School. The more aware and nimble of the university drama teachers have taken hope from Brustein's call to arms: more and more schools are accepting the proposition that the stages on the college campus should be intimately related to the stages of life. Away with pompous fogies in ivory towers, dead souls uninterested in the angry, scarred world outside the academic enclosures!

Brustein is ideally fitted for his new role as the chief of the campus revolution in theatre. He was a probing professor of dramatic literature when he taught at Columbia University, one happy result of which was a seminal volume, *The Theatre of Revolt;* as drama critic for *The New Republic,* he has fought the Broadway Establishment with wit, grace, and unerring aim. In his youth, he himself was a student at the Yale Drama School but dropped out in disgust over its antediluvian ways. As a graduate student at Columbia, he was deeply influenced by Lionel Trilling, who taught him, he once noted, "to look at literature as an expression, in a broad sense, of culture." He spent seven seasons as a member of a summer-stock company called Group 20 at Wellesley, Massachusetts, along with Ellis Rabb and Rosemary Harris, and later made the frustrating rounds of Broadway agents as an unemployed actor. In the fifties he went abroad to observe European subsidy and then directed plays at the University of Nottingham.

Thus fortified by wide experience, the rebel moved to Yale in July, 1966, and immediately organized his campaign to provoke the Drama School into life after its prolonged siege of apathy. One of his early acts was symbolic: he painted the old Playhouse a saucy red. In a relatively short time, Brustein collected an impatient, quirky band of assistants, teachers, actors, lecturers, and playwrights around him, theatre partisans who in their turn created an ambience of gay revolt among the students. The princes and clowns, making unpredictable entrances and exits, included Gordon Rogoff, Larry Arrick, Jan Kott, Sam Shepard, Jean-Claude van Itallie, Alvin Epstein, Barbara Garson, Kenneth Brown, Richard Gilman, Mildred Dunnock, Harvey Sabinson, and the inspired actress-teacher of indeterminate age, Stella Adler. In no time at all, the student applications had doubled.

Hamstrung by lack of funds and acting personnel during his first season, Brustein invited experimental groups from New York and Philadelphia to the Yale campus. A group from New York's Open Theatre performed Megan Terry's *Viet Rock*. The bittersweet antiwar opera born at Actors Studio, *Dynamite Tonite*, was also exhibited. This was directed by Paul Sills, a restless, searching graduate of the Second City troupe who employed children's games to develop ensemble feeling among actors. There were also productions of two classics, Jonson's *Volpone* and Aeschylus' *Prometheus Bound*, that were neither academic nor genteel. *Volpone*, in particular, was randy with sex and scatology. The richly textured and very free adaptation of *Prometheus Bound* was infused with modern existential and political ruminations by poet Robert Lowell, himself as rebellious as the drama's hero. Nothing on Broadway equaled it in quality and relevance. The director was London's intellectual provocateur Jonathan Miller, who tried to dispense with the "ghastly piety" (in his own words) surrounding most productions of classic Greek drama.

During that first historic season, letters cascaded onto the desks of Yale's president and other university officials. Most of the accusers heatedly charged Brustein with obscenity and bad taste. Members of the local Chamber of Commerce vigorously complained about the brief masturbatory motions of Hamm and Clov in *Endgame*, as though masturbation were unusual or un-American. Brustein was in open warfare against the deeply conservative nature of his New Haven audiences. The idea that theatre was a lusty, living event related to their own everyday lives was foreign to them. Brustein himself put it bluntly: "The New Haven theatre is dominated by Helen Hokinson ladies who taste plays in the same spirit they nibble mints after dinner."

During the second season (1967–68), Brustein proceeded with a more long-term goal than mere provocation: to create a conservatory atmosphere at Yale by developing a resident professional

[244]

repertory company. The company members also doubled as class-room teachers, and students and professionals alike learned from each other. Extra monies from foundations and other sources (including a $50,000 check from a fellow Yale dropout, actor Paul Newman) were welcome aid to Brustein. Such adroit actors as Stacy Keach (who played the title role in the New York *MacBird*), Kenneth Haigh (the original Jimmy Porter in Osborne's *Look Back in Anger*), Anthony Holland (from the Second City improvisers), John McCurry (from the original production of *The Connection*), and Ron Liebman (an Actors Studio member with an astonishingly wide range of body and vocal skills) were infinitely helpful in imparting a sheen and strength to campus productions. In December of 1967, Brustein presented the world premiere of *We Bombed in New Haven*, the first play by Joseph Heller, author of the best-selling novel *Catch-22*. Here was a flippant, funny-sad look at war as practiced by the officers and men of the U.S. Air Force, and here were all the obscenities of military life, actual and symbolic. (Incidentally, this black comedy reached Broadway in the fall of 1968, with Jason Robards and Diana Sands in the leads.) The season at Yale also included a somewhat conventional production of Shakespeare's *Coriolanus* and an impressive revival of Pirandello's *Henry IV* in an Eric Bentley translation.

In the spring of 1968, the Drama School published a new magazine, *yale/theatre*. Advertised as a "journal of ferment reflecting the excitement of the young in theatre" and issued three times a year, its pocket-sized pages have been garlanded with contributions by Susan Sontag, Jan Kott, Peter Weiss, Rochelle Owens, and Jean-Louis Barrault. In a nation woefully lacking in challenging drama magazines, *yale/theatre* may have revolutionary reverberations.

Another campus where professional theatre has been enthusiastically pursued is that of the University of Michigan. Under the energetic supervision of Robert Schnitzer, who has been a Broadway actor and stage manager, and his wife Marcella Cisney, a former television network director, the theatre program at Ann Arbor has been one of America's most promising. Bolstered by a playwright-in-residence plan which enables authors to participate in rehearsals and get paid for it, the Schnitzers have presented an unusual number of new plays. The premieres have included Studs Terkel's *Amazing Grace*, Alice Childress' *Wedding Band*, poet David Hall's dramatization of the work of another poet, *An Evening's Frost*, and Paul Shyre's *The Child Buyer*, based on John Hersey's novel. Broadway theatregoers have never been given an opportunity to view any of these fascinating dramas. The eclectic Schnitzers provide something for everybody, however, and the campus has been the scene, for example, of both *Hogan's Goat* and *The Impossible Years*.

The Michigan program was begun auspiciously in the early sixties when the Schnitzers offered shelter, financial aid, affection, and an appreciative audience to Ellis Rabb's wandering troupe, the Association of Producing Artists. This warm embrace between a university and a professional repertory has set a dramatic precedent, and many schools are now copying the idea. Were it not for the university's largesse, the APA might well have folded. Though the APA is now internationally celebrated and has its own home on Broadway, the grateful company returns to Michigan each year for a brief season of plays. Other repertory companies, including the American Conservatory Theatre and Canada's Stratford, have paid visits to the campus. Such exchanges could herald a healthy new turn for both regional and university theatres. Ann Arbor's educators have shown no signs of sagging interest in theatre. Indeed, a handsome new theatre will be completed, hopefully, in late 1969; for it, Jo Mielziner has designed a combination thrust-proscenium stage not unlike his platform for New York's Vivian Beaumont.

Since 1966, Brandeis University in Waltham, a suburb of Boston, has emerged as one of the more important theatre forces, primarily through the presence on campus of Howard Bay, a scenic designer and director of exceptional power. One of the outstanding directors in the Federal Theatre Project of the 1930's, Bay has since favored Broadway many times with his set designs, most recently for *Man of La Mancha*. The productions at Brandeis' beautifully equipped, 750-seat Spingold Theatre are performed by a company of professional artists-in-residence, who also teach, and by graduate drama students. The Massachusetts school is not content merely to present revivals. The American premiere of Bertolt Brecht's *Schweyk in the Second World War* was given here as well as the American premieres of two John Arden plays, *The Waters of Babylon* and *The Workhouse Donkey*. Incidentally, these plays have yet to come to Broadway. In May of 1968, the university offered the premiere of *Fire!* by an exciting new American playwright, John Roc. He was first presented in England by Peter Hall of the Royal Shakespeare Company, but Brandeis introduced him to the United States. A shocking and mystifying expressionist drama bursting with the rages and terrors that beset modern man in an uncertain world, *Fire!* was enthusiastically received by the local critics for its richly textured language and its volcanic theatricality. Brandeis brought the best of off-off-Broadway to Boston, too. The La Mama troupe performed there in the summer of 1968, and Tom O'Horgan conducted a six-week seminar.

Stanford University in Palo Alto, California, started a laudable Repertory Theatre in 1965, the pivot for its graduate program in drama. Gerald Hiken, a sterling actor given too few opportunities on Broadway, left New York to head the new troupe of professionals and graduate school apprentices. A grant from the Rockefeller Foundation sparked the first season. In 1966, the company presented a monumental *Prometheus Bound* under the direction of a guest from Holland, Erik Vos. Financing soon became difficult, however, and the size of the company has been drastically reduced. Stanford, like many another university around the nation, is learning a hard lesson: repertory is a precious cultural commodity that needs frequent and large injections of money.

Many schools do not possess resident professional companies but manage nevertheless to present arresting dramas. Jan Kott, that improbable Polish mixture of Marxism and existentialism, has jolted many students into stage action. Yale has not been his only stop on a tour of American campuses while he is on leave from the University of Warsaw. At the moment, his influence is as pervasive as that of Brecht, Artaud, and McLuhan. In the summer of 1967, Kott supervised a striking production of Stanislaw Ignacy Witkiewicz's *The Madman and the Nun* (or *There is Nothing Bad Which Could Not Turn into Something Worse*) at San Francisco State College.

It marked the somewhat belated American premiere of a Polish play written in 1923. In this updated version, a nun prays for a man in his asylum cell. Slide projections spell out his fantasies of Hitler, concentration camps, and Vietnam; films also indicate the nun's emotional interests, including flowers, happy children, nude statues, and finally close-ups of male genitals. Later the nun is down to her foundation garments and, before the conclusion of the drama, she is a topless nun grappling with the patient in his cell. Witkiewicz, father of the Polish avant-garde, painter, novelist, and philosopher, committed suicide the day Russia went into Poland. Perhaps through Kott's industry, more plays by Witkiewicz will be done in the United States.

At the University of California at Berkeley in March of 1968, Kott staged an amazing production of Euripides' *Orestes*. Sold out prior to its opening, the Greek classic was performed by a student cast at the Durham Theatre. Euripides wrote this play during the Peloponnesian Wars which marked the dissolution of Greek civilization. A year after he finished the script in 408 B.C., the disillusioned dramatist went into exile. Savant Kott thinks *Orestes* is acutely relevant to our times, and he chose Washington, D.C., as the setting because he deemed it appropriate to the madness and violence, both foreign and domestic, that is the theme of the play. Orestes was played as a bearded, beflowered hippie in jeans; Hermione wore a silver paper mini-dress; Helen of Troy was a swinging call girl. Protesters carried signs reading "We Are All Murderers," "Helen Is a Whore," and "Get Out of Troy, Now." There were slides of the Capitol in flames, and documentary films depicted the Vietnam war and the anti-draft demonstrations in Oakland. Would young drama students ever be the same after they met Jan Kott?

The 1960's may be remembered not only for Kott's invasion but also for the birth of a unique plan for the decentralization of American theatre. The American Playwrights Theatre, or APT, is a national non-profit service agency with headqarters at Ohio State University in Columbus, and it provides established playwrights frustrated by a declining Broadway with a direct line to national audiences. Through the APT the nation's regional and university theatres can present premieres of major works by leading playwrights *before* their possible production on Broadway. The idea was conceived in 1963 by two successful Broadway playwrights, Jerome Lawrence and Robert E. Lee, men deeply interested in the future of regional theatre and angered by Broadway's economic stranglehold. A university or civic theatre may become eligible for APT's services by paying an annual $50 subscription fee. The playwright, carefully chosen by the American Educational Theatre Association, the American National Theatre and Academy, and Ohio State, is guaranteed fifty productions at a minimum royalty fee of $200 and thus is assured of at least $10,000 for his efforts, more than he sometimes earns on hit-or-flop Broadway.

So far the bold idea has met with enormous success. The first APT production was Robert Anderson's *The Days Between*, given its world premiere by the Dallas Theatre Center in June of 1965. Anderson, who wearied of waiting for an improbably brilliant cast on Broadway, was enthusiastic about APT results. During the 1965–66 season, *The Days Between*, a probing, reflective drama about a professor-novelist and his desperate search for meaning in his insecure, second-rate existence, was given some three hundred performances by more than fifty APT member theatres, including the Center Stage in Baltimore, Maryland, the Civic Theatre in Portland, Oregon, the Playhouse in Oak Ridge, Tennessee, and the Civic Theatre in Binghamton, New York.

Since that auspicious beginning, other plays have included *And People All Around* by George Sklar and *Ivory Tower* by Jerome Weidman and James Yaffee. Sklar, who began his career as a member of Professor George Pierce Baker's class at the Yale Drama School, was remembered chiefly for his social-protest plays of the 1930's, including *Stevedore* and *Peace on Earth*. His new drama, based loosely on the 1964 murders of three civil rights workers in Philadelphia, Mississippi, was a pageant-like lament with choruses, civil rights songs, flashbacks, and interior monologues. The Sklar drama was a hit in such diverse playhouses as the Northridge Theatre Guild, a small community theatre in Los Angeles' San Fernando Valley, and the Meadow Brook Theatre, a superb professional repertory outpost at Oakland University near Detroit. When the play was produced at the State College in Towson, Maryland, there were demonstrations by the Ku Klux Klan and student counter-pickets. *Ivory Tower*, first performed in mid-1967 on the University of Michigan campus, was an unusual courtroom drama suggested by the case of poet Ezra Pound, who was accused of treason because of his broadcasts for the fascists in Italy during World War II. The APT chose *Summertree* for its 1968–69 season. This luminous work by newcomer Ron Cowen became the only APT play which had already been done in New York; it had been much admired at the Forum, a 299-seat off-Broadway showcase fostered by the Lincoln Center Repertory Company.

The success of these new plays around the nation might prove significant. All America may someday become a kind of improved Broadway, with eager new audiences everywhere attending premieres. Leading dramatists may then write primarily for audiences west of the Hudson River. Whether their plays are ever done on Broadway may then not be a vital question. The APT may become an alternative to Broadway, an important clue to the future.

CHAPTER 16

FUTURE STAGES

THEATRE IS THE dance of life, transfigured reality become art. It is nothing less than the true story of mankind. And so, of course, there can be no final chapter in or out of this book. The curtain rings down on individual performers, but the theatre itself is immortal, a stylized ritual that will endure—if man learns to control his toys of annihilation. Instead of ringing finalities, I can only offer exhortations, lamentations, speculations, and dreams, an uncertain view of a mistier time.

The future of American drama is intricately entwined with the American Dream. Indeed there is little point in discussing the theatre's future unless one is also talking about the overall quality of life in tomorrow's America. However tenuous it might seem to those trained to see life piecemeal, a connection does exist between shabby drama and urban blight. The fact of our shriveled and mean-spirited theatre reflects the bleeding nation outside. Art and life are not only inseparable: each endlessly affects the other. (We are, of course, all kin, for we see [or can, if we have the money and inclination] the same bad plays; we also breathe the same polluted air, periodically get mugged and robbed with the same impartiality, reap the bitter riots of the dispossessed, and go off to war to kill or be killed.) Americans must come to recognize the relatedness of things, for it is this lack of social vision, this absence of community, that is most appalling in the United States. The qualities of the solutions to both a demoralized theatre and a nation at war with itself are similar. The theatre arts must become pervasively collaborative. Our dreams for the stage must somehow

[251]

merge with the dreams for a profoundly cooperative and very different kind of America. On the actors' stages, shallow, cheap and selfish commercialism must be transformed into art; on the stages of life, poverty and murder (in war and in peace) must be transformed into abundance and communion.

There is, unfortunately, no infallible prescription for a sick theatre or, for that matter, a sick society. The issues are complex. I can only suggest a number of directions that theatre might take. But first I must sweep away one monstrous myth that has been dangerously blocking progress in the theatre and the other performing arts—the myth of a "cultural explosion." If America seriously believes that this country is enjoying an explosion or boom or renaissance or what-have-you, then the national goals are incredibly puny. The vapid assumptions and easy optimism surrounding the myth of a cultural explosion are sickening. A very slight resurgence in cultural affairs has been cheaply oversold under a false label by overzealous journalists. An edifice complex among the pampered does not constitute a boom.

Actually, the performing arts are in deep financial trouble, and their deficits will more than double by 1975. The theatre "income gap" (the difference between costs and income) is increasing at an alarming rate. True, the productivity of the economy as a whole (output per man-hour) has risen at a steady rate over the last half century. The performing arts, however, leave little room for labor-saving innovations, since the end-product is the labor of the performer. Increases in salaries in the arts—necessary and inevitable (many artists are grossly underpaid)—cannot be offset by higher productivity, and ticket prices cannot rise high enough or costs be cut sufficiently to eliminate the "income gap." These dismaying facts are capsuled from one of the most important statistical studies of the decade, *Performing Arts—The Economic Dilemma*. This authoritative and fact-packed analysis of the economic problems common to drama, opera, music and dance, published in the fall of 1966 under the auspices of the impressively impartial Twentieth Century Fund, is the result of three years of research by Princeton University economists William J. Baumol and William G. Bowen.

These clearheaded professors forever demolish loose talk about cultural booms: they point out that only a small minority, less than 3 per cent, of the American population attends as many as one live performance of any of the performing arts during the course of a year. These audiences are generally affluent, educated, and in no way representative of the entire nation. A shockingly disproportionate percentage of the audience is in New York City. The New York metropolitan area alone accounts for nearly 40 per cent of the receipts for all classical music performances and for more than 50 per cent of all theatre receipts in the United States. The citizenry, it turns out, is not really spending more on the performing arts. In 1929, 15 cents out of every $100 of disposable personal income went for tickets to performing events; in 1963, only 11 cents out of each $100 went to these presentations. In a time of enormous population growth, the Broadway commercial theatre has not increased its audience one whit. On the contrary, attendance has leveled off into a static statistic. These startling disclosures cannot be maneuvered, by any stretch of careless press-agentry, into a cultural explosion.

The performing arts will need millions of dollars annually to pay for the spiraling operating costs. They require permanent outside help to survive. These are grim and coldly statistical facts, and the knowledge is essential for the theatre. We must come to think of theatre in an entirely new way—as an art form and not as a business. It must be frankly considered a money-loser, not a money-maker. All the major symphonies, including the relatively rich New York Philharmonic, lose money annually. Though the Metropolitan Opera is regularly sold out, it operates—and expects to—at a deficit. This is equally true of our ballet companies. The opera and ballet are true repertory companies, with enormous staffs, a storehouse of sets and costumes, and a vast number of productions. They could not exist on the vagaries of the box office: they are not adventures for profit. Americans are slowly and somewhat painfully coming to understand that these extremely expensive forms of art are necessary to any self-respecting nation. Why must theatre be exempt from this intelligent approach to art? No permanent theatre company can survive for long at the mercy of the profit motive. For example, the Lincoln Center Repertory Company is in a constant state of financial crisis, although the troupe plays to 96 per cent capacity, a figure unequaled in any other regional theatre. The new resident theatres, whether in or out of New York, are now openly and proudly referring to themselves as nonprofit cultural institutions.

If then we must be prepared for ever-larger deficits in the theatre, who is to foot the bill? Only society's consistent willingness to help will keep the serious theatre alive. (Presumably Broadway, now devoted to light commercial fare, will somehow fend for itself.) Private philanthrophy is one important source. However, individual donors, corporations, and the foundations give most of their monies to organized religion, science and medicine, schools, and community-chest-type groups. A minuscule amount goes to the arts. In the 1960's, the foundations, particularly the Ford and Rockefeller Foundations, have given a larger share to theatre than had been customary, but it remains a trickle, sporadic, and at random. Most of it has been "seed" money to get new companies started. But what happens after these initial gifts are used up? The foundations will not continue forever to pour money into these ventures. The answer is government subsidy, on federal, state, county, and city levels. It must come in massive and ever-continuing amounts. America, with its prodigious resources, can provide its people with the theatre arts. It is quite possible, just as it is possible to eliminate slums and racism—if the nation really wishes to do so.

Many Americans fear subsidy in the theatre because it smacks of socialism, and they have been taught to fear socialism with ferocity. The National Theatre of Britain is subsidized, along with other English theatres, and yet the free-enterprise system is very much at home in that nation. Canada recently inaugurated a subsidized national theatre, the chief component of which is the Shakespeare Festival at Stratford, Ontario. Canada, however, has not deserted capitalism because of this salute to the arts of the stage.

We should study, without prejudice and in careful detail, the subsidized theatres of Berlin, Paris, Warsaw, Hamburg, Leningrad, and other large European cities. Actually, subsidy for American stages is not at all a question of wild-eyed revolt. It is simply a matter of catching up with the rest of the civilized world. We must completely rid ourselves of our Puritan heritage regarding subsidy, and adopt the saner European attitudes. The very idea that serious theatre should be required to show a profit would seem ridiculous in Czechoslovakia, France, or Denmark. Napoleon was not too immersed in his military misadventures in Russia to dispatch a letter home ruling that the state-subsidized Comédie Française must always keep low-priced seats available for the poor. Many lands now designate an enormous—some reactionaries would call it frightening—slice of their annual national budgets for the arts. Austria, for example, spends $5.50 per capita for the arts in its annual budget, as compared with America's 5 cents per capita. Subsidies to the state and municipal theatres throughout Germany, East and West, make American government aid, proportionately, seem miserly. In Moscow, thirty-seven resident repertory companies each average four different plays a week. Prague, with a population of little more than a million, has more than sixteen locally or nationally subsidized theatre groups, all of them repertory companies, exhibiting both the classics and contemporary plays, including American ones. And the government sees to it that the seats are inexpensive.

Subsidy has finally limped into American reality in the 1960's. The revolutionary (hopefully) Arts and Humanities Act was made law by Congress in 1965. One statement in Section 5 of the Act is particularly noble: "While no government can call a great artist or scholar into existence, it is necessary and appropriate for the Federal government to help create and sustain not only a climate encouraging freedom of thought, imagination, and inquiry, but also the material conditions facilitating the release of this creative talent." Whenever know-nothing politicians attempt to revoke this new law (and fight it they will), they must be reminded of this profoundly democratic passage. Under the pioneering law, a National Endowment of the Arts was created, with a twenty-six-member National Council on the Arts chosen to approve the grants. This Federal subsidy plan, however, has been woefully inadequate. A few thousand dollars has been awarded a number of resident companies, including the Arena Stage, the Alley Theatre, the

Minneapolis Repertory, and Theatre Atlanta. All monies are, of course, welcome, but these token amounts have little relevance to the theatre other than window-dressing before the rest of the world. The total grants for all the arts, including music, sculpture, painting, dance, film, television, architecture, and literature as well as theatre, have averaged considerably less than $10,000,000 a year. At any time, Congress may cut back these annual appropriations: indeed, it has already done so. It is ironic when one realizes that the equivalent of one week's expenditure for napalming Vietnamese peasants would give us an annual arts program surpassing that of any other nation.

Though 1965 is the year to remember for Federal subsidy, an even earlier date marks the first subsidies granted by a state government. In 1960 the New York State Legislature created a Council on the Arts under the leadership of Governor Nelson A. Rockefeller, a most unusual politician in that his personal commitment to the arts is ardent and catholic. The New York budget for all the arts is now well over $1,000,000, with an average of $300,000 set aside for theatre, mostly for a statewide touring program. I have felt honored to serve as an adviser to this state council, and I have observed with satisfaction the remarkable work it has accomplished. But the budget is indecent. To be fully effective, the theatre division alone must be allotted three or four million, not a few thousand dollars. Following New York's lead, every state in the union now has a council on the arts. None has either the imagination or the money of the New York organization: some are merely on paper and spend no more than $20,000 or $30,000 on all the arts. In the seventies, perhaps more city and county arts councils will be established to augment state aid to the ailing theatre. Municipal support has been paltry indeed, and sometimes the cities have been fantastically wrongheaded about the dramatic arts. The Tyrone Guthrie Theatre in Minneapolis has resorted to the courts in a bitter fight against the city government. Incredibly, Minneapolis imposed a real-estate tax of about $75,000 a year on a theatre that has brought the city international hosannahs!

Subsidy, if it be truly generous, will guarantee security and continuity, the necessary ingredients for the development of repertory

tion must be paid to their demands and suggestions. These great-grandchildren of Isadora Duncan have created a new life-style out of their own guts. More and more they are transforming their earlier bleak nihilism into a sharp-eyed, lusty, and joyous defiance of entrenched inanities. There is a moral beauty in their revolt against the brainwashing, hucksterism, and hypocrisy around them. Thanks to the young, the 1960's might be called the Decade of Rising Dissent. These insurgents have contributed priceless gifts to the theatre, and in the seventies, their explorations will become more and more heralded on both the non-profit and the commercial stages. They must be an integral part of any subsidy system, or else subsidy will be an empty gesture and the new regional theatres merely mausoleums.

The rebels of today are determined to make the word "culture" come alive—relevant, subversive, and unfettered. They are trying to subvert the all-American belief that Culture is something for well-off, proper, elderly ladies with blue rinses. To paraphrase a wise essay by Harold J. Laski, they have discovered the dangers inherent in being a gentleman, the pitfalls of "good taste." The new directors have adopted Antonin Artaud's cry of "No more masterpieces," and they are gleefully dusting off Shakespeare and the Greek classics and restoring them to their original vitality. Plays, liberated from libraries and museums, should live for *now*.

Perhaps the young's cardinal contribution to the theatre is their principled battle to destroy the last vestiges of Puritanism and middle-class sanctity. They are fighting for a return to that freedom of expression that was stomped on by the Puritans and finally murdered by the Victorians; by clearing away taboos and probing into our secret psychic experiences, they are adding a new vitality to theatre. Their revolt is total, not just economic and political. They are certain that in struggle one can retain a rich humanity and that one need not become congealed into one-dimensional dogmatism. They see more clearly than any other generation that revolution can sour into just another form of tyranny, a censorship of the mind and body. Without true democracy, socialism can be murderous. The new iconoclasts are painfully aware of yesterday's doctrinaire leftists and their peculiar strain of Puritanism. One must

theatre. When we finally arrive at repertory in the United States, we shall see a kind of character acting we never knew existed. It is simply not to be found anywhere in the nation today, for our theatre is a short-term effort, built on quick returns. Most of the companies in America which bill themselves as repertory are not the real thing. True repertory includes a year-round company, a permanent home, an artistic policy, and a change in program nightly or every few nights. To understand the nature of repertory, one must study a major ballet company. The systems are very similar. The repertory actor not only plays a number of roles in different productions each week, but he sometimes alternates roles within the same drama. If a new production fails in a subsidized repertory company, it is not catastrophic. It can continue for a while and possibly find a larger audience in time. Or it might be temporarily shelved and reworked. Chekhov's *The Sea Gull* was a box-office fiasco when it was first produced commercially in St. Petersburg. Luckily, it was taken over by the Moscow Art Theatre. Although it was not at first a financial success at the Moscow Art, it became popular after a passage of time. Masterpieces are not always recognized at first viewing. Only a fool could fail to see how the repertory system enriches the actor, the playwright, and the audience. But a repertory company must be supported with lavish subsidies, for repertory is a very expensive mistress.

But our dreams must extend beyond the ledgers of finance. Back in 1915, Lady Gregory, that determined den mother of Dublin's Abbey Theatre, expressed our dreams for us. At Andover, Massachusetts, during a cross-country lecture tour, she talked about a possible National Theatre: "I am still full of the idea that one will be started in America—a tree with a root in every state." Someday I envision at least a dozen great city- and state-subsidized repertory theatres in New York City. Since this city is really the nation's cultural capital, there should also be a splendid National Theatre, federally subsidized. Every state in the union must have at least one subsidized stage, and certainly the sixty or seventy major cities in the United States should have permanent showcases. National pride in theatre should be so intense that a city without a repertory company would feel acute embarrassment, just as it would if there were no symphony orchestra or art museum in town. Existing side by side with these great state theatres might be commercial Broadway-type ventures as well as smaller, avant-garde arenas of protest and exploration. Repertory across America—is this too bold a dream for the richest nation on earth? We have all dreamed too little. I suggest that it is not utopian to hope that Americans might someday visit Buffalo, Des Moines, or Seattle as one would journey to Prague or London or Berlin to enjoy the cultural life and, above all, to view its great theatres.

But again these dreams seem circumscribed. Eventually theatre and indeed all culture should be free. Or at least theatre tickets should be priced at some nominal fee, perhaps the cost of a loaf of bread. England's Kenneth Tynan and France's André Malraux have raised these issues in their own countries. They must be discussed here. One is not required to pay to enter public libraries, public schools, and most art museums—these are free cultural services and the right of every citizen. It is our Puritan heritage which prevents us from demanding that great theatre should be one of the inalienable rights of man. There has been much talk of a guaranteed minimum family income. Why not guaranteed culture for all? Governments are presumably interested in the citizens' health, education, housing, and employment. Why not an interest in their cultural pursuits, their leisure time? We must learn to see theatre as a social service, a social necessity. Sooner or later there must be a Secretary of Leisure and the Arts or a Secretary of Culture in the President's Cabinet. Perhaps a first step toward free theatre might be government-subsidized tickets for the country's teachers and students. (Some non-profit theatres like the Repertory Theatre at Lincoln Center have long offered tickets to students at nominal costs.) Or perhaps the government might subsidize tickets so that none cost more than two or three dollars.

A worry crops up immediately. With this massive aid, will theatre any longer be intellectually free? Will the politicians dictate what we see and hear? Will it be all *Life with Father* and *Oklahoma!* and no *MacBird* and *Hair*? Will the subsidies be poured into safe museums with no interest in dissent and controversy?

Must we then sneak into basements and backrooms to view the La Mamas and the Living Theatres? Or, for that matter, will we be insured a truly international repertory—not only a diet of English literature but also dramas from Eastern Europe, Africa, and the Orient? A shocking ignorance of the theatre arts by members of Congress was displayed during the Federal Theatre Project and the McCarthy periods. More recently, Representative Edna F. Kelly from Brooklyn yelled loudly about some "erotic" dances by Martha Graham. Mrs. Kelly happened to see Miss Graham dance in Europe when that great lady was touring under State Department auspices; the rectitudinous Representative was scandalized at what her tax dollar was going for. Even more recently (July of 1968), Senator Strom Thurmond of South Carolina viciously "exposed" Clive Barnes, a distinguished visitor from England and the drama critic for *The New York Times*, for writing a "depraved" review. The specific crime of which Barnes was publicly pronounced guilty on the Senate floor was his praise of the Broadway musical *Hair*, a romp which the Senator admitted he had not seen. The critic's review was printed intact in *The Congressional Record* in order that it might be read by the entire nation in its "full perversity." Far from incidentally, *Hair* celebrated miscegenation in audaciously explicit lyrics. We want no commissars from Al Capp's Lower Slobbovia controlling our cultural lives. This is precisely what happened in bureaucratic Russia under Stalinist Socialist Realism.

There are, of course, no pat answers or reassurances. Perhaps nationwide subsidized repertory stages devoted to world drama will somehow change our provincial ways of thinking about theatre. At any rate, we must fight any tendency to domesticate our rebels. Indeed, the subsidized theatre might even offer special grants to people who write plays against the government. Within the repertory houses, moreover, we must see to it that artistic directors are fully in charge and not hamstrung by dilettante boards of directors.

Special subsidies should be awarded avant-garde workshops so that the young unknowns can always vie with the safe and established artists. The young need not be worshipped, but close atten-

theatre. When we finally arrive at repertory in the United States, we shall see a kind of character acting we never knew existed. It is simply not to be found anywhere in the nation today, for our theatre is a short-term effort, built on quick returns. Most of the companies in America which bill themselves as repertory are not the real thing. True repertory includes a year-round company, a permanent home, an artistic policy, and a change in program nightly or every few nights. To understand the nature of repertory, one must study a major ballet company. The systems are very similar. The repertory actor not only plays a number of roles in different productions each week, but he sometimes alternates roles within the same drama. If a new production fails in a subsidized repertory company, it is not catastrophic. It can continue for a while and possibly find a larger audience in time. Or it might be temporarily shelved and reworked. Chekhov's *The Sea Gull* was a box-office fiasco when it was first produced commercially in St. Petersburg. Luckily, it was taken over by the Moscow Art Theatre. Although it was not at first a financial success at the Moscow Art, it became popular after a passage of time. Masterpieces are not always recognized at first viewing. Only a fool could fail to see how the repertory system enriches the actor, the playwright, and the audience. But a repertory company must be supported with lavish subsidies, for repertory is a very expensive mistress.

But our dreams must extend beyond the ledgers of finance. Back in 1915, Lady Gregory, that determined den mother of Dublin's Abbey Theatre, expressed our dreams for us. At Andover, Massachusetts, during a cross-country lecture tour, she talked about a possible National Theatre: "I am still full of the idea that one will be started in America—a tree with a root in every state." Someday I envision at least a dozen great city- and state-subsidized repertory theatres in New York City. Since this city is really the nation's cultural capital, there should also be a splendid National Theatre, federally subsidized. Every state in the union must have at least one subsidized stage, and certainly the sixty or seventy major cities in the United States should have permanent showcases. National pride in theatre should be so intense that a city without a repertory company would feel acute embarrassment, just as it would if there were no symphony orchestra or art museum in town. Existing side by side with these great state theatres might be commercial Broadway-type ventures as well as smaller, avant-garde arenas of protest and exploration. Repertory across America—is this too bold a dream for the richest nation on earth? We have all dreamed too little. I suggest that it is not utopian to hope that Americans might someday visit Buffalo, Des Moines, or Seattle as one would journey to Prague or London or Berlin to enjoy the cultural life and, above all, to view its great theatres.

But again these dreams seem circumscribed. Eventually theatre and indeed all culture should be free. Or at least theatre tickets should be priced at some nominal fee, perhaps the cost of a loaf of bread. England's Kenneth Tynan and France's André Malraux have raised these issues in their own countries. They must be discussed here. One is not required to pay to enter public libraries, public schools, and most art museums—these are free cultural services and the right of every citizen. It is our Puritan heritage which prevents us from demanding that great theatre should be one of the inalienable rights of man. There has been much talk of a guaranteed minimum family income. Why not guaranteed culture for all? Governments are presumably interested in the citizens' health, education, housing, and employment. Why not an interest in their cultural pursuits, their leisure time? We must learn to see theatre as a social service, a social necessity. Sooner or later there must be a Secretary of Leisure and the Arts or a Secretary of Culture in the President's Cabinet. Perhaps a first step toward free theatre might be government-subsidized tickets for the country's teachers and students. (Some non-profit theatres like the Repertory Theatre at Lincoln Center have long offered tickets to students at nominal costs.) Or perhaps the government might subsidize tickets so that none cost more than two or three dollars.

A worry crops up immediately. With this massive aid, will theatre any longer be intellectually free? Will the politicians dictate what we see and hear? Will it be all *Life with Father* and *Oklahoma!* and no *MacBird* and *Hair?* Will the subsidies be poured into safe museums with no interest in dissent and controversy?

Must we then sneak into basements and backrooms to view the La Mamas and the Living Theatres? Or, for that matter, will we be insured a truly international repertory—not only a diet of English literature but also dramas from Eastern Europe, Africa, and the Orient? A shocking ignorance of the theatre arts by members of Congress was displayed during the Federal Theatre Project and the McCarthy periods. More recently, Representative Edna F. Kelly from Brooklyn yelled loudly about some "erotic" dances by Martha Graham. Mrs. Kelly happened to see Miss Graham dance in Europe when that great lady was touring under State Department auspices; the rectitudinous Representative was scandalized at what her tax dollar was going for. Even more recently (July of 1968), Senator Strom Thurmond of South Carolina viciously "exposed" Clive Barnes, a distinguished visitor from England and the drama critic for *The New York Times,* for writing a "depraved" review. The specific crime of which Barnes was publicly pronounced guilty on the Senate floor was his praise of the Broadway musical *Hair,* a romp which the Senator admitted he had not seen. The critic's review was printed intact in *The Congressional Record* in order that it might be read by the entire nation in its "full perversity." Far from incidentally, *Hair* celebrated miscegenation in audaciously explicit lyrics. We want no commissars from Al Capp's Lower Slobbovia controlling our cultural lives. This is precisely what happened in bureaucratic Russia under Stalinist Socialist Realism.

There are, of course, no pat answers or reassurances. Perhaps nationwide subsidized repertory stages devoted to world drama will somehow change our provincial ways of thinking about theatre. At any rate, we must fight any tendency to domesticate our rebels. Indeed, the subsidized theatre might even offer special grants to people who write plays against the government. Within the repertory houses, moreover, we must see to it that artistic directors are fully in charge and not hamstrung by dilettante boards of directors.

Special subsidies should be awarded avant-garde workshops so that the young unknowns can always vie with the safe and established artists. The young need not be worshipped, but close attention must be paid to their demands and suggestions. These great-grandchildren of Isadora Duncan have created a new life-style out of their own guts. More and more they are transforming their earlier bleak nihilism into a sharp-eyed, lusty, and joyous defiance of entrenched inanities. There is a moral beauty in their revolt against the brainwashing, hucksterism, and hypocrisy around them. Thanks to the young, the 1960's might be called the Decade of Rising Dissent. These insurgents have contributed priceless gifts to the theatre, and in the seventies, their explorations will become more and more heralded on both the non-profit and the commercial stages. They must be an integral part of any subsidy system, or else subsidy will be an empty gesture and the new regional theatres merely mausoleums.

The rebels of today are determined to make the word "culture" come alive—relevant, subversive, and unfettered. They are trying to subvert the all-American belief that Culture is something for well-off, proper, elderly ladies with blue rinses. To paraphrase a wise essay by Harold J. Laski, they have discovered the dangers inherent in being a gentleman, the pitfalls of "good taste." The new directors have adopted Antonin Artaud's cry of "No more masterpieces," and they are gleefully dusting off Shakespeare and the Greek classics and restoring them to their original vitality. Plays, liberated from libraries and museums, should live for *now*.

Perhaps the young's cardinal contribution to the theatre is their principled battle to destroy the last vestiges of Puritanism and middle-class sanctity. They are fighting for a return to that freedom of expression that was stomped on by the Puritans and finally murdered by the Victorians; by clearing away taboos and probing into our secret psychic experiences, they are adding a new vitality to theatre. Their revolt is total, not just economic and political. They are certain that in struggle one can retain a rich humanity and that one need not become congealed into one-dimensional dogmatism. They see more clearly than any other generation that revolution can sour into just another form of tyranny, a censorship of the mind and body. Without true democracy, socialism can be murderous. The new iconoclasts are painfully aware of yesterday's doctrinaire leftists and their peculiar strain of Puritanism. One must see life whole, balls and all, not just as a clenched fist. The Russian Revolution graphically illustrates this point, for in that giant land sweeping economic change was accompanied by a stringent Victorian morality with viciously authoritarian restrictions on the personal sex lives of the citizenry. Today's revolutionists see the connection in all countries between political and sexual censorship. The young playwrights of the Other Theatre are not just naughty boys writing "fuck" on the walls. The freer use of four-letter words is part of the new esthetics all over the world. Curiously, these words are also part of a new morality.

However, youth is committed to more than freedom to use four-letter words. The experimenters in the off-off-Broadway workshops are engaged in profound research for theatre forms more pertinent to the modern world. They are utterly disdainful of mere reproduction of life on the stage—that's a job for the camera; they are attracted instead to expressionist, poetic and musical theatre. Multi-media forms, often with several screens and multiple track recordings, are being used on stage in exciting new ways, and the possibilities have only just begun to be pursued. Never have the avant-gardists been so busy—or so passionate. Tom O'Horgan particularly is evolving a style all his own, a Theatre of Impulse, a Subliminal Theatre, employing ritual, dance incantation, acrobatics, and music played onstage by the actors themselves.

These modern frontiersmen do not stop with form. They are frustrated by the very shape of old-fashioned theatre, going far beyond the earlier cry for thrust stages and theatres in the round. Deeply influenced by the work of the avant-garde in Eastern Europe and especially the experiments of Jerzy Grotowski in his Polish Lab Theatre, many Americans are searching for a new environmental theatre. Grotowski's persuasive argument is that there should be fresh spatial arrangements for each production. Both actors and audience must be totally enmeshed and immersed in a specially created environment. In one drama about the imprisonment of the human mind, Grotowski placed his audience and actors in a network of cells enclosed by wire mesh. The audience was led into particular cells and then watched the action of the play taking place in another cell centrally located. For Marlowe's

Doctor Faustus, the imaginative young director constructed an enormous horseshoe-shaped medieval dining table, with the audience seated at table with Faustus. The play becomes a flashback inside Faustus' last great monologue, and the spectators thus become guests at Faustus' last supper.

In America the environmental idea has been enriched by "happenings," a direction developed by painters and sculptors and promoted by the art galleries. The word was coined in 1959 by painter Allan Kaprow in a Rutgers University literary review. The happening has extended the boundaries of theatre. These art events soon moved out of the galleries into lofts, brewery cellars, wholesale meat storerooms, and other unlikely places, with the audience placed at random among the performers. Scripts were bare outlines, and much was left to chance and improvisation (key words in today's culture.) There are those partisans who see religious worship, political rallies and conventions, race riots, and all gatherings of people as happenings. All life is thus viewed as theatre spectacle, and the eye, heretofore blinded by habit and dogma, is miraculously awakened. Or so the philosophers of happenings argue. Perhaps this is true. However, I feel that the disciplined Grotowski environments, each carefully planned within the confines of a particular script, offer a more rewarding direction for theatre.

Whatever shape the New Theatre finally assumes in the future, the spectacle that envelops and sometimes engulfs the spectator made exciting and disputatious theatre talk in the late sixties. Megan Terry's *Changes* was an overwhelming assault on the senses. Performed in early 1968 at New York's seedy Central Plaza, a series of halls and meeting rooms used by social clubs and political groups, Miss Terry's wild happening was directed by La Mama's resident genius Tom O'Horgan. The audience was led from an assembly point across the street into the building. In the first room, the spectator removed his clothes and donned a floor-length shapeless garment with a woman's name on it; in another room, he was blindfolded and placed into a kind of wheelchair. He was harangued, pushed, shoved, and mauled as he was wheeled from place to place. Someone sucked his toe. He felt a naked girl; he suddenly found himself on a bed with several people. The argument was endless in the cafés: was it theatre or not? In June of 1968, Richard Schechner, the editor of *The Drama Review* and briefly a student with Jerzy Grotowski, put his own environmental theories into practice in an old garage in an off-beat New York location. His engrossing, irritating, and sometimes successful *Dionysus in 69* was labeled as "somewhat like Euripides' *The Bacchae.*" Schechner started with Euripides' text, but then added and subtracted at will, inserting contemporary jargon and topical references. The audience, deprived of seats, was dispersed all over the garage. The action was everywhere. The actors (the boys reduced to jockstraps and the girls to abbreviated tunics) writhed along the floor in sexual embraces. Often they attempted to involve the audience in dances and other stage actions.

It is easy to laugh off these happenings as cultist activities of collegians, but that would be a spectacularly obtuse interpretation. The young are fervently searching for new forms, and they are profoundly discontented with the old proscenium theatre.

But such experimentation has remained fun and games for a very small group of imaginative young people in New York City. It has not remotely touched most American citizens. And so the young have embarked on another adventure, the search for an ever-larger and more representative theatre audience. The vast majority of Americans have never attended a professional theatre performance in their entire lives. The soaring ticket prices and the seasonal subscription lists are among the many disadvantages that have effectively kept them out of the auditoriums. The theatre must somehow be made part of the lives of the poor, the disinherited, the unschooled. In this decade Michael Harrington has shocked many citizens with his *The Other America: Poverty in the U.S.* His controlled rage, backed by sober fact, has perhaps had an even greater impact than an earlier conscience-pricking document, Jacob Riis's *How the Other Half Lives*, first published in 1890. Even President Kennedy quoted from Harrington's eloquent volume in his political speeches. But the provocative book must have yet another meaning for dedicated theatre people: an audience exists that has never known the glory of the stage. How can we even talk about the successes of our theatre when it has reached such a minuscule portion of the American people? Though Americans seem to do the least about it, the problem of democratizing the theatre is not unique with America. France's crusading Roger Planchon, in his heavily government-subsidized theatre in Lyons, has successfully campaigned to win a working class audience, charging no more than $1 for some of the best seats. He has even sent his actors into the poorest districts and the factories to sell tickets. I also envy the Soviet Union its eager, attentive, and truly representative audiences. Theatre is immensely popular there, and everybody goes, from the street cleaner to the factory foreman. We must make it equally true in the United States.

Our theatre must become a majority theatre. Now many of my friends argue that this is Whitmanesque piffle. Proud and unbending elitists, they believe that quality theatre will always be for a highly educated and affluent handful; they readily agree with Mr. Samuel Goldwyn & Co. that the majority do not want quality and should be left in peace with their mass entertainment junk. I cannot accept this. A country without an artistic soul is a dangerous country. The welfare and the culture of each man affects every other man: we are separate but we are also one. The argument that the majority would not know good theatre if they saw it has never been properly tested. In recent years, I have entertained many visitors from all over the country, sometimes people who have seen little or no theatre. They invariably preferred something like Euripides' *The Trojan Women* or Weiss's *Marat/Sade* to the more familiar television-style comedies.

The gallant, single-minded Joseph Papp has pioneered in the United States in the battle for audiences. One of the rare times one can see a wonderfully diverse audience is at a Papp free Shakespeare-in-the-Park production. Here are all classes, colors, ages, and occupations, perhaps the closest to an Elizabethan audience we have anywhere in America. Papp also tours the New York parks and playgrounds in ghetto areas. The search for new audiences has led Patricia Reynolds and Phoebe Brand, actress wife of Morris Carnovsky, onto the streets of New York. Starting in the summer of 1962, their peripatetic company of minstrels has annually toured the poor neighborhoods of New York during the day-

[264]

light hours. With a rented truck and a portable stage which can be assembled quickly, the Theatre in the Street has offered such diverse fare as Chekhov's *The Marriage Proposal,* Goldoni's *A Servant of Two Masters, The Drunkard,* and dramatized African folk-tales. Bilingual, they perform in both English and Spanish. When they set up on a chosen side-street or alley, the actors apply their make-up in full view of the spectators, some of whom are watching intently from tenement windows and fire escapes. Various philanthropic groups have awarded the Theatre in the Street a driblet of financial aid, but it is never enough. This admirable non-profit troupe needs a hundred times more than the money it somehow musters up for each summer's performances.

Another group which has performed on New York's streets is Peter Schumann's brilliant Bread and Puppet Theatre, with its grotesque Bosch portraits of our mad modern world and its mystic, messianic parables. This theatre group employs puppets of all sizes, from enormous ones nineteen feet high to hand puppets. Expressionist in style, the company is fond of dance, mime, masks, and atonal music. The audiences have responded warmly to such themes as high rent, lack of heat, and the rat invasion. The group has been most successful with an antiwar play about Vietnam, *A Man Says Goodbye to His Mother.* No one gets paid in the Bread and Puppet Theatre. The company charges $1 admission when it appears indoors, nothing on the slum streets. The players hand out free bread during or after a show. Street permits are difficult to obtain, however, and these artists continue against enormous odds. Such theatres, richly and lovingly subsidized, should exist all over America. In mid-1968, the company toured Europe, performing in art galleries, factories, schoolyards, housing projects, and in the streets, as well as in more conventional theatres.

Hippie communal groups like the Diggers (enthusiastically backed by Richard Schechner in the pages of *The Drama Review*) have long argued for a free guerilla theatre, a radical theatre in the streets. In 1967 the flower-decked Diggers presented a script of sorts in Wall Street, burning money on the sidewalks and dramatically showering startled Stock Exchange officials with dollar bills thrown from an interior balcony. Schechner once suggested performing the Stations of the Cross in the subway, with the actions performed at fourteen different subway stops. He has also mentioned street corners, supermarkets, and cafeterias as suitable theatres. Robert Reed's *Kill Vietcong* (the script was published in *The Drama Review*) was acted on the city streets in 1967 at several locations. Bystanders were given plastic pistols and told to shoot young boys.

The San Francisco Mime Troupe, handsome, talented, and impatient, stays off the streets but likes to play in the parks. Since 1961 the company has invaded dozens of San Francisco's parks, and it has thrived despite poverty (no foundation or government money), police harassment (jail is a familiar home), and periodic press blackouts. Committed to making theatre, in content and style, "a living radical force," the Mime Troupe was started by a small group within the Actor's Workshop. They make ends meet by taking up a collection after each performance. They have been hailed by the young in whistle-stops across America, including colleges and universities, such favored underground theatres as the Minneapolis Firehouse, and even New York's Central Park. Nonrealist in approach, the actors have evolved a broad *commedia dell'arte* style, not neglecting masks and dance and music. Their sardonic minstrel show, *Civil Rights in a Cracker Barrel*, was both a scandal and a success. *L'Amant Militaire*, adapted from a Carlo Goldoni play, was transformed into a biting antiwar satire about Vietnam. At the end of the first act, the young audiences always chanted back at the actors: "Hell, no, we won't go."

El Teatro Campesino was started by Luis Miguel Valdes, a former member of the San Francisco Mime Troupe, in the fall of 1965. The actors are former farmworkers, and their company is the theatrical arm of the Delano, California, grape pickers' union. With the financial aid and blessings of the United Farmworkers Organizing Committee, AFL-CIO, which has organized the marginal laborers in the fields and has led the Delano strike, the actors have toured the nation, performing in both Spanish and English. Valdes uses stock slapstick characters out of *commedia dell'arte*, adapting them to "La Huelga," the strike. A scab is converted by a striker, for example, and a boss gets his comeuppance. It is earthy, vivid, and immensely likable, with a dash of Brecht and more than a little Mack Sennett. In general, the unions of the 1960's have been callous to cultural concerns, but El Teatro Campesino is a shining exception. American unions should be financing theatrical ventures in every major city, and their foot-dragging is one of the social paradoxes in the search for new audiences.

The motto of the Free Southern Theatre is brief and direct— "For those who have no theatre." This is a New Orleans-based company that tirelessly travels the rural areas of the South to bring drama to black Americans who have never attended any live theatre. These are the truly neglected audiences. With several cars and trucks, these intrepid black actors have toured the backwoods towns of Louisiana, Mississippi, Texas, Alabama, Tennessee, and Georgia. It has been perilous on occasion. Once the troupe was arrested by a sheriff who tipped off the Ku Klux Klan upon their release. They hid in the bushes while the Klansmen searched for them on the highways leading out of town. The Free Southern Theatre was organized in 1963 by John O'Neal and Gilbert Moses. O'Neal majored in English and philosophy at Southern Illinois University, and shortly after graduation decided that theory must be united with practice; Moses, who had acted at Cleveland's interracial Karamu Playhouse, was a fledgling playwright. His *Roots*, a farce about a Mississippi Negro couple, the wife shrewish with trashy, materialist values and the husband hardworking but passive, tickled the fancies of the Southern audiences, most especially the young. The company has offered free performances of Beckett's *Waiting for Godot*, Brecht's *The Rifles of Señora Carrar*, Duberman's *In White America*, Ossie Davis' *Purlie Victorious*, and Douglas Turner Ward's *Happy Ending*. Though it has received one fairly generous Rockefeller Foundation grant, it needs money desperately to support a year-round workshop in New Orleans, with classes in writing, acting, and stagecraft.

These tales of actors in the city slums and on the Southern "tobacco roads" are inspiring vignettes of sacrifice and courage. They are also profoundly depressing stories, for they point to what has not been done and what needs to be done on a gigantic scale. The U.S. Government should have brought theatre to the forgotten citizens decades ago. The Federal Theatre Project should have been enlarged, not murdered.

Another area in which Americans have conducted themselves in shameful fashion is children's theatre. Aside from a few productions by middle-class dance schools, there are few accomplishments in this field. There should be permanent and subsidized professional theatres for children all over America. You will find them in most of the cities of Europe, especially the Eastern European capitals. With their imposing buildings, large staffs, and lavish subsidies, they put America to shame. Our children are—hopefully—our guarantee for a more gracious tomorrow. Wit and compassion must be implanted early in life. Yet we ignore theatre for all children, just as we symbolically murder thousands of them in our slums every year. Two of the best companies in New York City—Mara, with her spell-weaving spectacles and richly detailed settings and costumes from the Orient, and the droll Paper Bag Players—exist precariously, with a pitiful pittance from a few farseeing philanthropists and an occasional crumb from the government. Their trip to London in early 1968 should have made America proud of its Paper Bags. When they appeared at the Royal Court, scene of the earlier historic *Look Back in Anger*, the English press uncharacteristically raved without restraint. The august London *Times* called the group "genius in the theatre" and wondered in print how these artfully carefree rubber-faced dolls could so deftly turn such everyday objects as paper bags and cardboard boxes into real and surreal props, costumes, and scenery.

Subsidy, repertory, welcome dissent by the young in both content and form, the persistent nurturing, financially and artistically, of new and more representative audiences—these are a few of the possible directions in theatre. If these dreams were pursued with enthusiasm and persistence, what a flowering of the theatre arts might occur! With thriving repertory theatres in most of our cities, truly significant American dramatists and dramas, a national passion for the international classics as well as audacious contemporary scripts, we might come to know what fervor and splendor can be.

But the nation is not ready to take theatre seriously. Everywhere there is a studied evasion of reality. Willy Loman is not the only man who wants to be well-liked. Business peculations go unchallenged. The truth of our city jungles seldom gets on the stages and when it does, it is smothered in sentimentality and half-baked Freudianism. Even the young are sometimes dangerously sentimental in their "love me" clichés. Tragically adrift, they must be shown that there is a precious American heritage of theatre revolt dating from the tens, twenties, and thirties to which they can relate in one way or another.

Before we find communion, we must foster a rising swell of dissent, a theatre of protest, or, better still, a *théâtre engagé*. We must recover a significant belief that has been lost: the stages of the theatre *can* change the stages of life. Perhaps the newest voices in the smaller workshops will provide the openly defiant drama we so desperately need. Many look for a new Odets, but perhaps the visionary playwrights will come unexpectedly through a back door. New social goals can be expressed in a variety of ways, through irony, shock, black comedy, parable, or even sheer joyous impudence.

Theatre represents, at its best, a victory of civilization over barbarism. Or it may merely be a way of boring ourselves as the world ends.

INDEX